"Ron Sider displays a thoughtful commitment to the cause of justice for the poor from a thoroughly biblical perspective. . . . This is a book we have needed for a long time."

—Roberta Hestenes, senior pastor,
Solana Beach Presbyterian Church

"If the poor were such a big deal to Jesus, and they were, shouldn't they be to us as well? *Just Generosity* offers understanding and concrete recommendations of how we can help."

—Gordon England, director of evangelism,
Promise Keepers

"Dispels the myths about poverty with facts and replaces pious rhetoric with practical action."

—Wesley Granberg-Michaelson, general secretary,
Reformed Church in America

"Ron Sider knows how to lift up people in need, transform their lives, and liberate them from material and spiritual poverty. The answers are in his important and challenging book. Ron's message of conquering poverty with spiritual tools cuts across traditional political and social boundaries. He will challenge you to consider what your role should be in helping the poor."

—John Ashcroft, U.S. Senator (R-Missouri)

"Sider has added another poverty-fighting book to the evangelical arsenal."

—Jim Skillen, executive director, Center for Public Justice

"Drawing creatively from both 'conservatives' and 'liberals,' Sider issues a powerful biblical call to end the scandal of widespread poverty in the richest nation on earth."

—David Beckmann, president, Bread for the World

"Asks the toughest and most significant question of all: Do Christians care enough to really do something about poverty? I hope every Christian will read this book and give a resounding answer of YES."

—Jim Wallis, convener, Call to Renewal

"How refreshing! Ron Sider's new book emphasizes the importance of both private and public responsibility in ending poverty. . . . Ron gets the balance right and then shows us how we can make a difference."

—Tony P. Hall, U.S. Congressman (D-Ohio)

"Sider's call for a holistic comprehensive framework is worthy of protracted consideration by those who would be faithful to the Jesus who had a special affection, ministry, and identification with the poor."

—Joan Brown Campbell, general secretary,
National Council of the Churches of Christ in the USA

"Lively, readable, and believable. . . . A convincing and workable answer to the question: What should we do?"

—Harvey Cox, Thomas Professor of Divinity,
Harvard Divinity School

"Ron Sider effectively engages the crucial economic and moral question of our times: How can our poor and marginalized participate in the American Dream? . . . His book not only makes this case but also provides useful examples of how to transform these problems."

—J. McDonald Williams, chairman,
Trammell Crow Company

"In his best book yet, Sider incisively identifies what is right and wrong in the approaches of both the Right and Left to poverty and presents a hopeful vision for a potentially historic ideological convergence."

—Don Eberly, founder, National Fatherhood Initiative

"A provocative and compelling mix of 'liberal' and 'conservative' solutions in presenting specific and comprehensive proposals for combating poverty."

—David Saperstein, director and counsel,
Religious Action Center of Reform Judaism

"Bold and daring proposals that are also practical and comprehensive. This is a must read volume for all Christians who are concerned about overcoming poverty in a rich nation."

—J. Deotis Roberts, research professor of Christian theology,
Duke University Divinity School

"I am excited by his work and look forward to seeing many of his policies implemented."

—Jeremiah A. Wright Jr., senior pastor,
Trinity United Church of Christ

"We have a biblical mandate to do justice. In *Just Generosity*, Ron Sider shows us how."

—Tom Pelton, president, March for Jesus USA

"Caring for the poor, the orphans, widows, prisoners, and homeless of the world is part of the Great Commission. . . . In this controversial book, you will become better acquainted with the poor, whom Jesus loved and with whom he identified."

—Bill Bright, founder and president,
Campus Crusade for Christ International

Just Generosity

A New Vision
for Overcoming Poverty in America

Ronald J. Sider

Foreword by Charles W. Colson
and John J. Dilulio Jr.

Afterword by Eugene F. Rivers, 3rd

Baker Books

A Division of Baker Book House Co
Grand Rapids, Michigan 49516

Published by Baker Books
a division of Baker Book House Company
P.O. Box 6287, Grand Rapids, MI 49516-6287

Printed in the United States of America

Library of Congress Cataloging-in-Publication Data

Sider, Ronald J.
    Just generosity : a new vision for overcoming poverty in America / Ronald J. Sider ; foreword by Charles W. Colson, and John J. DiIulio, Jr. ; afterword by Eugene Rivers.
        p.   cm.
    Includes index.
    ISBN 0-8010-6015-X
    1. Poverty—United States. 2. Poor—United States. 3. Distributive justice.
4. United States—Social conditions. 5. United States—Economic conditions.
6. Economics—Religious aspects—Christianity. I. Title.
HC110.P63S524 1999
362.5'8'0973—dc21   99-16360

Unless otherwise indicated, Scripture quotations are from the Revised Standard Version of the Bible, copyright 1946, 1952, 1971 by the Division of Christian Education of the National Council of the Churches of Christ in the USA. Used by permission.

Scripture quotations identified NCV are from the New Century Version. Copyright © 1987 by Worthy Publishing. Used by permission.

Scripture quotations identified NIV are from the HOLY BIBLE, NEW INTERNATIONAL VERSION®. NIV®. Copyright © 1973, 1978, 1984 by International Bible Society. Used by permission of Zondervan Publishing House. All rights reserved.

Scripture quotations identified NRSV are from the New Revised Standard Version of the Bible, copyright 1989 by the Division of Christian Education of the National Council of the Churches of Christ in the USA. Used by permission.

Figures 1, 2, and 3 are from Rebecca M. Blank, IT TAKES A NATION. Copyright © 1997 by Princeton University Press. Reprinted by permission.

Figure 4 is from Isaac Shapiro and Robert Greenstein, "Trends in the Distribution of After-Tax Income," Center on Budget and Policy Priorities, 14 August 1997. Used by permission.

Figure 6 is from Kathryn Porter, Wendell Primus, Lynette Rawlings, and Esther Rosenbaum, *Strengths of the Safety Net* (Washington, D.C.: Center on Budget and Policy Priorities, 1998). Used by permission.

Figure 7 on p. 122 is reprinted by permission of the publisher from MILES TO GO by Patrick Moynihan, Cambridge, Mass.: Harvard University Press, Copyright © 1996 by the President and Fellows of Harvard College.

All royalties from this book are being donated to charitable causes.

For current information about all releases from Baker Book House, visit our web site:
http://www.bakerbooks.com

To
friends and neighbors
in North Philly and Germantown
who have taught me so much

Contents

Star Power

Foreword: The Least of These, the Rest of Us

"I was hungry and you gave me food, I was thirsty and you gave me something to drink. . . . I was in prison and you visited me. . . . Truly I tell you, just as you did it to one of the least of these who are members of my family, you did it to me" (Matt. 25:35–36, 40 NRSV). "Whoever is kind to the poor lends to the LORD" (Prov. 9:17 NRSV). "Listen, my beloved brothers and sisters. Has not God chosen the poor in the world to be rich in faith and to be heirs of the kingdom that he has promised to those who love him? But you have dishonored the poor" (James 2:5–6 NRSV).

We Americans enter the twenty-first century and the new millennium as the most economically prosperous people in the history of the world. By any historical, comparative, or cross-national measure, we Americans enjoy unprecedented private affluence and enormous national wealth. Despite huge gaps in income and high concentrations of wealth, most poor Americans today "are better housed and better fed and own more personal property than average Americans throughout much of this century."[1] In the light of history, there is a pardonable excessive optimism in the claim that, at least for present-day America's least of these, the "problem of poverty, defined as material scarcity, has been solved."[2] There is, however, no denying that, even today, a significant minority of Americans still struggle to survive under economic conditions that the vast majority of us would consider impoverished and find intolerable were we suddenly forced to trade places with them.

To be sure, America's poverty problem has been, if not solved, then reduced since the mid-1960s because Americans have done ever more to honor the poor. Each year, the country's civil sector, led by the nation's religious charities, congregations, and community-serving ministries, provides billions of dollars in cash assistance and social services for the poor. For example, the average big-city urban religious congregation, during the course of a year, provides over 5,300 hours (or 132 weeks) of volunteer support to needy people, and a total of about $144,000 a year in community programs that primarily serve the poor.[3] The public sector's federal-state anti-poverty programs for children and families (food stamps, Medicaid, and other programs) provide billions of dollars annually in cash assistance and social services for the poor.[4] Thanks to those efforts, by 1996 only 14 percent of all families with children were in poverty (over a third fewer families in poverty than would exist without government aid);[5] and in the year 2002, all persons age nineteen and younger will be eligible if in need for publicly financed health care.[6] Most hopeful, as a result of recent changes in federal law, it is possible that in the first decades of the next century we will witness greater cooperation between government and faith-based social-service delivery and anti-poverty efforts.[7]

We also honor the nation's poor by recognizing that most poor adult Americans are decent, law-abiding citizens who, if given half a chance, will choose work over welfare.[8] Amid a tremendous national economic boom, and with new welfare-to-work laws being implemented in most states, the total number of people on welfare in America fell from 14.1 million in January 1993 to 8.9 million in March 1998 (a 37 percent decline), with many states reporting promising trends in the percentages of former welfare recipients who are finding jobs.[9] Between 1994 and 1998, the welfare rolls in thirty of the largest American cities declined by 35 percent.[10]

Still, as Ronald J. Sider reminds us in this new, important, and provocative book, let no one suppose for a moment that we live in a post-poverty America. Yes, welfare caseloads are down dramatically, but state welfare caseloads are increasingly concentrated in minority big-city neighborhoods that the rest of the society has left behind.[11] Yes, more formerly dependent adults are working, but there is yet a rising tide of child-only welfare cases, "children being raised by grandparents or other relatives because their parents are in jail, are on drugs or have lost custody as a result of abuse or neglect."[12] Yes, recent rates of black poverty are the lowest ever recorded, but about 1 in 5 black children still lives in high-poverty neighborhoods where there are "fewer resources for families, fewer jobs, fewer successful role models . . . , more schools with lower academic achievement, and a greater exposure to crime, drugs, alcohol, and violence."[13] Both of us know this to be true because we encounter it daily in our ministries.

Sider, nationally known as the president of the Philadelphia-based Evangelicals for Social Action, is a politically progressive yet steadfastly prolife evangelical Christian who has spent much of his adult life living and working among and on behalf of the poor. Over the years, and despite the differences of public policy vision and theological understanding we have with him, each of us has gotten to know Sider as a brother in Christ and to admire him as one who practices what he preaches about the biblical imperative to serve the poor.

For decades, Sider has argued forthrightly that prayers and spiritual deliverance, not programs and social service delivery, must be ever at the heart of Christian anti-poverty efforts. "Are we not naive," he asked in 1974, "if we suppose that evangelical social activists will be any more effective than were liberals unless we totally immerse our concern and activity in prayer to the Father? In short, the first agenda item for evangelical social activists in the seventies is prayer."[14] Twenty years later, he lamented that the Christian churches and ministries most engaged in meeting people's material needs "seldom get around to explicitly inviting people to Christ. People do not come to Christ automatically. They come to Christ when the people who serve them also long to share their dearest treasure, Jesus Christ the Savior, and therefore regularly pray for and watch for opportunities to encourage people to believe and obey Him."[15]

"Evangelism," Sider insisted once again in 1997, "is central to social change. Nothing so transforms the self-identity, self-worth, and initiative of a poor, oppressed person as a personal, living relationship with God in Christ."[16] Earlier this year, he recounted "stories of churches leading people to Christ and ministering to the needs of hurting people. I long for the day when every village, town, and city has congregations of Christians so in love with Jesus Christ that they lead scores of people to accept him as personal Savior and Lord every year—and so sensitive to the cry of the poor and oppressed that they work vigorously for justice, peace, and freedom."[17]

Just Generosity: A New Vision for Overcoming Poverty in America is primarily a work of public policy analysis rather than of theological exegesis or of Christian apologetics. Just the same, in this book Sider rightly acknowledges that helping the poor requires both a spiritual and a structural response. His policy-oriented yet deeply Christian perspective on poverty in America is bound to challenge readers of every religious, political, and ideological persuasion. As he writes on page 85, "Especially in the case of persons caught in a destructive environment that makes misguided decisions about drugs, sex, school, and single parenthood extremely easy, religious conversion is important. An inward transformation of values and character produces a radical transformation of outward behavior. While secular agencies and government programs cannot bring about such transformation, evidence clearly indicates that faith-based programs can and do."

As Sider explains, poverty is not the lone or leading cause of America's other social ills, and poverty is often the consequence of an individual's own morally myopic life choices (for example, dropping out of school, experimenting with illegal drugs, having sex outside of marriage, abandoning one's children). Yet, from the streets of north central Philadelphia to the streets of south central Los Angeles, there is no denying what he terms America's "poverty amidst abundance." Each of us would debate or disagree with certain of his empirical analyses and policy prescriptions. In the end, however, we are at one with Sider in his recognition that the problem of poverty in America is not merely economic but existential, not merely social but spiritual.

Whatever our worldly understanding of America's poverty problem, whatever our favorite public policy remedies, Sider's book reminds us that there is no way for us Christian citizens of the Great Republic to honor our faith should we "dishonor the poor," no way for us to share his love should we shirk responsibility for the needy in our very midst. "How does God's love abide in anyone who has the world's goods and sees a brother or sister in need and yet refuses help? Little children, let us love, not in word or speech, but in truth and action" (1 John 3:17–18 NRSV).

As literally hundreds of studies have documented, persons in the custody of the criminal justice system as well as crime victims are disproportionately drawn from low-income populations, especially poor and minority urban populations. In joyful "truth and action," the mission of Prison Fellowship is to exhort, equip, and assist the body of Christ in its ministry to prisoners, ex-prisoners, victims, and their families, and to promote biblical standards of justice in the criminal justice system. In Sider and his new book, we recognize a sharp mind and a kindred Christian spirit dedicated to showing how the rest of us can and should serve the least of these.

Charles W. Colson is founder and chairman of the board of Prison Fellowship (PF), a syndicated radio commentator, author of fifteen books, and winner of the 1993 Templeton Prize for Progress in Religion. John J. DiIulio Jr., a PF board member, is Fox Leadership Professor of Politics, Religion, and Civil Society at the University of Pennsylvania, senior fellow of the Manhattan Institute and the Brookings Institution, and winner of the Kershaw Award of the American Association of Policy Analysis and Management.

Preface

Living among the poor and the lower middle class in North Philadelphia and then the lower Germantown section of Philadelphia for the last thirty years has shaped this book in far more ways than even I understand.

My wife, Arbutus, and I have joined our neighbors to shut down a drug house a few doors up the street. We have added locks and helped organize our block to help residents feel more secure.

We have watched moms and dads do battle with their drug addiction for the sake of their kids. We have held those children in their pain as mom or dad let them down. We have cheered on dramatic transformation rooted in spiritual conversion, and we have watched helpless while others lost the struggle.

We have listened with sadness and resentment as members of our church looked in vain for a job to help them care for their family. We have muttered in anger as cancer suddenly overwhelmed a hardworking and temporarily jobless, and therefore, uninsured fellow elder in our church with $100,000 in medical bills that he knew he could never pay.

We have watched in amazed admiration as some fought incredible odds to obtain an education and a decent future. And we have puzzled over others who seemed paralyzed by inner doubts and invisible demons, unable in spite of encouragement and support to make what seemed like normal efforts at self-help.

We have walked with our two sons as they almost singlehandedly integrated an inner-city public school, talking through their struggles and eventually transferring them to a much more integrated public school. We have also worked hard to help found a private Christian high school in North Philadelphia so struggling families would have an alternative to failing public schools.

We have labored long at crossing racial barriers, growing inner-city churches, and fostering holistic community development. We have worked furiously, prayed frantically, failed frequently, despaired sometimes, and, thank God, on occasion succeeded. We have learned enough to know that overcoming poverty requires more than youthful idealism and a few good ideas—even from my best books.

Since I am an evangelical Protestant (of a distinct Mennonite and Wesleyan flavor), my first instinct has always been to ask what Jesus and biblical revelation have to say to present problems. I believe passionately that the Scriptures, faithfully interpreted and lived, can provide the vision and motivation to dramatically reduce poverty in this richest nation on earth. That is why biblical exploration is central to this book—and why I hope evangelicals will be among the first to wrestle hard with its content.

At the same time, I welcome and expect many readers from a wide variety of other traditions. I am deeply grateful for the many people of goodwill from other religions who are searching for better ways to empower the poor. To a large extent, the framework I work with here is one that anyone committed to a broadly Judeo-Christian understanding can embrace. It is certainly one that Christians generally share.

I know, of course, that different Christian communities approach the Bible in somewhat different ways. A mainline Protestant or a Roman Catholic would not write chapter 2, "A Biblical Foundation," in exactly the way this Anabaptist, Wesleyan, evangelical (teaching at a Baptist seminary) has. At the same time, in my many years of dialogue and cooperation with Catholic, Orthodox, and mainline Protestant Christians, I have regularly found that starting with a biblical foundation is a good way to build common ground. After all, we all believe that God has spoken uniquely and authoritatively through the Bible.

My years of academic study and activist engagement have taught me two other things. First, you have to know more than biblical norms, and second, you must dare to specify concretely what should be done. The Bible does not say a word about whether we should raise the minimum wage or adopt a particular proposal for universal health insurance. We must combine solid, sophisticated socioeconomic analysis with normative biblical principles of justice if we are to formulate wise, effective social policy.

I have also learned—sometimes from painful personal experience—that good Christians don't always get their politics right. Not only are they sometimes dead wrong, they are regularly in vigorous if not angry disagreement. Some conclude that Christians ought to abandon all attempts to make concrete policy suggestions based on biblical faith. We should just stick to general biblical principles. But everybody favors justice in general. It is only when one dares to suggest that perhaps biblical principles require public policies that strengthen two-parent families, implement universal health insurance, make divorce far more difficult, and enforce a living wage that one becomes helpful to real people trying to figure out how to vote and speak to their politicians. At that point, too, of course, one becomes controversial. Good Christians disagree about those things.

Knowing all that, I have nonetheless presumed to include in this book not just as careful a discussion of biblical norms as I can manage, but also (even though I am a theologian) careful grappling with the best socioeconomic data available from both liberals and conservatives. And then I have even dared to spell out a concrete set of proposals for a new social policy that I truly believe could dramatically reduce poverty.

Do I think you are morally degenerate or un-Christian if you disagree with my specific proposals? Not at all. But please don't call me names. Just explain clearly to me how the normative biblical framework I spell out is not adequately scriptural, or that I have misread the socioeconomic data, or that my combination of the norms and the data to arrive at concrete conclusions really does not follow from the norms and the data.

Above all, remember that I by no means claim the same authority for these three levels of discussion. I would want to make the strongest claims for the biblical framework, although I am painfully aware that this finite, imperfectly sanctified Christian seriously misunderstands parts of the Bible. I would, of course, gladly correct any distortions if I knew where they were because my deepest desire is unconditional submission to Jesus Christ and Scripture.

I offer my socioeconomic analysis with still more qualification. I am not a trained economist or sociologist, although I try hard to listen to the best data, even when it challenges my prejudices.

I want my readers to view my specific policy proposals still more tentatively than my sketch of the biblical framework and discussion of the socioeconomic data. Until others help me see why the specific proposals are misguided, however, I will work hard to implement them, because God probably knew what he was doing when he asked finite, imperfect sons and daughters to be his stewards in shaping societies that feed the hungry, clothe the naked, and heal the sick. Together, let's figure out how to do that more justly and more wisely in the next century than we have in the past.

Acknowledgments

Every book is a cooperative effort. In this case, however, an unusually large number of people have made significant contributions.

Without Patricia Bauman and the Bauman Foundation, this book never would have seen the light of day. The generous support of the Bauman Foundation made possible a two-year process, bringing together approximately twenty scholars to ask one basic question: If this society chose to empower the poor in the United States, what would a successful, comprehensive agenda look like? The result is the scholarly volume titled *Toward a Just and Caring Society: Christian Responses to Poverty in America*, edited by David P. Gushee and published simultaneously with this more popularly written book, *Just Generosity*.

To all of my colleagues who wrote the scholarly articles for *Toward a Just and Caring Society* and thereby provided invaluable research for the present book, I say a special thanks: Stephen Charles Mott, Stephen V. Monsma, James Halteman, Ashley Woodiwiss, Kurt C. Schaefer, George N. Monsma, Timothy Slaper, Clarke E. Cochran, John E. Anderson, Charles L. Glenn, John D. Mason, Helene Slessarev, Joseph A. Maciariello, Stanley W. Carlson-Thies, and David P. Gushee. My good friend Dave Gushee worked long and superbly administering the project and editing the scholarly volume.

Several groups of people provided much-appreciated feedback on an early draft of the manuscript. Mary Jo Bane and Richard Parker from the Kennedy School of Government and Jim Wallis and Brent B. Coffin from the Center for the Study of Values in Public Life spent several hours one spring afternoon at Harvard providing invaluable critique. Tom Atwood, Deanna Carlson, Jennifer Marshall, Robert W. Patterson, Bob Morrison, and Alan Crippen provided lunch and very stimulating discussion of the manuscript at the Family Research Council in Washington. Bread for the World's president David Beckmann and seven of his colleagues (Jim Riker, Joel Underwood, Kim Wade, Lynette Engelhardt, Elena McCollim, Alice Benson, and Barbara Howell) read various chapters and offered probing questions and suggestions during a lively exchange at their office. My active participation with Jim Wallis, Duane Shank, and many other good friends in Call to Renewal has also contributed significantly to my developing thought and provided a setting to hammer out some of the concrete policy proposals.

A large number of scholars and friends commented on one or more of the various chapters and/or provided suggestions: William Lockhart, Rick Chamiec-Case, Amy Sherman, Paul Gorman, David Richardson, Lawrence K. Jensen, Wesley Nord, Wendell Primus, Phyllis Bennett, Andrea Beck, John E. Stapleford, Cathy Brechtelsbauer, Diana R. Garland, Art Simon, Dwight Ozard, Janis Balda, John L. Carr, Don Hammond, Harry A. Dawkins III, and Janet E. de Young.

I owe a special debt to John J. DiIulio Jr., who has become a special friend and treasured colleague. Even in a frantically busy schedule, he found time to offer counsel on almost everything connected with this book, including a critique of the manuscript. John, a very special thanks.

I am especially grateful for the people who agreed to let me tell their stories or helped point me to the stories of others: Ron Tinsley, Bob George, Wayne Gordon, Mary Nelson, Onita Styles, Brian Mast, Skip Long, Nefretiri Cooley, Carl Holland, Kathy Dudley, Maria Rodriguez-Winter—and those who remain anonymous.

A special word of appreciation to my friends at Baker Book House. It was publisher Dwight Baker's personal interest in the things I have felt called to write about that sealed my interest in publishing with Baker Books. Editors Bob Hosack and Melinda Van Engen have become friends and much-appreciated partners in all the details of bringing a book to press.

For twenty-one years, Eastern Seminary has provided a supportive friendly "home base" for my ministry of teaching, writing, lecturing, and organizing. This and many other books I have written would have been much more difficult if not impossible had I not enjoyed supportive understanding of the many demands on my time. To President Scott Rodin, Dean

Eric Ohlmann, former president Manfred Brauch, and faculty colleagues, I say a special thanks.

For twenty-six years, Evangelicals for Social Action has played a central role in my life. Without ESA's outstanding staff, this book and so many things I do simply would not be possible. Cliff Benzel, ESA's executive vice president, has been an invaluable partner and very dear friend the last six wonderful years as God has allowed us to work closely together. The sacrificial gift of his wisdom and talents to the ministry of ESA will be forever appreciated. To all my other colleagues at ESA (Monya Cooper, Phil Olson, Rodney Clapp, Fred Clark, Stan LeQuire, Scott Althouse, and Ed Jeffcoat) I express appreciation for your partnership in this book and much more.

My research assistants, Merid Seifu and Joan Hoppe-Spink, have been faithful in tracking down a host of pesky details. Naomi Miller, my gifted secretary/administrative assistant for sixteen years, not only demonstrated her near flawless mastery of my original handwritten text as she typed and retyped the manuscript but also managed to continue her friendly, highly competent management of much of my public life.

To my wife, Arbutus, with whom I have now shared not only thirty-eight wonderful years of marriage but a mutual passion to share God's concern for the needy, I say thank you, darling, for all the ways you have encouraged my ministry and brought joy to my life.

None of the above are responsible for the mistakes that remain in this book, but they certainly have helped me avoid and/or repent of many that would otherwise be present.

Introduction

What would it be like to live in the United States on $16,530 a year? That's the poverty level for a family of four. In the richest nation on earth, 36 million people struggle to survive at or below this level.

Try to imagine what your family, or the family of four you know best, would need to give up to exist on $16,530 a year.

Begin by selling your house and moving to a modest two-bedroom apartment ($525 a month including heat). No more study, rec room, bedroom for each child, second bathroom, backyard, or porch. If you are willing to live in a lower-income, multiracial neighborhood, you might be able to buy a small house.

Next, sell all your cars. You don't have a garage anyway. You can get around on public transportation, or perhaps you can afford an old car, if you have a friend who can make necessary repairs and you purchase only liability insurance. Either way, you will be able to spend only $45 a week on transportation.[1]

Forget about being in fashion. New clothes each season are unthinkable; Nike sneakers are out of the question. If you visit the local thrift store for most things, buy sturdy shoes, and use winter coats for several years, you can probably get by on $380 per person per year.

You will no longer be able to afford to eat at restaurants.

You will have to figure out how to avoid hunger and stay healthy on just a little more than $1 per meal for each person.

No more regular telephone calls to Grandma, other relatives, or friends in other cities. Your telephone budget is just $25 a month. And be sure to turn off the lights when you leave a room because you have only $40 a month for all utilities not included in your rent.

Let's look at the totals.

Table 1

Living at the Poverty Level (Family of Four)

housing	6,300
utilities	780
food	4,800
transportation	2,340
clothing	1,520
Social Security taxes	788
(for a full-time worker earning minimum wage)	
	16,528

What is the total? $16,528. The 1998 poverty level was about $16,530, so you have two dollars for a call to Grandma once a year on her birthday.

Notice what this budget does *not* include. No household appliances, no vacations, no toiletries, no birthday or Christmas gifts, no recreation, no visits to the dentist, no private health insurance, no donations for church, no child care, no movies, no travel outside the city, no private music lessons, no sports equipment for the children. Poor people, of course, do have some of these things. However unthinkable from a middle-class perspective, somehow they manage to spend less on some of the other items or receive help from family, friends, or church.

Any volunteers? No, I don't mean for three years of graduate school while you prepare for a secure middle-class livelihood. I mean year after year with little hope for improvement. That's what millions of our neighbors struggle with in our affluent nation.

Life at the poverty level is tough. In addition to scraping by financially, poor people feel excluded from the community. Many poor people face terrible schools, widespread crime, and a lack of quality health care. More than 43 million persons in the United States do not even have health insurance.

That's the bad news. But the bad news gets even worse when we realize that many of our best people in public policy now acknowledge that they do not know how to reduce poverty and the related escalation of single parenthood, inner-city crime, and failing urban schools. At the end of a powerful book outlining the inadequacy of U.S. social policy of the last several decades, Senator Daniel Moynihan confesses: "The problem . . . is that no one has a clue as to what it would take for public policy to be *sufficient*."[2] Both the liberal and the conservative policies of the past few decades have failed to solve the problem of poverty in the richest nation in the world.

The good news is that both liberals and conservatives seem ready to try something new. Both sides seem eager to explore a holistic approach that enables people of deep religious faith to contribute what they do best to solving social decay and poverty. In the media, in Washington think tanks, and in the halls of Congress, religion is suddenly "in." Religion's role in public policy is the hottest topic at Harvard's Kennedy School of Government.

The most striking illustration of this astonishing change can be found in the June 1, 1998, issue of *Newsweek* with Rev. Eugene Rivers on the cover. The caption? "God vs. Gangs." Inside, *Newsweek* reporters relate the remarkable story of how Rivers's TenPoint Coalition in Boston has dramatically reduced gang violence through a combination of prayer and faith in action in the streets. Just perhaps, the story suggests, God, religious transformation, and people of faith can succeed where several decades of government programs have failed miserably.

Is that good news? Certainly not if people conclude that government can slash social programs because religious institutions will take care of all the problems. That is simply nonsense. There is, however, another possibility. The present situation offers an unusually fluid moment when this nation has the opportunity to work out a new vision of how religious institutions, government, and other sectors of society can best work together. If we can come up with the right approach to helping the poor in which churches and other faith communities, businesses, the media, and government all contribute what each does best, we could dramatically reduce poverty.

Why is the right combination so important? Because of human nature. For several decades, secular policy elites have, explicitly or implicitly, worked on the assumption that persons are essentially economic/materialistic machines. Both liberals and conservatives thought that all we had to do to get the right behavior was switch the economic incentives and change the external environment. Just increase (or decrease) welfare payments, raise (or lower) the minimum wage, and subsidize more (or less) low-income housing and we can produce the desired behavior. People immersed in the Judeo-Christian tradition know this is much too simplistic. The Bible clearly teaches that persons are both spiritual and material beings. Both unjust social structures and bad moral choices together create social problems. Solutions, therefore, require both inner, moral, spiritual change and outer, socioeconomic, structural change.

The good news is that for the first time in decades, the larger institutions of society are astonishingly ready to welcome the contribution of religion to solving our most desperate social problems. Christians and other people of faith have a historic opportunity that has not existed for decades.

To seize this opportunity, we need a comprehensive, holistic vision of how to overcome the complex problems of intolerable poverty in our country today. We must combine a biblical framework of values with careful social analysis to create a holistic vision and an effective, comprehensive agenda of integrated policy proposals for reducing poverty. Of equal if not more importance, we must motivate millions of Christians—and other people of faith as well—to care as much about the poor as Jesus did. Only then will we have enough generous, compassionate citizens to implement what biblical faith and empirical analysis demand.

A quick comparison of *Just Generosity* with three earlier influential books on poverty in the United States underlines the unique approach of *Just Generosity.*

In 1962, Michael Harrington published a book that is widely credited with significantly influencing the Kennedy-Johnson War on Poverty. In *The Other America,* Harrington focused on the structural and environmental causes of poverty and concluded that "there is only one institution in the society capable of acting to abolish poverty. That is the Federal Government." A private, charitable approach simply "does not work."[3] There is not a hint in Harrington's liberal analysis that faith-based strategies might be helpful. Harrington understood that the broken families and broken spirits of the poor would make it difficult to overcome the "culture of poverty," but his only hope was government. For a decade and more, our brightest policy specialists in Washington and our top universities shared Harrington's optimistic belief that the right government policies could end poverty.

By the early eighties, this liberal dream was collapsing. In fact, conservative analyst Charles Murray argued in *Losing Ground* (1984) that the expensive government programs had actually made things much worse.[4] Government policy had been offering all the wrong incentives and disincentives. Welfare grants, food stamps, lenient courts, and affirmative action programs offered incentives that undermined the family, increased crime, and weakened responsibility and work. His solution? Different *government* policies! Just abolish welfare payments, food stamps, and so on, and force people to make it by their own effort.

In 1992, an evangelical journalist offered a different approach. In *The Tragedy of American Compassion,* a book that Republican Speaker Newt Gingrich was soon to warmly endorse, Marvin Olasky argued that American social history proves that private, charitable, faith-based programs are the best way to reduce poverty.[5] That, I believe, was an important contribution to the debate. But in his discussion of the causes of poverty, Olasky stresses the misguided choices and destructive behaviors of the poor with hardly a hint that structural, economic factors might also be important.

Just Generosity builds on and offers an alternative vision to Harrington, Murray, and Olasky. To point only to structural causes and governmental solutions (whether in a liberal or a conservative vein) is just as one-sided as emphasizing only the moral and spiritual causes and solutions. Olasky is half right and his partial truth is important—but economic, structural factors are also crucial. It is time for a comprehensive, integrated vision that gets beyond the one-sided analyses and programs that clearly have failed.

This book seeks to define the problem of poverty, sketch a biblical framework within which to address the issue, outline a comprehensive vision for addressing it, and then develop a concrete agenda for ending the scandal of widespread poverty in the richest nation on earth.

Part 1

Poverty
amidst Abundance

1

What Does Poverty Look Like?

> How would I feel if I were a poor person living in the richest nation on earth and knew my comfortable neighbors simply did not care enough to offer me real opportunity?

In the United States, over 35,000,000 people live in poverty in the richest society in human history.[1] Their income actually dropped form 1974 to 1996. That is true both in comparison to the well-to-do majority and also in absolute terms. From 1974 to 1996, the bottom 20 percent lost 10 percent in real income (i.e., after taking inflation into account). The top 20 percent gained 39 percent, and the top 5 percent gained 65 percent.

Who are the poor? Where do they live? What causes poverty in this land of unprecedented abundance?

Mrs. Onita Styles is a sixty-eight-year-old widow living in Dallas, Texas. In early 1997, she was in despair. The house that she and her deceased husband had owned since 1944 was collapsing around her, and she was barely able to survive on her monthly Social Security check.

Mrs. Styles had worked in the kitchen and laundry in two Dallas hotels for over twenty years, but when her employers discovered she had developed serious lead poisoning from the cleaning fluid used to polish the silverware, she was forced to leave. After that, she struggled but usually found full-time work in private homes, cooking and cleaning. Still, her modest income was not enough to keep her house in good repair. So in the early 1980s, Mrs. Styles took out a $3,500 loan from a nonprofit organization that contracted to do much-needed repairs. The company began the repairs, pulling up the floor, but never completed the job. Unfortunately, they never returned any of the money! When that organization went out of business, the city took over the loan. Tragically, Mrs. Styles did not know her way through the system well enough to renegotiate the loan. She just kept making monthly payments as her house got worse and worse.

When my friend Kathy Dudley of the Dallas Leadership Foundation first visited Mrs. Styles in early 1997, her house was a wreck. The foundation was collapsing. Sections of the floor had rotted. The walls and ceiling were cracked. The tub and toilet had sunk below the floor level and were unusable, and there was no running water. Mrs. Styles cooked with a hot plate and carried water in gallon jugs from a neighbor's house.

That's what poverty means to one of our 36,000,000 poor neighbors. Fortunately, this story has a happy ending.[2] Volunteers mobilized by Kathy's Dallas Leadership Foundation gave over $50,000 and hundreds of hours of donated labor to renovate Mrs. Styles's home in 1998. Most of the poor are not that fortunate.

In 1997, 35.6 million persons—13.3 percent of the U.S. population—fell below the official poverty line. For a married couple with two children, the poverty level in 1998 was $16,530.[3] This seems like a lot of money. In fact, it is if you compare it to the one dollar a day on which 1.3 billion people in the developing world live. On the other hand, the mean family income in the United States in 1997 was $56,902![4] I explained in the introduction what it means to scrape by on $16,530 a year in the United States. Financially, it means stretching every penny and having no budget for many things such as furniture, vacations, recreation, private health insurance, and so on that most of us take for granted. Poor people, of course, do have some of these things. Somehow, they manage to spend less on food and housing, beg from family and friends, or do part-time work that is never reported to the IRS.

This is what it means financially to live *at* the official U.S. poverty level. The vast majority of the 36 million people in the United States who are poor live *below* the poverty level. Forty percent of all poor families have incomes under 50 percent of the poverty level.[5] Imagine a family of four living on $8,265 a year!

There are weaknesses, as many scholars have shown, in the way the government calculates the official poverty rate.[6] The official calculation does not count noncash benefits such as food stamps (it should). Nor does it deduct taxes (it should also do that). Using a more precise measure of poverty recommended by the National Academy of Sciences, the poverty rate would be a little lower—11.5 percent (1996).[7] But that still adds up to 30.5 million poor persons in ever more affluent America.

Almost anybody reading this book would find it almost unthinkable to care for a family of four on $16,530 a year. Whether the number of people trapped in that agony is 30 million or 36 million, it is fundamentally unacceptable for anybody who cares about God's concern for the poor.[8] Even if there were only 15 million, that kind of poverty in the richest nation on earth is morally intolerable.

Living at the official U.S. poverty level also means poorer education, higher risk of crime, lower self-esteem, and for many, no health insurance—and the fear that if illness strikes, one may not receive proper medical treatment. In 1997, 43.4 million people in the United States had no health insurance. Twenty-seven percent of the uninsured were poor. More than half of all workers who worked full-time but still fell below the poverty level in 1996 lacked health insurance.[9] Poverty is dangerous to one's health.

Sam and Jane Mitchell are hardworking people whose British ancestors came to this country over 150 years ago.[10] For decades, Sam and Jane worked hard and acted responsibly, but they still ended up with a huge medical bill they simply cannot repay.

Sam and Jane both enjoyed excellent health for most of their thirty-six years of marriage. Their modest income did not allow many luxuries, but they raised their two children, helped both finish college, and slowly paid off the mortgage on a nice little house they had lived in for twenty-five years.

Since 1986, they have operated a small furniture repair business. Until 1991, they were able to purchase health insurance, but after that they simply could not afford the escalating premiums on their modest income. When the premiums reached $800 a month, they simply had to drop their coverage.

Last year, disaster struck. The doctors discovered that Sam had cancer. Within twelve months, their medical debt climbed to $37,000. Sam and Jane have always paid their bills faithfully, so a huge debt weighed heavily on them. There was no way they or their children could pay off this high medical bill—and there will almost certainly be additional medical bills they cannot pay because at fifty-seven, Sam has eight more years before he is eligible for Medicare.[11]

Does our rich society really want to allow millions of hardworking poor people like Sam and Jane to struggle with that kind of agony?

Who Are the Poor?

Mention poverty and many people in the United States instantly think of a single, black mom living in an urban ghetto with a bunch of little kids. Wrong.

Only 12 percent of the poor live in urban ghettos; only 27 percent are African American. In reality, 34.9 percent of the poor live in families headed by a married couple.[12] Twenty percent of poor families have an adult working full-time year-round, and still they live in poverty.[13] 37.2 percent of all poor children in the United States live in a family in which at least one parent is working full-time.[14]

The elderly used to suffer the highest poverty rates (see fig. 1). Now it is our children. In 1960, one-third of the elderly were poor. Now—thanks to Social Security and SSI—only about 9 percent are poor.[15] But 20.5 percent of all our children—that means 14.5 million!—live in poverty.[16]

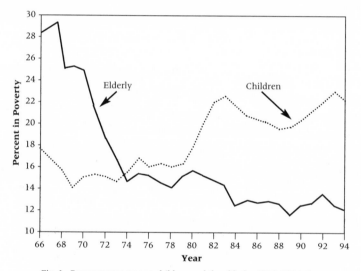

Fig. 1. Poverty rates among children and the elderly, 1966–1994. *Source:* U.S. Bureau of the Census, 1995a,b, from Rebecca M. Blank, *It Takes a Nation: A New Agenda for Fighting Poverty* (Princeton, N.J.: Princeton Univ. Press, 1997), 19.

Thirty years ago, half of the poor lived in rural areas. Today, only 25 percent do. Poverty is growing fairly rapidly in the suburbs (especially the inner suburbs) where 33 percent of the poor now live. The largest group live in our cities (43 percent), mostly in mixed-income neighborhoods. Only 12 percent of the poor live in urban ghettos—defined as an area in which at least 40 percent of all the residents are poor.[17]

Mr. and Mrs. Perez live in Maricopa County, Arizona—one of the fastest-growing counties in the United States—filled with million-dollar houses, manicured golf courses, and magnificent malls. But the Perez family lives in Maricopa County's Guadalupe, a very poor town populated mostly by Yaqui Indians and Latinos, tucked in between wealthy neighbors like Phoenix, Tempe, Paradise Valley, and Scottsdale.

The Perez family lives in a shack of the sort we expect to see only in a poor third-world country. The walls are old doors, tar paper, chicken wire, and rotting boards. The ground provides a dirt floor. There is no bathroom, no running water, no electricity, no heat. Their toilet is a reeking outhouse across the street.

Andrew Cuomo, the U.S. Secretary of Housing and Urban Development, visited the Perez's dilapidated home recently. He wanted to dramatize his plea to comfortable Americans to use this time of fantastic economic boom and the largest budget surplus in our history to reach out to those left behind in hidden places in Appalachia, Indian reservations, inner cities, and poverty-stricken towns tucked away in the middle of an affluent country.

Before he left, Cuomo asked Mrs. Perez if she had ever heard of the Dow Jones stock index, which had just roared past 10,000. "The Dow Jones?" she asked. "What does that mean?"[18]

Although less than half of the poor are black and Latino, poverty rates for minorities are more than double those for whites. 28.4 percent of all African Americans and 29.4 percent of all Latinos were poor in 1996, while only 11.2 percent of whites were poor.[19]

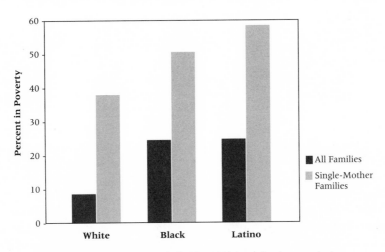

Fig. 2. Poverty rates by race and ethnicity, 1994, in total and among single-mother families. *Source:* U.S. Bureau of the Census, 1995b, from Rebecca M. Blank, *It Takes a Nation: A New Agenda for Fighting Poverty* (Princeton, N.J.: Princeton Univ. Press, 1997), 19.

The largest single block of poor people (43 percent) live in single-parent families with children. Twenty-two percent of the poor are single adults not living with children. But that still leaves one-third (35 percent) of all the poor living in married-couple families.[20] Figure 2 underlines the close connection between single parenthood and poverty. In 1996, only 8.7 percent of all married-couple families were poor, but 44.3 percent of all female-headed households with children were in poverty.[21] And the rates were even higher for single moms who are black (45 percent) and Latino (49 percent).[22] This important correlation between poverty and single parenthood is one we will explore in more depth in chapter 5.

The length of time a person or family experiences poverty significantly determines how much harm poverty causes. At any given time, about 6 percent of the poor are full-time students freely choosing a *temporarily* low income for future gain.[23] A recent study showed that from 1979 to 1991, 66.4 percent of all people in the United States were never poor. Seventeen percent were poor for only one to three years. Only 5 percent experienced poverty for ten or more years. The figures, unfortunately, are radically different for African Americans. Almost two-thirds of all African Americans—but only one-quarter of whites—suffer at least one year of poverty. Seventeen percent of all blacks—but only 2 percent of whites—struggle with poverty for ten or more years.[24]

Is Poverty a Myth?

The picture just outlined reflects the mainstream analysis of U.S. poverty today. But some, especially Robert Rector at the Heritage Foundation, have argued that the notion of widespread poverty in America is a myth. If poverty means not having enough nutritious food, clothing, and a place to live, according to Rector, "There are few poor persons remaining in the United States."[25]

Rector cites much interesting data from U.S. government agencies about people below the official poverty line. In 1995, 41 percent of poor households owned their own homes. Seventy percent of poor households owned a car. Ninety-seven percent had a color TV, and two-thirds had air conditioning. *Poor* Americans have a lot more living space per person than the *average* person in Paris, Athens, Tokyo, or Warsaw. On average, poor children in the United States consume about the same amount of protein, vitamins, and minerals as middle-class children. Poor women are more likely to be overweight than middle-class women.

The Census Bureau (which develops the figures on poverty rates) only counts cash income. Using these figures, the lowest fifth of all households received $8,350 in income in 1995. But the U.S. Department of Labor reported in 1995 that the lowest fifth of all households actually spent $14,607—indicating substantial unreported income. Furthermore, the Labor Department does not include housing subsidies and government medical programs. If those are added, the total "expenditures" of the bottom fifth of households rises to $20,335 in 1995. Hardly poverty, Rector concludes.

The real problem, Rector argues, is "behavioral poverty"—single parenthood, a declining work ethic, and accompanying social decay due to drugs and crime. In *America's Failed $5.4 Trillion War on Poverty,* Rector argues that it is precisely the government's anti-poverty (welfare) programs that have destroyed the family, the work ethic, and poor communities.[26]

Finally, Rector claims that the anti-poverty programs have not reduced poverty. Testifying before Congress, he said, "Since the onset of the War on Poverty, the U.S. has spent over $5.3 trillion on welfare. But during the same period, the official poverty rate has remained virtually unchanged."[27]

Is Rector right? His statistics are largely accurate—provided one understands that he is talking not only about what people popularly mean by "welfare" but rather about all means-tested programs (i.e., all programs in which the amount of the grant or service depends on the person's income and/or assets). But his argument is internally inconsistent, he ignores important data, and his conclusions are fundamentally flawed.

For starters, Rector's use of the word *welfare* is not accurate. Most people use that word to refer to the old Aid to Families with Dependent Children plus related housing, job training, medical, and food stamps benefits. *All* those programs together make up one-quarter of the cost of all federal means-tested entitlement programs. Government spending for low-income elderly and disabled—which few people consider welfare or want to abolish—makes up almost one-half of all means-tested entitlement costs. Furthermore, many means-tested programs provide benefits to people above the poverty level.[28] Rector's language confuses rather than clarifies.

Second, even if there were only a third or a quarter as many people living in poverty as the official figures suggest, it would still be a tragic injustice that we must correct rather than explain away. According to Rector himself, however, one-fifth of all households spent only $14,607 in 1995. That means—according to his calculations—that tens of millions of our neighbors in this rich land were at or below the official poverty level, which as we have seen means incredible hardship.

Third, Rector wants to include government medical programs in his calculation of income for the poor. We could do that, but then we would also have to raise the poverty level by the same amount.[29] When middle-class citizens calculate their income for the IRS, they do not include health insurance premiums paid by their employers. Poverty guidelines have never taken health care into account.[30] Therefore, adding medical assistance to the income of the poor confuses and distorts the discussion.

Fourth, Rector's charge that the official poverty level has remained "virtually unchanged" since the beginning of the War on Poverty in 1964 is simply untrue. It fell dramatically from 1964 to 1973 and then increased when the economy ran into trouble and President Reagan reduced benefits for the poor (see p. 39).

Fifth, Rector's blanket attack on government anti-poverty programs is simplistic and blind to careful research data. Some government programs have failed, but Rector blatantly ignores data that demonstrates that some have been highly effective. The Earned Income Tax Credit *increases* work effort (see p. 104). Serious malnutrition has largely disappeared in this country precisely because of food stamps, the Women-Infant-Children feeding program (WIC), and other government nutrition programs. In fact, every federal dollar spent on prenatal care for mothers in the WIC program saves from $1.77 to $3.13 in Medicaid costs.[31] Without Social Security, 50 percent of all elderly Americans today would be mired in poverty. Thanks to Social Security, less than 10 percent are poor.[32] Because of government programs, especially Medicaid, the poor receive much better medical care than they did thirty years ago, and they are healthier.[33]

Sixth, the millions of poor neighbors living in households that Rector himself says spent only $14,607 in 1995 had this much income in part because of the very government programs that Rector denounces and wants to abolish. It is an astonishing argument to call for abolishing anti-poverty programs because there is allegedly no poverty when in fact it is precisely those very programs that have significantly reduced poverty.

Part of Rector's concern, to be sure, is valid and important. There is a tragic correlation between single parenthood, poverty, and a long list of social disorders that liberals have too often ignored. We must face this reality honestly.

To imply, however, that the entire government effort to combat poverty in the last thirty years has been a disaster is plainly false. So is the suggestion that the problem of poverty has essentially disappeared in the United States. Until Mr. Rector is ready to have his family join the bottom one-fifth of households who, he calculates, have $14,607 a year, we need not take seriously his suggestion that living at the official poverty level is not much of a hardship.

What Causes Poverty?

In the last few decades, political liberals and conservatives have fought harsh ideological battles over the causes of poverty. Liberals traditionally argued that structural changes and systematic injustice caused most poverty. They explained how globalization, technological change, and the shift from a manufacturing to a service and information economy reduced the demand for low-skill, well-paying jobs. Robots and machines replaced many factory workers. When possible, companies moved labor-intensive operations to developing countries where wages were dramatically lower. In addition, many jobs moved from central cities to the suburbs. Suburban industrial parks replaced crowded factories in decaying urban neighborhoods. Retail jobs moved to new suburban malls, and new suburban office complexes emerged closer to suburbanites' homes. Since public transportation to suburban locations was inadequate and the urban poor often lacked cars, there were simply not enough good jobs available to the urban poor.[34] Woven through everything else was continuing racism.

Conservatives disagreed.[35] Poverty has resulted from wrong moral choices exacerbated by bad government policy. They loved to point out that only a very small percentage of those who finished high school and avoided having children out of wedlock were poor. Soaring illegitimate births, divorce rates, and single-parent families—along with bad choices about drugs, alcohol, work, and sex—were the primary causes of poverty. And generous government welfare programs that allowed the state to replace fathers as the breadwinners simply made things worse.

Who is right? Both are partly right. I have lived and worshiped with the poor far too long to side either with the liberal who quickly dismisses the way personal choices contribute to poverty or with the conservative who ignores the way complicated structural barriers make it difficult for many hardworking people to escape poverty. If your factory closes because global economic forces prompted management to move production to Mexico and you can only find a much-lower-paying job, the problem is not lack of personal responsibility. On the other hand, if you lose your job because of poor work habits, drugs, or alcohol, personal choices are more clearly central to the problem. What Harvard's distinguished African American scholar Henry Louis Gates Jr. says of the black community is generally true across racial lines today in the United States: "The causes of poverty within the black community are both structural and behavioral."[36]

It is also essential to see how these two sets of causes are intertwined. In a recent essay, Glenn Loury rejects liberal attempts to explain inner-city poverty and inequality between blacks and whites exclusively or primarily in terms of economic factors, arguing that social and cultural factors are also important. But Loury insists that a long history of unjust political, economic, and racist structures are tightly interrelated with unhelpful cultural and behavioral patterns today.[37] William Julius Wilson, on the other hand, is more inclined to emphasize the economic causes of inner-city poverty, but he also insists that "there is much that these factors do not explain."

"Cultural factors do play a role. . . . We need a broader vision that includes *all* of the major variables."[38]

I will argue that there are four broad causes of poverty: structural causes; personal decisions and misguided behavioral patterns; sudden catastrophes; and permanent disabilities. When analyzing nonstructural causes of poverty, it is important to distinguish between a basically healthy family who experiences a temporary setback (e.g., because of the death or extended illness of the breadwinner) and a family that has a complex set of destructive behaviors (e.g., drug use, abuse of alcohol, poor school performance, out-of-wedlock births, violence) and remains mired in poverty for years. We can help the first family with short-term cash assistance, job training, and new work opportunities. In fact, over 50 percent of all people who ever get public welfare receive it for three years or less, and 27 percent use it for only one year or less.[39] The average length of time a family spends on welfare is approximately two years. Temporary assistance helps them move on to self-sufficiency. Twenty-three percent of all welfare recipients, however, stay on welfare for ten or more years. Over 50 percent of the heads of households below the poverty line are not working at all.[40] The multiple causes of their poverty go well beyond temporary setbacks, and a long-term solution will require personal transformation as well as structural change and temporary assistance.

Structural Causes

Decreasing number of low-skill, well-paying jobs. Harvard sociologist William Julius Wilson is surely correct in seeing the loss of low-skill, decent-paying jobs as one major cause of poverty. Many formerly well-paying, low-skill, blue-collar jobs have moved to Mexico or China, and new service sector jobs often do not pay enough to support a family. Many employers have moved to the suburbs, but the public transportation system was not designed to enable inner-city residents to travel easily to such locations. The lack of jobs that pay a family wage, Wilson rightly argues, helps create absent fathers, increasing violence, and general social decay.[41]

Falling wages. Changes in the global economy and technological changes that caused people to be replaced with machines have also produced falling wages for low-skilled persons. Wages for men without a college degree have fallen dramatically in the last twenty years even when such men work full-time all year. From 1979 to 1993, high school male dropouts saw a 22.5 percent decrease in average weekly wages; high school graduates, an 11.9 percent decrease (see fig. 3). Even men with some post-high-school training lost 5.3 percent of their wages. On the other hand, college-educated men gained almost 10 percent, and those with a graduate degree enjoyed an increase of 22 percent.[42] The unemployment rate (which counts only people actively looking for work) is five times higher for high school dropouts than for college graduates.

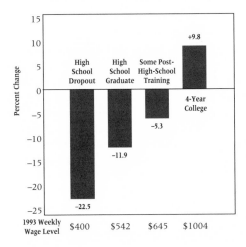

Fig. 3. Percent change in men's average weekly wages, for full-time, full-year workers, 1979–1993. *Source:* Rebecca M. Blank's tabulations from 1980 and 1994, March Current Population Surveys; *It Takes a Nation: A New Agenda for Fighting Poverty* (Princeton, N.J.: Princeton Univ. Press, 1997), 62.

Women have not fared as badly. Female high school dropouts saw a 6 percent decrease in their wages from 1979 to 1993. But female graduates gained a little (6 percent), those with some additional training gained more (11 percent), and female college graduates enjoyed a 27 percent increase in weekly wages.[43]

A growing economy no longer helps the less educated—especially men. The contrast between two similar periods of large economic growth is striking. In the 1960s, wages for everyone increased dramatically, and the poverty rate dropped from 22 percent to 13 percent. Every 1 percent expansion of the economy saw a jump in weekly wages of $2.18 for workers in low-income families. The economy expanded in a similar way from 1983 to 1989, but the poverty rate hardly declined at all. Even though people worked more hours, weekly wages for the poorest 18 percent actually *dropped* 32 cents for every 1 percent *increase* in the economy. The reason? Falling wages for less-skilled workers.[44]

Not surprisingly, low-skilled men are simply not working as much as in the past. In 1970, 86.8 percent of all male high school dropouts were working or looking for work. By 1993, the number was only 72.3 percent. The trend for women is slightly different. Female high school dropouts earned less per week in 1993 than in 1970, but there was a slight increase (1.6 percent) in the number of those working. But female college grads, who were earning much more in 1993, were also far more likely (18.3 percent) to be working. Low pay discourages work.[45]

Why this dramatic decline in wages for low-skilled people? We have already noted several crucial factors. Because of technological changes, machines have replaced many low-skilled workers, so businesses need fewer such workers. Because of the globalization of the economy, low-skilled American workers are competing with workers in China, Indonesia, or Mexico, where salaries are vastly lower.[46]

Minimum wage. The falling real value of the minimum wage is another structural cause of poverty. When the minimum wage remains the same while inflation reduces each dollar's purchasing power, the real value of the minimum wage falls lower and lower. In both 1968 and 1975, a full-time, year-round worker paid at the minimum wage earned a salary at least equal to the poverty level for a family of three. By 1991, that same person's wages were only 74 percent of the poverty level, and in 1997, that same full-time worker's wages were just 84 percent of the poverty level.[47]

One implication of falling wages for workers with low skills and, consequently, increasing poverty, is clear: It is no longer possible to solve the problem of poverty for less-educated people simply by expanding the economy. There are simply not enough jobs available that pay a family wage.

Welfare. The worsening situation for the poorest 20 percent of the population is also related to the fact that those dependent on welfare payments saw their income drop dramatically in the last two decades. The average monthly welfare payment per family (in 1996 dollars) fell from $734 in 1970 to $523 in 1980 to $470 in 1990 to $374 in 1996![48]

Unions and part-time workers. Other causes of declining wages have also played a part in the growth of poverty. Unions, which historically have been successful at raising wages, have lost members and power in the last few decades. In 1953, 26.9 percent of the U.S. labor force belonged to a union; by 1998, only about one-half that many (13.9 percent) were unionized.[49] Some scholars estimate that 20 percent of the increase in inequality in men's earnings in the 1980s is connected to this decline in the strength of unions.[50] Also important is the fact that employers have consciously increased the number of part-time workers to avoid paying benefits.

Racism. The extent to which continuing racism contributes to poverty is difficult to measure, but it is certainly the case that the lingering effects of our racist past and racial prejudice in the present play a role in the poverty of minorities.[51] A racist history means that African Americans inherit less wealth. Ongoing discrimination in housing, education, employment, and law enforcement limit their opportunities and lower their earnings. One study suggested that if we simply reduced discrimination in the sale and rental of housing by 13 percent, we would narrow the gap between blacks and whites in earnings and education by 33 percent.[52]

Job audits provide one of the clearest indications of persistent racism in hiring. In a job audit, a white and black person with equal skills apply for the same job. The white person is 10 percent more likely to get an interview. If both are interviewed, 50 percent of whites—but only 11 percent of blacks—receive a job offer. When both receive a job offer, the salary is 15 cents per hour higher for whites.[53] Racism obviously still contributes to black poverty.

A quick review of the years from the mid-1960s to mid-1980s shows how broad structural factors reduce or increase poverty. After President Johnson launched the War on Poverty in 1964, several important programs quickly followed: Food Stamp Act (1964), Economic Opportunity Act (1964), Medicare and Medicaid (1965). The economy was also booming. The result? The poverty rate fell from 19 percent (1964) to 11 percent (1973).

Then the huge jump in oil prices in 1973 and the severe recession of 1974 to 1975 halted economic growth. In 1981, President Reagan cut taxes, as well as social programs for the poor. The effective federal income tax rate for the poorest 20 percent *increased* from 8.1 percent to 10.4 percent from 1980 to 1985, and it *dropped* from 29.7 percent to 24.4 percent for the richest 5 percent. Reagan also restricted welfare benefits. What happened? From 1979 to 1983, the child poverty rate climbed from 16.4 percent to 22.3 percent.[54] Structural factors obviously play a large role in the existence and perpetuation of poverty.

Personal Decisions and Misguided Behavioral Patterns

While the structural causes of poverty are many and varied, they alone do not explain all poverty. In fact, structural causes are often intertwined with personal decisions and misguided behavioral patterns. A young unmarried teenager who is sexually active, gets pregnant, and then drops out of school is certainly making personal choices that will very likely condemn her to extended poverty. But how much was her action shaped by the fact that her father had left her mother when he lost his job because the factory he worked in moved to Mexico, by the fact that subtle racism helped create an inferior high school, and by the fact that the best-paying job available to her boyfriend was selling drugs? Keep in mind this interconnectedness as we examine some of the personal decisions and behaviors that lead to poverty.

An increase in the number of single-parent families. Skyrocketing single parenthood is one of the major causes of growing poverty in the United States. Single-mom families are the poorest people in our nation. Half of all families headed by an unmarried mother have total cash income of less than

$12,400.[55] In 1996, 44.3 percent of all single-parent, female-headed families were poor; only 8.7 percent of all married-couple families were poor.[56]

Single moms have always been poor, but now they represent a much higher percentage of the total population. This is due to a number of factors. The percentage of single *adult* women who have a child has not increased much for several decades, but far more women today decide never to marry, and married women have fewer children. At the same time, higher divorce rates are creating more single moms, and more teenagers than ever are having children today, and fewer are marrying the father of their child.[57] The result is a skyrocketing number of single-parent families. In 1970, a single mom was the head of 11.5 percent of all families. By 1995, that number had jumped to almost 25 percent. And in the African American community, it escalated from 33 percent to 60 percent during the same years.[58]

Out-of-wedlock births are the most important contributing factor to the growth of single-parent families. In 1960, 85 percent of all teenagers who bore children were married; by 1995, only 25 percent were.[59] Of all the families in 1970 headed by a single mother, only 7 percent were this way due to out-of-wedlock births. By 1995, however, according to the U.S. Bureau of the Census, 34.6 percent of all children in single-mom families lived with a mother who had never married. (The figure was 54.7 percent for black children and 37.3 percent for Latinos.) The poverty rate for all single-mom families is high, but it is higher for families in which Mom never married than for families in which Dad died or the marriage ended in divorce.[60]

Why this escalation in out-of-wedlock births? Society's abandonment of historic Judeo-Christian sexual moral standards—thanks in part to TV, popular music, and the movies—is one important reason.[61] Decreasing job opportunities and lower wages for low-skilled men—especially inner-city minorities—is another. A recent poll discovered that 77 percent of women listed a well-paying job as an essential requirement for a husband.[62] Unfortunately, as William Julius Wilson points out, that is precisely what an increasing number of young minority men do not have.

Many of the reasons female-headed households experience more poverty are painfully obvious. Absent fathers provide little child support. With only one person to care for the children, there is less time to earn a living. When women do work, they get paid less per hour than men.

The poor single men who make up 9 percent of the poor also face a host of problems that contribute to the growing number of poor single-parent families. Many have fathered children out of wedlock and pay little or no child support. They are more likely than single women to be homeless and involved in drugs, crime, and violence. Thirty-seven percent of all black men between the ages of eighteen and thirty-four are under the supervision of our jails or courts.[63]

The impact on children of single parenthood and poverty is staggering. Growing up in a poor home frequently means inadequate health care, deficient nutrition, poor housing, bad schools, unsafe neighborhoods, extra stress, and diminished hopes. With one-fifth of all our children living in poverty, we are damaging millions of kids and undermining our nation's future.

Other behavioral patterns. The decisions and behaviors that lead to single parenthood are not the only ones that contribute to the existence of poverty. Drug use and sexual abuse are also important factors. A small but significant number of families are poor because one or both parents use illegal drugs or abuse alcohol. There is also a high correlation between sexual abuse and teen pregnancy. One study found that 61 percent of all teenagers who were pregnant or parenting had suffered sexual abuse earlier in life.[64] Abuse creates low self-esteem, which fosters excessive craving for male affection. Poverty also increases the likelihood of sexual abuse. Female-headed households are more likely to have transient boyfriends who in turn often feel powerless and hopeless and sometimes compensate by asserting power over girls in the family. Tragically, that abuse increases teen pregnancy, which increases the chances of poverty.

Wrong choices, not merely unjust structures, cause poverty. As James Q. Wilson, one of America's premier political scientists insists, "A variety of public problems can only be understood—and perhaps addressed—if they are seen as arising out of a defect in character formation."[65]

Sudden Catastrophes

Sometimes disaster strikes fast. Every day accidents on the road or at work kill or disable the principal breadwinner in solid lower-middle-class families. Every day long-term illness hits a person who, along with tens of millions of other people in the United States, lacks health insurance. Too often, the result is poverty. In these and similar cases, the cause is neither broader structural change nor misguided personal choices. But the result can be devastating poverty.

Permanent Disabilities

Finally, some people are poor simply because (often through no fault of their own) they have a condition that prevents them from working. This is true of the mentally and physically disabled. It is also true of the elderly who can no longer work but were not able to save enough money for retirement. Without government disability payments or retirement benefits via Social Security, they would be desperately poor. Even with those government benefits, they often struggle.

Distribution of Income and Wealth

Not only are 36 million people in the United States poor in the midst of enormous wealth, *they are becoming poorer while the rich grow richer.*

Growing Inequality

Table 2 shows that in 1974, the bottom 20 percent of the population received only 5.7 percent of the total national income, while the top 20 percent enjoyed 40.6 percent. In the next twenty-plus years, the inequality became worse. The bottom share dropped to 4.2 percent, while the top share expanded to 46.8 percent. In 1974, the richest fifth enjoyed seven times as much income as the poorest fifth. Twenty-two years later, the rich had *eleven* times as much!

Table 2
Income of Families in the United States[66]

	Percent of Total Income		Mean Income (1996 dollars)		
	1974	1996	1974	1996	Change
lowest fifth	5.7%	4.2%	$12,697	$11,388	−10%
second fifth	12.0%	10.0%	26,803	26,847	0%
third fifth	17.6%	15.8%	39,191	42,467	+8%
fourth fifth	24.1%	23.1%	53,612	62,052	+16%
top fifth	40.6%	46.8%	90,337	125,627	+39%
top 5 percent	14.8%	20.3%	131,766	217,355	+65%

Source: U.S. Census Bureau, from George N. Monsma, "Income Distribution in the United States," in *Toward a Just and Caring Society: Christian Responses to Poverty in America,* ed. David P. Gushee (Grand Rapids: Baker, 1999), chap. 6.

Nor is it just the poor who are seeing their share of income decline. From 1979 through 1997, only the top 20 percent saw their share of income grow. Everyone else—the other 80 percent!—saw their share of income fall.[67]

One could make a moral case for growing inequality if it were the most effective way to improve the lot of the poorest. But the reverse happened.

The poorest lost ground not only in comparison to the richest but also in real dollars. The income of the bottom fifth declined 10 percent and the second fifth made no progress, while the top 5 percent gained 65 percent.

Another way to describe what happened in this same period is by examining the bottom 20 percent's adjusted household income in terms of the federal poverty level. In 1979, the poorest 20 percent had an average income almost equal to the poverty level (96 percent), but by 1994, their average income had declined to 89 percent of the poverty level.[68]

An even more striking picture emerges from a comparison of after-tax income for the years 1977 to 1994. Figure 4 shows how much the after-tax income of different groups fell or rose in these years. The bottom three-fifths all lose ground! But the top 1 percent gains 72 percent. In 1994, the richest 1 percent (2.6 million) enjoyed as much after-tax income as the bottom 35 percent (88 million). The top 20 percent received almost as much as the remaining 80 percent of Americans.[69]

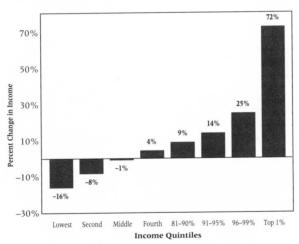

Fig. 4. Percent change in after-tax income, 1977–1994. *Source:* Congressional Budget Office, from Isaac Shapiro and Robert Greenstein, "Trends in the Distribution of After-Tax Income," Center on Budget and Policy Priorities, 14 August 1997, 2–3.

What about the distribution of *wealth*? Wealth and income are often confused, but they are quite distinct. Looking at a family's wealth (all assets, including money, stocks, houses, cars, pension rights, and so on, minus debts) is a better way to predict their long-term financial security than measuring their income (earnings) in a given year.[70]

The distribution of wealth is vastly more unequal than the distribution of income. According to a study by John Weicher published by the con-

servative American Enterprise Institute, the richest 1 percent of U.S. households in 1989 owned 35 percent of all American wealth. The top 20 percent owned 80 percent.[71] The distribution of wealth became even more
unequal in the next decade. By 1997, the share of the top 20 percent had
increased to over 84 percent of all wealth. In fact, the top 1 percent had
more wealth than all of us in the bottom *90* percent![72]

Figure 5 shows what has happened to the distribution of wealth since
1962. From 1962 to 1983, there was not much change in the share of the
wealth that each fifth enjoyed. From 1983 to 1997, however, the top 20
percent saw their share increase from 81 percent of all wealth to 84.3 percent, and the bottom 80 percent saw their share fall from 19 percent to
15.7 percent.

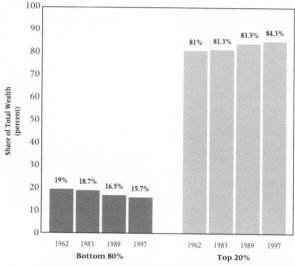

Fig. 5. Distribution of wealth, 1962–1977. *Source:* Adapted from table 5.5
in Lawrence Mishel, Jared Bernstein, and John Schmitt, *The State of Working America, 1998–1999* (Ithaca, N.Y.: Cornell Univ. Press, 1999), 262.

Many people think that growing participation in the stock market in the
last decade or two has democratized the ownership of wealth. There has,
in fact, been a modest expansion of the number of households who own
stock in the last decade. But in 1995, 60 percent of all households owned
absolutely no stock. The top 10 percent owned 88 percent of all stock, and
the bottom 90 percent had just 12 percent. Eighty-six percent of the profits from stocks in the stock boom from 1989 to 1997 went to the top 10
percent.[73]

Measured by the distribution of wealth, the gap between the haves and
the have-nots in the United States is greater today than at any time since

1929. We used to think of Europe as a class-based society in which aristo-crats owned most of the wealth. Today, wealth distribution is more equal in Europe than in the "land of the free."[74]

The United States has the greatest income inequality of all developed nations.[75] On average, of course, U.S. residents have higher incomes than persons in almost all developed nations. Does that mean that the poorest 10 percent of Americans are better off than the poorest 10 percent in other developed countries in spite of the great inequality here? Not at all. Because of higher wages and more generous support programs for the poor, the poorest Germans, for example, are 13 percent better off in absolute terms than the poorest Americans—even though the *median* income in Germany is much less than that of the United States. In fact, the poorest 10 percent in this country are worse off economically than the poorest 10 percent in every developed country except the United Kingdom.[76]

Is there at least greater economic mobility here than in Europe? Is it eas-ier in the United States for those in the bottom fifth to move up to the sec-ond or third fifth over the course of a decade or two or three? Again, the answer is no. Mobility in the United States is no greater than in France, Italy, or Scandinavia, where the inequality is much less and the poorest are economically better off. In fact, as U.S. inequality increased in the 1980s, mobility decreased.[77]

The United States has a far higher percentage of very low-income fam-ilies than Western European nations. The number is more than three times that of Germany and the Netherlands and more than twice that of France and the United Kingdom.[78]

CEOs versus Their Workers

In 1965, CEOs made approximately forty-four times the salary of the average factory worker. Thirty years later, the CEOs received 209 times the average factory worker's salary.[79]

The contrast between increases in CEO pay, company profits, inflation, and factory wages is striking. CEO salaries jumped 499 percent between 1980 and 1995, but company profits only increased 145 percent. The aver-age factory worker saw a pay raise of only 70 percent—not even enough to keep up with the increase in inflation (85 percent). If factory workers had received pay raises comparable to those of their CEOs between 1980 and 1995, they would have earned $90,000 a year by 1995, and the min-imum-wage worker would have earned $39,000 a year![80]

The United States has the most unequal distribution of disposable income among all the wealthy countries in the Organization for Economic Cooperation and Development.[81] Again, the inequality might be acceptable if the poor reaped substantial benefits, but the opposite has occurred.

Campaign Contributions

People with wealth have an enormous impact on the political campaigns of both parties. According to the non-partisan Center for Responsive Politics, 96 percent of all Americans make no political contributions at all. The 4 percent who do are largely the richest members of society. All direct, individual contributions of $200 or more to congressional candidates (for the U.S. House and Senate) are given by a mere one-third of 1 percent of the American people. Eighty percent of all money for congressional campaigns comes from: (1) $200-plus donations from a tiny wealthy minority; (2) Political Action Committees (PACs) (mostly business PACs—business outspends labor seven to one); and (3) personal contributions of wealthy candidates.[82] That is concentrated power—and probably helps explain why economic inequality has grown in the last few decades.

Conclusion

Poverty is alive and well in the United States at the peak of one of the longest boom economies in our history. Over 35 million Americans experience this unnecessary trauma. Over 14 million of our children suffer poverty's destructive effects. Over 43 million lack health insurance. For the poor, the schools do not work and their jobs do not pay. For the richest nation on earth, this situation is unnecessary. For Christians, it is immoral.

I wish every middle-class person in the United States would spend half an hour honestly grappling with one simple question: How would I feel if I were a poor person living in the richest nation on earth and knew my comfortable neighbors simply did not care enough to offer me real opportunity?

The rest of this book offers a comprehensive vision of how a committed movement of people with a Judeo-Christian perspective could dramatically reduce agony and injustice by offering the poor genuine opportunities to work their way out of poverty.

Part 2

A Holistic, Biblical Vision for Empowering the Poor

2

A Biblical Foundation

They thrust the poor off the road; the poor of the earth all hide themselves. . . . They lie all night naked, without clothing, and have no covering in the cold. . . . (There are those who snatch the fatherless child from the breast, and take in pledge the infant of the poor.) . . . Hungry, they carry the sheaves. . . . They tread the wine presses, but suffer thirst. From out of the city the dying groan.

Job 24:4–12

They shall all sit under their own vines and under their own fig trees.

Micah 4:4 NRSV

How should Christians respond to the fact that agonizing poverty and astonishing affluence stand side by side in the United States today? This stark contrast raises tough questions. Does the growing inequality matter? Is justice satisfied as long as the laws are applied honestly, even if the outcome is poverty for some and affluence for others? Is equality the ideal, or does fairness (equity) actually demand unequal shares of the economic pie?

What kind of program to change things would fit with who persons really are? Would changing the economic structures and incentives end poverty? Or is inner spiritual transformation the key?

If something must be done, who should do it? Family? Churches and other voluntary associations? Government?

Clearly, any proposal to change the situation described in chapter 1 requires answers to these questions. Just as clearly, these questions are ultimately moral and religious questions. We need more than economic analysis; we need a normative framework.

For Christians, that means searching Scripture for biblical help with these questions. Many Christians, of course, do not do that.[1] Often unconsciously, they take their cue for economic life from secular sources, whether left or right. If we want to be biblical, however, we must submit to scriptural norms even when they contradict our inherited biases and ideological preferences.

But how can the Bible help us solve the problem of poverty today? Nowhere in Scripture do we find a systematic biblical treatise on poverty and economics. What we do find are hundreds of biblical texts scattered throughout the Bible that offer essential clues. When we combine these biblical teachings into a comprehensive summary, we discover that biblical faith offers a powerful paradigm for solving our problems.

Four questions are especially important when attempting to construct a biblical approach to helping the poor.[2]

1. What is the relevant foundational framework for approaching the issue of poverty?
2. According to the Bible, does justice require only honest courts and fair procedures, or does it also insist on specific outcomes?
3. What is the biblical definition of equality (or equity)?
4. Who—government, family, churches—should care for the poor?

A Conceptual Framework

Many foundational biblical truths are essential parts of the normative framework we need. The God we worship is Lord of all, including economics. The biblical understanding of the world and history, the nature of persons, the creation of wealth, the glory of work, and the reality of sin all significantly deepen our understanding of how to conquer poverty.

The Lord of Economics

The one and only God, sovereign over all, is the only absolute owner (Lev. 25:23). We are merely stewards summoned to use the wealth God allows us to enjoy for the glory of God and the good of our neighbor. We cannot worship God and mammon. Excessive preoccupation with material abundance is idolatry. God's righteous demands for justice stand in judgment on every economic system. As the Lord of history, God works now—with and through human co-workers—to create more wholesome economies that respect and nurture the dignity and worth of every human being.

The Importance of the World and History

Because it is created out of nothing *(ex nihilo)* by a loving, almighty Creator, the material world and history are finite, good, and full of meaning.

Many modern secular thinkers absolutize the historical process even while they pronounce it meaningless. (Even if life is absurd, our time here is all we have.) Some Eastern thinkers consider the world an illusion to escape. Some Christians do almost the same thing, viewing earthly life as a mere preparation for eternity. Take, for instance, the old gospel song, "This world is not my home, I'm just a-passing through."

According to the Bible, this material world is so good that the Creator of the galaxies became flesh and even promised at the second coming to restore the groaning creation to wholeness (Rom. 8:19–23). God promises to bring the glory of the nations (Rev. 21:24, 26) into the New Jerusalem and assures us that eventually the kingdoms of this world will become the kingdom of our Lord (Rev. 11:15).

The biblical vision of the world calls human beings to revel in the goodness of the material world rather than seek to escape it. It invites persons to use the nonhuman world to create wealth and construct complex civilizations—always, of course, in a way that does not destroy the rest of creation and thereby prevent it from offering its own independent hymn of praise to the Creator. Finally, it calls persons to overcome oppression and correct injustice, knowing that the Lord Jesus will complete the victory over every evil at his return.

The Nature of Persons

Created in the image of God and fashioned as body-soul unities formed for community, persons possess inestimable dignity and value that transcend any economic process or system.

Because our bodies are a fundamental part of our created goodness, a generous sufficiency of material things is essential to human goodness. Any economic structure that prevents persons from producing and enjoying material well-being violates our God-given dignity.

Because our spiritual nature and destiny are so important that it is better to lose even the entire world than one's relationship with God, any economic system that tries to explain persons only as economic actors or that offers material abundance as the exclusive or primary way to human fulfillment contradicts the essence of human nature. Any economic structure that subordinates labor to capital thereby subordinates spiritual reality to material reality in contradiction of the biblical view of persons. Any program for comprehensive social change that deals only with the material side of persons and ignores spiritual transformation is doomed to failure. For persons invited to live forever with the living God, no material abundance, however splendid, can satisfy the human heart.

People are made both for personal freedom and communal solidarity. The God who cares so much about each person that the incarnate Creator died for the sins of the whole world and invites every person to respond in freedom to the gift of salvation demands that human economic and political systems acknowledge and protect the dignity and freedom of each individual. Any economic order that denies economic freedom to individuals or reduces them to a factor of production subordinated to mere economic goals violates their individual dignity and freedom.

Since persons are free, their choices have consequences. Obedient, diligent use of our gifts normally produces sufficiency of material things (unless powerful people oppress us). Disobedient, lazy neglect of our responsibilities normally increases the danger of poverty. As a result, completely equal economic outcomes are not compatible with human freedom.

The first few chapters of Genesis underline the fact that we are also created for community. Until Eve arrived, Adam was restless. Mutual fulfillment resulted when the two became one flesh. God punished Cain for violating community by killing his brother, Abel, but God still allowed Cain to enjoy the human community of family and city (Genesis 4). As social beings, we are physically, emotionally, and rationally interdependent. Mutual responsibility and collective decision making are essential to every form of human life. Therefore, economic and political institutions are not merely a consequence of the fall.

Because our communal nature demands attention to the common good, individual rights, whether of freedom of speech or private property, cannot be absolute. The right to private property dare not undermine the general welfare. Only God is an absolute owner. We are merely stewards of our property called to balance personal rights with the common good.

Our communal nature is grounded in God. Since persons are created in the image of the triune personal God, who is Father, Son, and Holy Spirit, "being a person means being united to other persons in mutual love."[3] Any economic system that emphasizes the freedom of individuals without an equal concern for mutual love, cooperation, and responsibility neglects the complex balance of the biblical picture of persons. Any economic system that exaggerates the individual right of private property at the expense of mutual responsibility for the common good defies the Creator's design for human beings.

The biblical view of persons means that economic injustice is a family problem. Since we are all "God's offspring" (Acts 17:29; cf. all of vv. 24–29), we all have the same Father. Therefore, all human beings are sisters and brothers. "Exploitation is a brother or sister treating another brother or sister as a mere object."[4] Poverty is wrong not just because it means financial hardship but also because it involves exclusion from community.

Human rights specify minimal demands for how we should treat people to whom God has given such dignity and worth. Human institutions cannot create human rights; they can only recognize and protect the inestimable value of every person that flows from the central truths of the biblical story: Every person is made in the image of God; every person is a child of the heavenly Father; every person is so loved by God that the eternal Son suffered crucifixion because God does not desire that any should perish (2 Peter 3:9); every person who accepts Christ, regardless of race, gender, or class, is justified on exactly the same basis—namely, unmerited grace offered through the cross. Since this is the way God views people, this is the way we should treat each other. Since persons are created as body-soul unities, a biblical understanding of human rights must include both freedom rights and socioeconomic rights.

Statements of human rights spell out for individuals and communities the fixed duties that implement love for our neighbors in typical situations of competing claims. Rights extend the response of love from spontaneous responses to individual needs to structured patterns of fair treatment for everyone. Vigorous commitment to human rights for all helps societies respect the immeasurable dignity and worth that the Creator has bestowed on every person.

The Creation of Wealth

The ability to create wealth is a gift from God. The one in whose image we are made creates astounding abundance and variety. Unlike God, we cannot create out of nothing; we can only retrace the divine design. But by giving us minds that can study and imitate his handiwork, God has blessed human beings with awesome power not only to reshape the earth but to produce new things that have never been.

The Creator could have directly created poetry, plays, sonatas, cities, and computers. Instead, God assigned that task to us, expecting us to cultivate the earth (Gen. 2:15), create new things, and expand human possibilities and wealth. Adam and Eve surely enjoyed a generous sufficiency. Just as surely, the Creator intended their descendants to probe and use the astoundingly intricate earth placed in their care to acquire the knowledge, power, and wealth necessary, for example, to build vast telescopes that we can use to scan the billions of galaxies about which Adam and Eve knew nothing. In a real sense, God purposely created human beings with very little so that they could imitate and glorify their Creator by producing vast knowledge and wealth. Indeed, Jesus' parable of the talents sharply rebukes those who fail to use their skills to multiply their resources. Just, responsible creation of wealth is one important way persons obey and honor the Creator.

The Glory of Work

God works (Gen. 2:1–2). God incarnate was a carpenter. St. Paul mended tents. Even before the fall, God summoned Adam to cultivate the earth and name the animals (Gen. 2:15–20). Work is not only the way we meet our basic needs. It is both the way we express our basic nature as co-workers with God and also a crucial avenue for loving our neighbors. Meaningful work by which persons express their creative ability is essential for human dignity. Any able person who fails to work disgraces and corrodes his or her very being. Any system that could but does not offer every person the opportunity for meaningful work violates and crushes the human dignity bestowed by the Creator.

The Reality of Sin

Nothing on God's good earth has escaped sin's marauding presence. Sin has twisted both individual persons and the ideas and institutions we create. Exaggerating our own importance, we regularly create economic systems—complete with sophisticated rationalizations—that oppress our neighbors. Workable economic structures must both appeal to persons' better instincts that sin has not quite managed to obliterate and also hold in check and turn to positive use the pervasive selfishness that corrupts every act. Because sin has become embedded in socioeconomic structures, justice requires structural change. And because the problem lies deeper than mere social systems and is located finally in distorted human hearts, personal spiritual conversion is also essential for long-term societal improvement.

This biblical understanding of God, the world and history, the nature of persons, wealth, work, and sin provides the best framework for designing successful programs to overcome poverty.

Is Justice More Than Fair Procedures?

Fair procedures are certainly at the heart of biblical justice. Scripture frequently demands honest courts unbiased toward either rich or poor (Exod. 23:3; Lev. 19:15; Deut. 10:17–18). Equally clear is the insistence on honest weights and measures for fair commercial exchange (Lev. 19:35–36; Prov. 11:1; Amos 8:5). Without a doubt these two types of justice—which scholars sometimes call procedural justice and commutative justice—are biblical imperatives.

But is that all? According to the biblical perspective, is distributive justice (the fair distribution of wealth, resources, and power) satisfied as long as the procedures are fair, even if many people are quite poor and others are very rich? Some Christians like Calvin Beisner say yes. Economic justice is present, no matter how poor some are, as long as the laws prevent fraud, theft, and violence.

> Justice in economic relationships requires that people be permitted to exchange and use what they own—including their own time and energy and intellect as well as material objects—freely so long as in so doing they do not violate others' rights. Such things as minimum-wage laws, legally mandated racial quotas in employment, legal restrictions on import and export, laws requiring "equal pay for equal work," and all other regulations of economic activity other than those necessary to prohibit, prevent, and punish fraud, theft, and violence are therefore unjust.[5]

Others argue that the biblical materials understand justice to include a dynamic, community-building character. Rather than having primarily a minimal, punitive, and restraining function, biblical justice also has a crucial restorative character. It identifies and corrects areas of material need.

To treat people equally, those who hold to this second view argue, justice looks for barriers that interfere with a person's access to the productive resources needed for them to acquire the basic goods of society or to be dignified, participating members of the community. Justice takes into consideration handicaps that hinder the pursuit of opportunities for wholesome life in community.[6] The handicaps that justice considers go beyond individual physical disabilities and personal tragedies. Significant handicaps can be found in poverty or prejudice. A just society removes any discrimination that prevents equality of opportunity. Distributive justice gives special consideration to disadvantaged groups by providing basic social and economic opportunities and resources.

Biblical teaching points to the second, broader, rather than the first, narrower, exclusively procedural, understanding of justice.[7] Four aspects of this teaching are especially important:

1. Frequently the words *love* and *justice* appear together in close relationship.
2. Biblical justice has a dynamic, restorative character.
3. The special concern for the poor running through Scripture moves beyond a concern for unbiased procedures.
4. Restoration to community—including the benefit rights that dignified participation in community require—is a central feature of biblical thinking about justice.

Love and Justice Together

In many texts we discover the words *love* and *justice* in close association. "Sow for yourselves justice, reap the fruit of steadfast love" (Hosea 10:12).[8] Sometimes, love and justice are interchangeable: "[It is the LORD] who executes justice *[mišpāt]* for the orphan and the widow, and who loves the strangers, providing them food and clothing" (Deut. 10:18 NRSV; cf. Isa. 30:18).[9]

Justice's Dynamic, Restorative Character

The terms for *justice* are frequently associated with the words for deliverance and salvation: "God arose to establish justice *[mišpāt]* to save *[hôšîaᶜ]* all the oppressed of the earth" (Ps. 76:9; cf. Isa. 63:1).[10] "Give justice to the weak" and "maintain the right of the lowly" are parallel to "rescue the weak and the needy; deliver them from the hand of the wicked" (Ps. 82:3–4 NRSV).[11]

The words for *justice* are used to describe the deliverance of the people from political and economic oppressors (Judg. 5:11),[12] from slavery (1 Sam. 12:7–8; Micah 6:4), and from captivity (Isa. 41:1–11 [cf. v. 2 for *sedeq*]; Jer. 51:10). Providing for the needy means ending their oppression, setting them back on their feet, giving them a home, and leading them to prosperity and restoration (Pss. 10:15–18; 68:5–10).[13] Biblical justice does not mean we should merely help victims cope with oppression; it teaches us to remove it. Biblical justice does not merely require fair procedures for the poor; it demands new opportunity!

God's Special Concern for the Poor

Hundreds of biblical verses show that God is especially attentive to the poor and needy.[14] God is not biased. Because of unequal needs, however, equal provision of basic rights requires justice to be partial in order to be impartial. (Good firefighters do not spend equal time at every house; they are "partial" to homes on fire.) Partiality to the weak is the most striking characteristic of biblical justice.[15] In the raging social struggles in which the poor are perennially victims of injustice, God and God's people take up the cause of the weak.[16] Rulers and leaders have a special obligation to do justice for the weak and powerless.[17] This partiality to the poor provides strong evidence that in biblical thought, justice is concerned with more than fair procedures.

Scripture speaks of God's special concern for the poor in at least four ways.[18]

1. Repeatedly, the Bible says that the Sovereign of history works to lift up the poor and oppressed (Exod. 3:7–8; 6:5–7; Deut. 26:6–8). "Because the poor are despoiled, because the needy groan, I will now rise up," says the LORD (Ps. 12:5).

2. Sometimes the Lord of history tears down rich and powerful people. Mary's song is shocking: "My soul glorifies the Lord. . . . He has filled the hungry with good things but has sent the rich away empty" (Luke 1:46, 53 NIV). James is even more blunt: "Now listen, you rich people, weep and wail because of the misery that is coming upon you" (James 5:1 NIV).

Since God calls us to create wealth and is not biased against the rich, why does Scripture warn again and again that God sometimes works in history to destroy the rich? The Bible has a simple answer: The rich sometimes get rich by oppressing the poor, or they have plenty and neglect the needy. In either case, God is furious.

James warned the rich harshly because they had hoarded wealth and refused to pay their workers (5:2–6). Repeatedly, the prophets said the same thing (Ps. 10; Isa. 3:14–25; Jer. 22:13–19). "Among my people are wicked men who lie in wait like men who snare birds and like those who set traps to catch men. Like cages full of birds, their houses are full of deceit; they have become rich and powerful and have grown fat and sleek. . . . They do not defend the rights of the poor. Should I not punish them for this?" (Jer. 5:26–29 NIV). The prophets warned that God was so outraged that he would destroy the nations of Israel and Judah. Because of the way they "trample on the heads of the poor . . . and deny justice to the oppressed" (2:7 NIV), Amos predicted terrible captivity (5:11; 6:4, 7; 7:11, 17). So did Isaiah and Micah (Isa. 10:1–3; Micah 2:2; 3:12). And it happened just as they foretold. According to both the Old and New Testaments, God destroys people and societies that get rich by oppressing the poor.

But what if we work hard and create wealth in just ways? That is good—as long as we do not forget to share. No matter how justly we have acquired our wealth, God demands that we act generously toward the poor. When we do not, God treats us in a similar way to those who oppress the poor. There is not a hint in Jesus' story of the rich man and Lazarus that the rich man exploited Lazarus to acquire wealth. He simply neglected to share. So God punished him (Luke 16:19–31; cf. Ezek. 16:49–50).

The Bible is clear. If we get rich by oppressing the poor or if we have wealth and do not reach out generously to the needy, the Lord of history moves against us. God judges societies by what they do to the people at the bottom.

3. God identifies with the poor so strongly that caring for them is almost like helping God. "He who is kind to the poor lends to the Lord" (Prov. 19:17 NIV). On the other hand, one "who oppresses the poor shows contempt for their Maker" (Prov. 14:31 NIV).

Jesus' parable of the sheep and goats is the ultimate commentary on these two proverbs. Jesus surprises those on the right with his insistence that they had fed and clothed him when he was cold and hungry. When they protested that they could not remember ever doing so, Jesus replied, "Whatever you did for one of the least of these brothers of mine, you did for me" (Matt. 25:40 NIV). If we believe his words, we look on the poor and neglected with entirely new eyes.

4. Finally, God demands that God's people share God's special concern for the poor. Repeatedly, the Bible calls on God's people to treat the poor in the same generous way that God has treated them (Exod. 22:21–24; Deut. 15:13–15; 2 Cor. 8:9).

The Bible, however, goes one shocking step further. God insists that if we do not imitate God's concern for the poor, we are not really God's people—no matter how frequent our worship or how orthodox our creeds. Because Israel failed to correct oppression and defend poor widows, Isaiah insisted that Israel was really the pagan people of Gomorrah (Isa. 1:10–17). God despised their fasting because they tried to worship God and oppress their workers at the same time (Isa. 58:3–7). Jeremiah 22:13–19 teaches that knowing God is *inseparable* from caring for the poor. Through Amos, the Lord shouted in fury that the very religious festivals God had ordained made him angry and sick. Why? Because the rich and powerful were mixing worship and oppression of the poor (Amos 5:21–24). Jesus was even harsher. At the last judgment, some who expect to enter heaven will learn that their failure to feed the hungry condemns them to hell (Matt. 25:31–46). If we do not care for the needy brother or sister, God's love does not abide in us (1 John 3:17).

One thing is crystal clear from these biblical texts: God and God's faithful people have a great concern for the poor.

But is God biased? Earlier we saw that God is partial to the poor but not biased. God does not love the poor any more than the rich. God has an equal concern for the well-being of every single person. Most rich and powerful people, however, are genuinely biased; they care a lot more about themselves than about their poor neighbors. By contrast with the genuine bias of most people, God's lack of bias makes God appear biased. God cares equally for everyone.

How then is God partial to the poor? Because in concrete, historical situations, equal concern for everyone requires special attention to specific people. In a family, loving parents do not provide equal tutorial time to a son struggling hard to scrape by with D's and a daughter easily making A's. Precisely in order to be "impartial" and love both equally, they devote extra time to helping the needier child. In situations (e.g., apartheid) in which some people oppress others, God's lack of bias does not mean neutrality. Precisely because God loves all equally, God works against oppressors and actively sides with the oppressed.

We see this connection precisely in the texts that declare God's lack of bias: "For the LORD your God is God of gods and LORD of lords, the great, the mighty, and the terrible God, who is not partial and takes no bribe. He executes justice for the fatherless and the widow, and loves the sojourner, giving him food and clothing" (Deut. 10:17–18; cf. also Lev. 19:10–15). Justice and love are virtual synonyms in this passage. There is no suggestion that loving the sojourner is a benevolent, voluntary act different from a legal demand to do justice to the fatherless. Furthermore, there is no indication in the text that those needing food and clothing are poor because of some violation of due process such as fraud or robbery. The text simply says they are poor, and therefore, God, who is not biased, pays special attention to them.

Precisely because God is not biased, God pays special attention to the poor. Consequently, an understanding of justice that reflects this biblical teaching must be concerned with more than procedural justice. Distributive justice that insists on special attention to the poor so they have opportunity to enjoy material well-being is also crucial.

Justice as Restoration to Community

In the Bible, justice includes restoration of the things people need for dignified participation in their community. Since persons are created for community, Scripture portrays the good life as sharing in the essential aspects of social life. It is hardly surprising, therefore, that biblical justice includes restoration to community. Justice includes helping people return to the kind of life in community that God intends for them. Leviticus 25:35–36 describes the poor as being on the verge of falling out of the community because of their economic distress. "If members of your community become poor in that their power slips *with you,* you shall make them strong . . . that they may live *with you*" (emphasis mine).[19] The word translated as *power* here is *hand* in Hebrew. *Hand (yōd)* metaphorically means *power.*[20] The solution is for those who are able, to correct the situation and thereby restore the poor to community. The poor in fact are their own flesh or kin (Isa. 58:7). Poverty is a family affair.

In order to restore the weak to participation in community, the community's responsibility to its diminished members is "to make them strong" again (Lev. 25:35). This translation is a literal rendering of the Hebrew, which is the word "to be strong," which is in the causative (Hiphil) conjugation, and therefore, means "cause him to be strong." The purpose of this empowerment is "that they may live *with you*" (v. 35, emphasis mine). According to Psalm 107, God's steadfast love leads God to care for the hungry so they are able to "establish a town to live in; they sow fields, and plant vineyards. . . . By his blessing they multiply greatly" (vv. 36–38 NRSV). Once more the hungry can be active, participating members of a community. The concern is for the whole person in community and what it takes to maintain persons in that relationship.

Community membership means the ability to share fully within one's capacity and potential in each essential aspect of community. Participation in community has multiple dimensions. It starts with physical life itself and the material resources necessary for a decent life. It also includes participation in decision making, social life, economic production, education, culture, and religion.

The basic material necessities of food and shelter are essential for communal participation. It is God "who executes justice for the oppressed; who gives food to the hungry" (Ps. 146:7 NRSV). The Lord "executes justice for the orphan and the widow, and . . . loves the strangers, providing them food and clothing" (Deut. 10:18 NRSV). "Food and clothing" is a Hebraism for what is indispensable.[21]

As we shall see in the next section, restoration to community involves much more than donating food and clothing to the poor. People in distress need empowerment at the point at which their participation in community has been undercut. That means restoring their productive capability. Therefore, restoration of the land, the basic productive resource in ancient Israel, is the way that Leviticus 25 commands the people to fulfill the call to "make them strong again" so "they may live with you" in the land (v. 35). As the poor return to their land, they receive a new power and dignity that restores their participation in the community.

There are also restrictions on the processes that tear people down so that their "power slips" and they cannot support themselves. Interest on loans was prohibited; food to the poor was not to be sold at profit (Lev. 25:36–37). A means of production such as a millstone (used to grind grain into flour) was not to be taken as collateral on a loan because that would be "taking a life in pledge" (Deut. 24:6 RSV). If a poor person gave an essential item of clothing as a pledge, the creditor had to return it before night came (Exod. 22:26). All these provisions are restrictions on individual economic freedom that go well beyond merely preventing fraud, theft, and violence. The law did, of course, support the rights of owners to benefit from their property, but the law placed limits on the owners' control of property and on the quest for profit. The common good of the community outweighed unrestricted economic freedom.

The fact that justice in Scripture includes benefit rights of the sort discussed above means that we must reject the claim that biblical justice is only or primarily procedural, and that, therefore, the state merely protects property, life, and equal access to the procedures of the community. That is by no means to deny that procedural justice is important. When we deny a person these protections, we cut them off from the political and civil community. Procedural justice is essential to protect people from fraud, theft, and violence.

Biblical justice, however, also includes positive rights, which are the responsibility of the community to guarantee. Biblical justice has both an economic and a legal focus. The goal of justice is not only integrity in the legal system, it also includes the restoration of the community as a place where all live together in wholeness.

The wrong to which justice responds is not merely an illegitimate process (like stealing). What is wrong is also an end result in which people are deprived of basic needs. Leviticus 19:13 condemns both stealing *and* withholding a poor person's salary for a day: "You shall not defraud your neighbor; you shall not steal; and you shall not keep for yourself the wages of a laborer until morning" (NRSV). Isaiah 5:8–10 condemns those who buy up field after field until only the rich person is left dwelling alone in his big, beautiful house. Significantly, however, the prophet here does not denounce the acquisition of the land as illegal. Through legal foreclosing of mortgages or through debt bondage, the property could be taken legally. Isaiah nevertheless condemns the rulers for permitting this injustice to the weak. He appeals to social justice above the technicalities of current law. Restoration to community is central to justice.

From the biblical perspective, justice demands both fair courts and fair economic structures. It includes both freedom rights and benefit rights. Precisely because of its equal concern for wholeness for everyone, it pays special attention to the needs of the weak and marginalized.

None of the above claims, however, offers a norm that describes the actual content of distributive justice. The next three sections seek to develop such a norm.

Equity as Adequate Access to Productive Resources

Equality has been one of the most powerful slogans of our century. But what does it mean? Does it mean equality before the law? One person, one vote? Equality of opportunity in education? Identical income shares? Or absolute identity as described in the satirical novel *Facial Justice*?[22]

As we saw earlier, equality of economic results is not compatible with human freedom and responsibility. Free choices have consequences; therefore, when immoral decisions reduce someone's earning power, we should, other things being equal, consider the result just. Even absolute equality of opportunity is impossible unless we prevent parents from passing on any of their knowledge or other capital to their children. (Proverbs 13:22 explicitly endorses such inheritance.)

So what definition of equality—or better, equity—do the biblical materials suggest?

Capital in an Agricultural Society[23]

The biblical material concerning Israel and the land offers important clues about what a biblical understanding of equity would look like. The contrast between early Israel and surrounding societies was striking. In Egypt, most of the land belonged to the pharaoh or the temples. In most other Near Eastern contexts, a feudal system of landholding prevailed. The king granted large tracts of land, worked by landless laborers, to a small number of elite royal vassals. Only at the theological level did this feudal system exist in early Israel. Yahweh the King owned all the land and made important demands on those to whom he gave it to use. Under Yahweh, however, each family had their own land. Israel's ideal was decentralized family "ownership," understood as stewardship under Yahweh's absolute ownership.

Land was the basic capital in early Israel's agricultural economy, and the law said the land was to be divided in such a way that each extended family had the resources to produce the things needed for a decent life.

Joshua 18 and Numbers 26 contain the two most important accounts of the division of the land[24] and represent Israel's social ideal with regard to the land. Originally, the land was divided among the tribes, clans, and families so that a relatively similar amount of land was available to all the family units. The larger tribes received a larger portion and the smaller tribes a smaller portion (Num. 26:54). By lot the land was further subdivided among the protective associations of families *(mišpāhâ),* and then the extended families *(bēth-ʾav)* (Joshua 18–19). The criterion of the division, according to Ezekiel's vision of a future time of justice, was equality. In this redistribution of the land, it was to be divided "equally" (literally, "each according to his brother" [Ezek. 47:14]). The concern, however, was not the implementation of an abstract ideal of equality but the empowerment of all the people.

The picture of land ownership in the time of the judges suggests some approximation of equality of land ownership—at least up to the point at which every family had enough to enjoy a decent, dignified life in the community if they acted responsibly.

We should not understand "necessities" as the minimum necessary to keep from starving. In the nonhierarchical, relatively egalitarian society of small farmers depicted in the Book of Judges, families possessed resources to earn a living that would have been considered reasonable and acceptable, not embarrassingly minimal. That is not to suggest that every family had exactly the same income. It does mean, however, that every family had an equality of economic opportunity up to the point that they had the resources to earn a living that would enable them not only to meet minimal needs of food, clothing, and housing but also to be respected participants in the community. Possessing their own land enabled each extended family to acquire the necessities for a decent life through responsible work.

Two astonishing biblical texts—Leviticus 25 and Deuteronomy 15—show how important this basic equality of opportunity was to God. The Jubilee text in Leviticus demanded that land return to its original owners every fifty years, and Deuteronomy 15 called for the release of debts every seven years.

The Year of Jubilee

Leviticus 25 is one of the most radical texts in all of Scripture,[25] at least to people committed either to communism or to unrestricted capitalism. Every fifty years, God said, land was to return to its original owners. Physical handicaps, death of a breadwinner, or lack of natural ability may lead some families to become poorer than others. But God did not want such disadvantages to lead to ever increasing extremes of wealth and poverty with the result that the poor eventually lacked the basic resources to earn a decent livelihood. God therefore gave his people a law to guarantee that no family would permanently lose its land. Every fifty years, land returned to its original owners so that every family had enough productive resources to function as dignified, participating members of the community (Lev. 25:10–24). Private property was not abolished. Regularly, however, the means of producing wealth were to be equalized—up to the point of every family having the resources to earn a decent living.

What is the theological basis for this startling command? Yahweh's ownership of everything: "The land shall not be sold in perpetuity, for the land is mine; for you are strangers and sojourners with me" (Lev. 25:23). God, the landowner, permits his people to sojourn on his good earth, cultivate it, eat its produce, and enjoy its beauty. But we are only stewards.

Before and after the Year of Jubilee, land could be "bought" or "sold." Actually, the buyer purchased a specific number of harvests, not the land itself (Lev. 25:16). And woe to the person who tried to get more than a just price for the intervening harvests from the date of purchase to the next Jubilee! "If the years are many you shall increase the price, and if the years are few you shall diminish the price, for it is the number of the crops that he is selling to you. You shall not wrong one another, but you shall fear your God; for I am the LORD your God" (Lev. 25:16–17).

Yahweh is Lord of all, even of economics. There is no hint here of a sacred law of supply and demand that operates independently of biblical ethics and the lordship of Yahweh. The people of God should submit to God, and God demands economic justice among his people.

The assumption in this text that people must suffer the consequences of wrong choices is also striking. An entire generation or more could suffer the loss of ancestral land. Every fifty years, however, the basic source of wealth returned to its original owners so that each family had the opportunity to provide for its basic needs.

Leviticus 25:25–28 implies that this equality of opportunity was of higher value than that of absolute property rights. If a person became poor and sold his land to a more prosperous neighbor but then recovered enough to buy back his land before the Jubilee, the new owner was obligated to return it. The original owner's right to have his ancestral land to earn his own way took precedence over the right of the second owner to maximize profits.

This passage prescribes justice in a way that haphazard handouts by wealthy philanthropists never will. The Year of Jubilee was an institutionalized structure that affected all Israelites automatically. It was the poor family's right to recover their inherited land at the Jubilee. Returning the land was not a charitable courtesy that the wealthy might extend if they pleased.

Interestingly, the principles of Jubilee challenge both unrestricted capitalism and communism in a fundamental way. Only God is an absolute owner. No one else has absolute property rights. The right of each family to have the means to earn a living takes priority over a purchaser's property rights or an unrestricted market economy. At the same time, Jubilee affirms not only the right but the importance of private property managed by families who understand that they are stewards responsible to God. This text does not point us in the direction of the communist model in which the state owns all the land. God wants each family to have the resources to produce its own livelihood. Why? To strengthen the family (this is a very important pro-family text), to give people the freedom to participate in shaping history, and to prevent the centralization of power—and totalitarianism, which almost always accompanies centralized ownership of land or capital by either the state or small elites.

It is not clear from the historical books how much the people of Israel implemented the Jubilee. Regardless of its antiquity or possible lack of implementation, however, Leviticus 25—and the social ideal it expresses—remains a part of God's authoritative Word.

The teaching of the prophets about the land underlines the principles of Leviticus 25. In the tenth to the eighth centuries b.c., major centralization of landholding occurred. Poorer farmers lost their land, becoming landless laborers or slaves. The prophets regularly denounced the bribery, political assassinations, and economic oppression that destroyed the earlier decentralized economy described above. Elijah condemned Ahab's seizure of Naboth's vineyard (1 Kings 21). Isaiah attacked rich landowners for adding field to field until they dwelt alone in the countryside because the smaller farmers had been destroyed (Isa. 5:8–9).

The prophets, however, did not merely condemn. They also expressed a powerful hope for a future day of justice when all would have their own land again. In the "latter days" (the future day of justice and wholeness), "they shall all sit under their own vines and under their own fig trees" (Micah 4:4 nrsv; cf. also Zech. 3:10). No longer will the leaders oppress the people; instead they will guarantee that all people will again enjoy their ancestral land (Ezek. 45:1–9, especially vv. 8–9).

In the original division of the land, the Jubilee provisions for maintaining that decentralized ownership, the prophets' denunciation of oppressors who seized the land of the poor, and the eschatological vision of a new day when once again all will delight in the fruits of their own land and labor we see a social ideal in which families are to have the economic means to earn their own way. A basic equality of economic opportunity up to the point that all can at least provide for their own basic needs through responsible work is the norm. Failure to act responsibly has economic consequences, so there is no assumption of equality. Central, however, is the demand that each family have the necessary capital (land) so that responsible stewardship will result in an economically decent life.[26] A friend of mine likes to summarize this biblical principle as follows: "According to the Bible, private property is so good that everybody ought to have some."

The Sabbatical Year

God's law also provided for liberation of soil, slaves, and debtors every seven years. Again the concern was justice for the poor and disadvantaged (as well as the well-being of the land). A central goal was to protect people against processes that would result in the loss of their productive resources and to restore productive resources after a time of loss.

Every seven years the land was to lie fallow (Exod. 23:10–11; Lev. 25:2–7). The purpose, apparently, was both ecological and humanitarian. Not planting any crops every seventh year helped to preserve the fertility of the soil. It also was God's way of showing his concern for the poor: "For six years you shall sow your land and gather in its yield; but the seventh year you shall let it rest and lie fallow, that the poor of your people may eat" (Exod. 23:10–11). In the seventh year the poor were free to gather for themselves whatever grew spontaneously in the fields and vineyards.

The sabbatical provision on loans (Deut. 15:1–6) called for cancellation of debts every seventh year.[27] Yahweh even added a footnote for those with a sharp eye for loopholes: It is sinful to refuse a loan to a poor person just because it is the sixth year and financial loss might occur in twelve months.

> Be careful that you do not entertain a mean thought, thinking, "The seventh year, the year of remission, is near," and therefore view your needy neighbor with hostility and give nothing; your neighbor might cry to the Lord against you, and you would incur guilt. Give liberally and be ungrudging when you do so, for on this account the Lord your God will bless you in all your work and in all that you undertake.
>
> Deuteronomy 15:9–10 NRSV

If followed, this provision would have protected small landowners from the exorbitant interest of moneylenders and thereby helped prevent them from losing their productive resources.

Hebrew slaves also received their freedom in the sabbatical year (Deut. 15:12–18). Poverty sometimes forced Israelites to sell themselves as slaves to more prosperous neighbors (Lev. 25:39–40). But this inequality and lack of property, God decreed, was not to be permanent. At the end of six years Hebrew slaves were to be set free, and masters were to share the proceeds of their joint labors with departing male slaves: "And when you let him go free from you, you shall not let him go empty-handed; you shall furnish him liberally out of your flock, out of your threshing floor, and out of your wine press; as the Lord your God has blessed you, you shall give to him" (Deut. 15:13–14; see also Exod. 21:2–6). As a consequence, the freed slave would again have some productive resources so he could earn his own way.

As in the case of the Year of Jubilee, this passage involves structured justice rather than mere charity. The sabbatical release of debts was an institutionalized mechanism to prevent economic divisions in which a few people possessed all the capital while others had no productive resources.

The sabbatical year, unfortunately, was practiced only sporadically. Some texts suggest that failure to obey this law was one reason for the Babylonian exile (Lev. 26:34–36; 2 Chron. 36:20–21). Disobedience, however, does not negate God's demand. Institutionalized structures to prevent poverty are central to God's will for his people.

The central normative principle that emerges from the biblical material concerning the land and the sabbatical release of debts is this: Justice demands that every person or family has access to productive resources (land, money, knowledge) so they have the opportunity to earn a generous sufficiency of material necessities and be dignified participating members of their community. This norm offers significant guidance for ways to shape the economy so that people normally have the opportunity to earn their own way.

Inequality and Power

Equality of income is not the biblical norm for equity. Biblical faith, however, demands something that goes well beyond what America—or any other society today—offers: namely, equality of opportunity up to the point that every person or family has the productive resources necessary to earn their own way and be dignified participants in their community. But meeting that goal would not preclude major differences in income and wealth between rich and poor.

Does that mean that biblical norms do not care about differences between rich and poor? Up to a point, the answer is, differences *are* morally acceptable, in fact, even morally necessary. In a moral universe, bad economic choices rightly produce negative economic consequences. That means differences in income and wealth. Furthermore, Scripture explicitly commends situations in which children inherit from righteous parents (Prov. 13:22). Hence, additional inequality.

Does that mean that biblical people should be indifferent to great extremes between rich and poor? Not at all. Precisely because of what Scripture tells us about sin and power, biblical people must always oppose great extremes of power. In a fallen world, powerful people will almost always take advantage of weak neighbors. And money, especially in a market economy, is power. Therefore, great extremes of poverty and wealth threaten justice and democracy.

The special attention that Scripture gives to the plight of the widow, the orphan, the poor, and the resident alien reflects the awareness in Scripture that when persons lack basic power, evil frequently follows. Thus, in the center of Job's declaration of the injustices to these groups is the statement: "The powerful possess the land" (Job 22:8 NRSV; cf. Job 35:9; Eccles. 4:1). In the real world since the fall, sinful actions against others pervert the intention of the Creator. Sinful persons and evil forces often prevent weak persons from being co-workers with God to shape their lives and world the way the Creator intended. This fallen use of power to oppose the Creator's intentions for the lives of others is exploitative power. Exploitative power allows lust to work its will. "Alas for those who devise wickedness and evil deeds on their beds! When the morning dawns, they perform it, because it is in their power. They covet . . . they oppress" (Micah 2:1–2 NRSV). Unequal power leads to exploitation.

The biblical understanding of human nature warns us about the potential for evil afforded by sharp differences in power among individuals and groups in society. John Calvin described a "rough equality" in the Mosaic law. In commenting on the canceling of debts in the sabbatical year, he wrote,

> In as much as God had given them the use of the franchise, the best way to preserve their liberty was by maintaining a condition of rough equality *[mediocrem statum]*, lest a few persons of immense wealth oppress the general body. Since, therefore, the rich if they had been permitted constantly to increase their wealth, would have tyrannized over the rest, God put a restraint on immoderate power by means of this law.[28]

A Christian political philosophy and economic theory accordingly must be based on a realism about sinful human nature. Because great imbalances of power almost inevitably lead to injustice, Christians must oppose great extremes of wealth and poverty.

To be sure, that norm is general. It does not tell us explicitly whether a ratio of 10 to 1 between the top and bottom 20 percent is dangerous and immoral. But the general warning against great extremes plus the clear demand that everyone have access to adequate productive resources does offer significant guidance. Certainly, whenever—as at present—the bottom 20 percent lack adequate productive resources and are losing ground, *and at the same time* the top 20 percent are rapidly expanding their share of total income, the ratio is seriously askew. In such times, biblical people should demand change.

But what should be done for those—whether the able-bodied who experience an emergency or dependents such as orphans, widows, and the disabled—who for shorter or longer periods simply cannot provide basic necessities through their own efforts alone?

Generous Care for Those Who Cannot Care for Themselves

Again the biblical material is helpful. Both in the Old Testament and the New Testament, we discover explicit teaching on the community's obligation to support those who cannot support themselves.

The Pentateuch provides at least five important provisions designed to help those who could not help themselves:[29]

1. The third year tithe was to go to poor widows, orphans, and sojourners, as well as the Levites (Deut. 14:28–29; 26:12).
2. Laws on gleaning stipulated that the corners of the grain fields and the sheaves and grapes that dropped were to be left for the poor, especially widows, orphans, and sojourners (Lev. 19:9–10; Deut. 24:19–21).
3. Every seventh year, fields were to remain fallow and the poor were allowed to reap the natural growth (Exod. 23:10–11; Lev. 25:1–7).
4. A zero-interest loan was to be available to the poor, and if the balance was not repaid by the sabbatical year, it was forgiven (Exod. 22:25; Lev. 25:35–38; Deut. 15:1–11).
5. Israelites who became slaves to repay debts went free in the seventh year (Exod. 21:1–11; Lev. 25:47–53; Deut. 15:12–18). And when the freed slaves left, God commanded, their temporary "master" was obligated to provide liberally, giving the former slaves cattle, grain, and wine (Deut. 15:14) so they could again earn their own way.

In his masterful essay on this topic, John Mason argues that the primary assistance to the able-bodied person was probably the no-interest loan. This would maintain the family unit, avoid stigmatizing people unnecessarily, and require work so that long-term dependency did not result.

Dependent poor such as widows and orphans received direct "transfer payments" through the third-year tithe. But other provisions such as those on gleaning required the poor to work for the "free" produce they gleaned. The widow Ruth, for example, labored in the fields to feed herself and her mother-in-law (Ruth 2:1–23).

It is important to note the ways in which the provisions for helping the needy point to what we now call "civil society." Not only did Ruth and other poor folk have to glean in the fields, wealthy landowners had the responsibility to leave the corners of the fields and the grapes that dropped. And in the story of Ruth, Boaz as the next of kin took responsibility for her well-being (chapters 3, 4). Laws such as these emphasize the role of the family and neighbors in meeting the needs of the poor.

The texts seem to assume a level of assistance best described as "sufficiency for need," "with a fairly liberal interpretation of need."[30] Deuteronomy 15:8 specifies that the poor brother receive a loan large enough to meet his need. Frequently, God commanded those with resources to treat their poor fellow Israelites with the same liberality that God showed them at the Exodus, in the wilderness, and in giving them their own land (Exod. 22:21; Lev. 25:38; Deut. 24:18, 22). God wanted those who could not care for themselves to receive a liberal sufficiency for need offered in a way that encouraged work and responsibility, strengthened the family, and helped the poor return to self-sufficiency.

Were those "welfare provisions" part of the law to be enforced by the community? Or were they merely suggestions for voluntary charity? The third-year tithe was gathered in a central location (Deut. 14:28) and then shared with the needy. Community leaders would have to act together to carry out such a centralized operation. In the Talmud, there is evidence that the proper community leaders had the right to demand contributions.[31] Nehemiah 5 deals explicitly with violations of the provisions concerning loans to the poor. The political leader would call an assembly, bring "charges against the nobles," and command that the situation be corrected (Neh. 5:7; cf. vv. 1–13). Old Testament texts often speak of the "rights" or "cause" of the poor. Since these terms have clear legal significance, they support the view that the provisions we have explored for assisting the poor would have been legally enforceable. "The clear fact is that the provisions for the impoverished were part of the Mosaic legislation, as much as other laws such as those dealing with murder and theft. Since nothing in the text allows us to consider them as different, they must be presumed to have been legally enforceable."[32]

The sociopolitical situation was dramatically different in the New Testament. The early church was a tiny religious minority with few political rights in a vast pagan Roman empire. But within the church, the standard was the same. Acts 2:43–47 and 4:32–37 record dramatic economic sharing in order to respond to those who could not care for themselves. The norm? "Distribution was made to each as any had need" (Acts 4:35). As a result, "there was not a needy person among them" (v. 34).

The great evangelist Paul spent much of his time over several years collecting an international offering for the impoverished Christians in Jerusalem (2 Corinthians 8–9). For his work, he found a norm (2 Cor. 8:13–15)—equality of basic necessities—articulated in the Exodus story of the manna in which every person ended up with "as much as each of them needed" (Exod. 16:18 NRSV).

Throughout Scripture we see the same standard. When people cannot care for themselves, their community must provide a liberal sufficiency so that their needs are met.

A Role for Government?

Thus far we have seen that the biblical paradigm calls for an economic order in which all who are able to work enjoy access to appropriate productive resources so they can be creative co-workers with God, create wealth to bless their family and neighbors, and be dignified participating members of their community. For those who cannot care for themselves, the biblical framework demands generous assistance so that everyone has a liberal sufficiency of basic necessities.

Institutions including the family, the church, the schools, and business have crucial obligations. Certainly government does not have sole responsibility. But what role should government play?

At different points in the biblical text it is clear that the family has the first obligation to help needy members. In the text on the Jubilee in Leviticus 25, the first responsibility to help the poor person forced by poverty to sell land is the next of kin in the extended family (Lev. 25:25, 35). But the poor person's help does not end with the family. Even if there are no family members to help, the poor person has the legal right to get his land back at the next Jubilee (25:28). Similarly, 1 Timothy 5:16 insists that a Christian widow's relatives should be her first means of support. Only when the family cannot help should the church step in. Any policy or political philosophy that immediately seeks governmental solutions for problems that could be solved just as well or better at the level of the family violates the biblical framework that stresses the central societal role of the family.

But is there a biblical basis for those who seek to exclude government almost completely from the area of the economy? Not at all. The state is not some evil to be endured like an appendectomy.[33] According to Romans 13, the state is a gift from God designed for our good. Hence, John Calvin denounced those who regarded magistrates "only as a kind of necessary evil." Calvin called civil authority "the most honorable of all callings in the whole life" of mortal human beings; its function among human beings is "no less than that of bread, water, sun, and air."[34]

The earlier discussion of the economic components of justice is central for a biblical view of the role of government: "The LORD . . . has made you king to execute justice and righteousness" (1 Kings 10:9 NRSV; cf. Jer. 22:15–16). And these two key words—*justice* and *righteousness*—as we have seen, refer not only to fair legal systems but also to just economic structures. Again and again the biblical texts call on the king to promote justice and righteousness.

The positive role of government in advancing economic justice is seen in the biblical materials that describe the ideal monarch. Both the royal psalms and the messianic prophecies shed light on this ideal ruler.

Psalm 72, one of the royal psalms, gives the following purpose for the ruler: "May he defend the cause of the poor of the people, give deliverance to the needy, and crush the oppressor" (v. 4 NRSV). And this task is identified as the work of justice (vv. 1–3, 7). In this passage, justice includes using power to deliver the needy and oppressed.

According to Psalm 72, there are oppressors of the poor separate from the state who need to be crushed. State power, despite its dangers, is necessary for society because of the evil power of such exploiting groups. "On the side of their oppressors there was power," Ecclesiastes 4:1 NRSV declares. Without governmental force to counter such oppressive power there is no one to comfort (Eccles. 4:1). Whether it is the monarch or the village elders (Amos 5:12, 15), governmental power should deliver the economically weak and guarantee the "rights of the poor" (Jer. 22:15–16; also Pss. 45:4–5; 101:8; Jer. 21:12).

Sin makes government intervention in the economy necessary. When selfish, powerful people deprive others of their rightful access to productive resources, the state rightly steps in with intervening power to correct the injustice. When other individuals and institutions in the community do not or cannot provide basic necessities for the needy, government rightly helps.

Prophecies about the coming messianic ruler also contribute to the picture of the ideal ruler. "With righteousness he shall judge the poor, and decide with equity for the meek of the earth; he shall strike the earth with the rod of his mouth, and with the breath of his lips he shall kill the wicked" (Isa. 11:4 NRSV). This ideal ruler will act like a shepherd in taking responsibility for the needs of the people. "He shall feed them and be their shepherd" (Ezek. 34:23 NRSV). Ezekiel 34:4 denounces the failure of the shepherds (i.e., the rulers) of Israel to "feed" the people. Then in verses 15–16, the same phrases are repeated to describe God's promise of justice:

> "And I will make them lie down," says the Lord GOD. "I will seek the lost, and I will bring back the strayed, and I will bind up the injured, and I will strengthen the weak, but the fat and the strong I will destroy. I will feed them with justice" (NRSV).

This promise will be fulfilled by the coming Davidic ruler (vv. 23–24). Similarly in Isaiah 32:1–8, the promised just and wise monarch is contrasted to the fool who leaves the hungry unsatisfied (v. 6).

This teaching on the role of government applies not just to Israel but to government everywhere. The ideal monarch was to be a channel of God's justice (Ps. 72:1), and God's justice extends to the whole world (e.g., Ps. 9:7–9). All legitimate rulers are instituted by God and are God's servants for human good (Rom. 13:1, 4). In this passage, Paul states a positive reason for government (government acts "for your good" [v. 4]) before he specifies its negative function ("to execute wrath on the wrongdoer" [v. 4]). Romans 13 is structurally similar to Psalm 72:1 in viewing the ruler as a channel of God's authority. All people everywhere can pray with the Israelites: "Give the king your justice, O God" (Ps. 72:1 NRSV).

Daniel 4:27 shows that the ideal of the monarch as the protector of the weak has universal application. God summons the Babylonian monarch no less than the Israelite king to bring "justice and . . . mercy to the oppressed." Similarly in Proverbs 31:9, King Lemuel (generally considered to be a northern Arabian monarch) is to "defend the rights of the poor and needy" (NRSV). "The general obligation of the Israelite king to see that persons otherwise not adequately protected or provided for should enjoy fair treatment in judicial proceedings and should receive the daily necessities of life is evidently understood as the duty of all kings."[35]

The teaching on the ideal, just monarch of Israel, whether in royal psalms or messianic prophecies, cannot be restricted to some future messianic reign. God demanded that the kings of Israel provide in their own time what the messianic ruler would eventually bring more completely: namely, justice that delivers the needy from oppression. God's concern in the present and in the future within Israel and outside of Israel is that there be a community in which the weak are strengthened and protected from their foes.

Government is an aspect of community and is inherent in human life as an expression of our created social nature. Governmental action to empower the poor is one way we promote the common good and implement the truth that economic justice is a family affair.

Frequently, of course, the state contributes to social cohesion by encouraging and enabling other institutions in the community—whether family, church, nongovernmental social agencies, and unions—to carry out their responsibilities to care for the economically dependent. Sometimes, however, the depth of social need exceeds the capacity of nongovernmental institutions. When indirect approaches are not effective in restraining economic injustice, providing economic opportunity to all, or in providing care for those who cannot care for themselves, the state rightly acts to demand patterns of justice and provide vital services.

Conclusion

Does the biblical material offer a norm for distributive justice today? Some would argue that the biblical material only applies to God's covenant community. But that is to ignore the fact that the biblical writers did not hesitate to apply revealed standards to persons and societies outside Israel. Amos announced divine punishment on the surrounding nations for their evil and injustice (Amos 1–2). Isaiah condemned Assyria for its pride and injustice (Isa. 10:12–19). The Book of Daniel shows that God removed pagan kings such as Nebuchadnezzar in the same way he destroyed Israel's rulers when they failed to show mercy to the oppressed (Dan. 4:27). God obliterated Sodom and Gomorrah no less than Israel and Judah because they neglected to aid the poor and feed the hungry (Ezek. 16:49). The Lord of history applies the same standards of social justice to all nations.

That does not mean, however, that we should try to apply the specific mechanisms of the Jubilee and the sabbatical release to late-twentieth-century global market economies. It is the basic paradigm that is normative for us today. Land, for example, has a very different function in an industrial economy. Appropriate application of these texts requires that we ask how their specific mechanisms functioned in Israelite culture and then determine what specific measures would fulfill a similar function in our very different society. Since land in Israelite society represented productive power, we must identify the forms of productive power in modern societies. In an industrial society the primary productive power is machinery, and in an information society it is knowledge. Faithful application of these biblical texts in such societies means finding mechanisms that offer everyone the opportunity to share in the ownership of these productive resources. If we start with the Jubilee's call for everyone to enjoy access to productive power, we must criticize all socioeconomic arrangements in which productive power is owned or controlled by only one class or group (whether bourgeoisie, aristocracy, or workers)—or by a state or party oligarchy. Indeed, we saw that the prophets protested the development of an economic system in which land ownership was shifted to a small group within society. Today we must develop appropriate intervening processes in society to restore access to productive resources to everyone.

The traditional criterion of distributive justice that comes closest to the biblical paradigm is distribution according to needs. That is not to ignore the important truth that bad choices rightly have negative economic consequences. Nor is it to forget that the able-bodied have an obligation to work to earn their way. But it does mean that a theory of distributive justice grounded in Scripture places much more emphasis on structural arrangements that guarantee basic needs for life in community than do other views. Other views of distributive justice place primary emphasis on birth, or might, or ability, or contract, or achievement.

To be sure, these other criteria of distributive justice are not all irrelevant. Indeed, some of them are at least assumed in the biblical approach. Achievement (e.g., ability in the market, so stressed in Western culture) has a legitimate role. It must be subordinate, however, to the central criterion of distribution according to needs for the sake of inclusion in community.

The biblical material provides at least three norms pertaining to distribution of resources to meet basic needs:

1. Normally, all people who can work should have access to the productive resources so that, if they act responsibly, they can produce or purchase an abundant sufficiency of all that is needed to enjoy a dignified, healthy life in community.
2. The difference in wealth between the rich and the poor dare not become so great that great inequalities of wealth and therefore power lead to oppression.
3. Those who cannot care for themselves should receive from their community a liberal sufficiency of the necessities of life provided in ways that preserve dignity, encourage responsibility, and strengthen the family.

Those three norms are modest in comparison with some ideals presented in the name of equality. At the same time they demand fundamental change in our nation.

If God's Word is true, then the United States today stands in blatant defiance of God's norms for society. Anyone who seeks to be biblical must demand an end to the scandal of poverty in the richest nation on earth. If the Bible teaches that private property is so good that everybody ought to have some, then biblical people will lead the way in offering new opportunity to the bottom 20 percent.

3

A Comprehensive Strategy

Every institution in society must do its share, and each one must do what it does best.

Call to Renewal

Once upon a time just a few decades ago in a city not far away, Tim Brown, a beautiful baby boy, was born to sixteen-year-old Mary. Mary tried hard to care for Tim and finish high school, but most of her friends dropped out of school when they became pregnant, and Mary soon joined them. Mary lived in an urban ghetto where life on her modest welfare check and food stamps was difficult and dull. Her neighborhood used to be one of the few places where African Americans could find housing. The police tolerated widespread crime and violence, and liquor stores, churches, and high-priced corner grocery stores seemed to be the only remaining neighborhood institutions that still worked. More and more, Mary found her only excitement in alcohol, drugs, and boyfriends.

Young Tim found his best babysitter in the TV and his closest family in the local gang. Tim initially hesitated to sell drugs and use guns, but his gang soon shamed him into taking part. In grade 9 Tim got to know Jim Moore, a tenth grader. Jim's dad was a famous black preacher at Eighth Memorial Baptist Church. Tim admired Jim's personal integrity, good grades, and plans for college, secretly wishing he could do the same. He even went to church with Jim a few times and felt drawn by the preacher's claim that Jesus could help young people say no to sex, drugs, and crime. But when Tim dared to mention all this to his friends in the gang, they laughed at him and dismissed Jim as an egghead. Tim stuck with his friends.

Life at Edison High School seemed pointless. The building was old. Most of the teachers didn't seem to think the kids could learn. Tim remembered some story about former glory days at Edison High when most of the students were white. But the city apparently had built a new high school in a new all-white section of the city, and the former name, trophies, and most of the good teachers had moved to the new school. Tim dropped out halfway through grade 11, abandoning his last lingering dreams about imitating Jim, who had just been admitted to Yale.

More alcohol, more girls, more drugs followed. Good money came easily if one was smart at drug running. Tim had several kids by several women, but he seldom saw them. One woman was different. Rosemary was beautiful and fun, with a haunting inner beauty that Tim found irresistible. They lived together for more than a year. They even talked of marriage. She would go off welfare, he would abandon the drug trade and get a job. Tim tried—twice. Tim was fired from his first job the third week because he often showed up late, frequently could not read instructions, and lost his temper when his boss challenged his mistakes. At the second job, the supervisor was openly racist. Tim left in anger. Besides, he had not been able to stop using drugs, even after trying a government-run drug and alcohol detox program. Desperate, Tim and Rosemary went to Jim Moore's church a couple times. They wondered if the preacher's invitation to "give their hearts to Jesus" (whatever that meant) might help. But they did not want to give up drugs and alcoholic binges, so they soon stopped going to church. One night after an especially nasty fight, Tim walked out on Rosemary.

Tim plunged deeper into selling and using drugs. He knew it was only a matter of time before either the police or a bullet from a rival gang member would get him. Fortunately, it was the police. Tim spent five years in prison for attempted homicide in a drug war over turf.

In prison, Tim did a lot of thinking. He explored Islam, and he read the Bible. He also found a way to get drugs. Then one day, to his astonishment, he saw a notice announcing that Rev. Jim Moore Jr., an assistant pastor at Eighth Memorial Baptist, was going to be preaching in the prison chapel. *Might this possibly be my old friend?* Tim mused. He had to find out.

As he listened to his former high school buddy talk about the way Jesus wanted to forgive and change even the most broken, Tim wept silently. At the end of the service, when Rev. Moore invited people to come forward to pray, Tim felt irresistibly drawn. Only toward the end of the time of prayer did Jim Moore recognize his old friend. They embraced, sat down, and for two long hours Tim poured out his painful story.

When he had finished, Jim Moore made Tim an offer. "Jesus can transform your life if you are willing," he promised. "I and my church will walk with you. In your remaining year and a half in prison, you can study the Bible, get your high school equivalency degree, and prepare for a different life." Every other choice Tim could imagine ended in despair and ruin. Somewhere, deep within, a glimmer of hope flickered dimly. Tim accepted the offer.

There were many days Tim almost gave up. Other prisoners mocked his changed lifestyle, and the temptation to return to his old ways almost overpowered him. He never would have made it if it wasn't for Jim's frequent visits and the love and prayers of a growing circle of believing prisoners nurtured by the prison ministry at Jim's church. Slowly, Tim began to sense a new set of values, even a transformed character, growing within him.

The day Tim walked free, both elation and fear flooded his being. For the first time in his life, a hopeful future seemed conceivable. But Tim reminded himself of the awful difficulties ahead. He had almost no skills, a criminal record, thousands of dollars in bills, and no family or friends to help him get started. The only people he knew were his old gang friends.

Rev. Jim had told Tim to wait for Deacon Bulford, who would pick him up from prison. Tim sat on the prison steps praying frantically that the deacon would not forget. He didn't, and after Deacon Bulford dropped him off at the church's Memorial Holistic Community Center, Tim could hardly believe what he heard. The people there spoke of a legal clinic that could help Tim with legal problems. The large health clinic would offer him free medical care until he found a job. He could stay in the halfway house for newly released prisoners, studying what it means to live a Christian life and taking a job training course. Later Tim learned that the word *holistic* in the center's name reflected the fact that the programs met both spiritual and physical needs.

The center was funded through an unusual new partnership between government, business, and several partner churches. The community center raised private dollars to fund the programs focusing on personal faith and character building. State funds (via a voucher program using federal dollars) were used for the job training component. Those who passed the job training course had a guaranteed job waiting for them at ServiceMaster, a large corporation that worked closely with the center.

Tim worked in a way he never had before in his life. After six months, he landed his first job. It paid only minimum wage, but he learned a great deal about being a responsible employee. Almost every day, at first, he felt like quitting, but the job readiness support group at the center kept him going. After six months, Tim got his first tiny raise and a promise of on-the-job training and future opportunities for promotion. The day he moved into his own small apartment, Tim finally believed deep in his heart that he could make it.

Tim started attending Eighth Memorial Baptist Church the first Sunday after he left prison. Regularly he left renewed and encouraged to face the week's struggles. Tim also loved the way the pastor's sermons and the faith and government committee helped him understand that the God who was changing his heart also demanded justice for the poor. With enthusiasm he joined those from the church who were organizing a large movement in the city to demand that politicians work harder to provide quality education, safe streets, and a living wage.

One Sunday, about eight weeks after Tim left prison, Rev. Moore Sr. asked him to share his story with the congregation. With a voice that lurched from joy to tears, he told the congregation that for the first time in his life he was beginning to live out the dreams of a different life he had secretly harbored ever since he met Rev. Jim Moore Jr. in grade 9.

Nothing, however, prepared him for the surprise he encountered at the end of the service. When he finally turned to greet the last person in a long line of members who welcomed him with hugs and prayers, he saw the smiling face of his old girlfriend Rosemary. Her embrace awoke a new hope. As they talked, Rosemary explained that her life had slowly degenerated into chaos after he left. But two years ago, in despair, she had remembered Rev. Moore's church. After a few Sundays, she had come to personal faith, and over the months, the preaching, prayers, and a supportive small group had slowly transformed her life. With the help of a federally funded job training program and state vouchers for child care at the church day care center, she had found a job and her own apartment.

Tim didn't even dare ask what he most wanted to know, but he looked for her at the next church fellowship group for singles. To his joy, she was there—and almost seemed to be looking for him. Over many months, they became close friends. Ten weeks of marriage counseling followed their engagement. On their wedding day, as Tim watched Rosemary walk down the aisle followed by her two children as flower girl and ring bearer, tears of joy overwhelmed him. Together as Tim and Rosemary listened to their wedding sermon about how Jesus and his body of believers can restore lives broken by bad choices and unfair environments, they wept for joy. By the power of God, Tim realized, his dreams were coming true.

Tim and Rosemary experienced joy and struggle during the years that followed. Ghosts from the past at times provoked painful struggles. For a time, before the promised promotions materialized, Tim's full-time job and Rosemary's part-time job at minimum wage barely provided enough income for them to slowly repay debts and offer their children a little of the opportunity they had never had. Fortunately, the federal Earned Income Tax Credit helped them keep their heads above water, and frequently, just when they began to despair, their church family came through with encouragement and, on occasion, a little financial help. Yes, indeed, Tim decided, his dreams had come true. And their children, he felt confident, could dream even bigger dreams.[1]

Everybody agrees that poverty is bad and that it ought to be reduced. But how? That is where the agreement ends. I am convinced, however, that the above story holds the key. We need better government programs, greatly expanded work by religious communities, and a new partnership between them and other institutions in society.

A Policy Impasse

The question of how to reduce poverty, of course, is intimately related to the question of what causes poverty. Until recently, as we saw in chapter 1, liberals and conservatives identified different causes and proposed different solutions, resulting in a policy impasse.[2] Each blocked the other's solutions, and the poor remained mired in their agony. Political liberals traditionally argued that structural changes and systemic injustice were responsible for most poverty. Obviously, then, modifying the structures—along with quality education, job training, and child care—ought to solve the problem. Conservatives disagreed. Poverty resulted from wrong moral choices exacerbated by bad government policy. The solution was to cut welfare, which created economic incentives for unethical behavior, reduce taxes, and let an expanding economy create more jobs. The market would encourage (or force) individuals to work to earn a living.

One essential step in breaking the impasse between liberal and conservative proposals is to see, as I argued in chapter 1, that both are partly right. Structural changes have caused poverty. So have wrong personal choices and the breakdown of the family.

In addition to ignoring each other's partly correct analyses, both liberals and conservatives, until recently, also overlooked a third crucial cause and solution: civil society. Robert Bellah has argued that both liberals and conservatives are individualists with an inadequate understanding of community and the common good. Liberals thought the individual would do fine if government played a dominant role. Conservatives expected individuals to flourish if government got out of the way and let the market do its magic.

Fortunately, both liberals and conservatives are beginning to place more emphasis on the crucial role of civil society in causing and reducing poverty. This emerging agreement offers a way out of the policy impasse.

The Indispensable Role of Civil Society

What is civil society? Some define it as that web of "relationships and institutions that are neither created nor controlled by the state."[3] Civil society, therefore, includes families, religious organizations, businesses, unions, and a vast array of smaller voluntary organizations. More helpful, perhaps, is Stephen Monsma's definition. Civil society includes all those institutions in which—to a greater or lesser degree—their members "are personally aware of each other and interact with each other, thereby giving their members a meaningful sense of belonging."[4] Families, local religious congregations, local service clubs, and hospital guilds are all typical examples.

Why is civil society important? Because persons are not just isolated autonomous individuals. We are social beings made for community. Only in warm, intimate, nurturing communities such as a wholesome family can we grow into the whole persons God intended. If we view persons merely as autonomous individuals who need only a free market in which to make self-centered decisions and an impersonal, bureaucratic state to provide essential services, we ignore a crucial part of our humanity. We need face-to-face, intimate, personal relationships that provide friendship, support, meaning, and obligations.

That is not to overlook the extremely important role of large, corporate—but nongovernmental—structures such as businesses, unions, and the media. They, too, lie between the individual and the state and, partly because of their independence from governmental control, contribute enormously to the freedom and well-being of society. But their large size and bureaucratic structure distinguish them from smaller, "face-to-face" institutions. I will speak of the former as "large, nongovernmental public institutions" and label the latter "civil society."

A Weak versus Strong Civil Society

How does a weak civil society contribute to poverty? Let's reflect on two contrasting situations.

Consider the most impoverished areas of our inner cities. Stable, two-parent families have almost disappeared. Single parenthood in some areas is more than 80 percent. The middle class and the civic institutions and social clubs they organized have fled to the suburbs. The only working institutions are liquor outlets and churches—and the churches are struggling. The odds of escaping poverty for a child like Tim Brown, growing up in a setting in which civil society is in such decay, are vastly reduced.

Consider, on the other hand, a closely knit community with strong families, vibrant churches or synagogues, and vigorous social clubs. In their family, their church, and a variety of lively youth clubs, children learn moral values, personal responsibility, and postponement of immediate gratification. Family and friends discourage sexual permissiveness, treasure education, and assist those hindered by less ability or crippling accident. Informal communal networks share job opportunities. Growing up in such a setting makes avoiding poverty much easier.

A strong, moral civil society has numerous positive benefits. First and most important, our primary moral teachers are located in civil society—especially in the family and religious institutions. "What is it," Mary Ann Glendon of Harvard Law School asks, "that causes individual men and women to keep their promises, to limit consumption, to stick with a spouse in sickness and health, to care for their children, . . . to reach out to the poor, to respect the rights of others?"[5] Neither bureaucratic government nor for-profit business is very good at teaching such things. But good families and faith communities are. When children do not learn these fundamental values from their family and religious community, violence, irresponsibility, single parenthood, and poverty all increase.

It is precisely the institutions of civil society that teach the attitudes of heart and mind that both prevent poverty in the first place and also help the poor escape poverty once they have fallen into it. One careful review of published research discovered that religious involvement reduces problems such as "sexual permissiveness, teen pregnancy, suicide, drug abuse, alcoholism, and to some extent deviant and delinquent acts, and increases self-esteem, family cohesiveness and general well being."[6] People who attend church just once a month are more than twice as likely to avoid divorce as persons who attend once a year or less.[7] In addition, religious faith is especially effective in transforming people trapped in the multitude of behaviors and attitudes that greatly contribute to poverty.

Second, civil society is important because its institutions provide crucial help and support. Children receive essential physical and emotional support in families. Family members and church friends provide emotional and economic support in times of unemployment, sickness, and death. If government tried to replace all the essential services provided by civil society, the cost would be staggering and the bureaucratic results would be cold and barren.

Third, a strong civil society can help those who are not poor develop the public attitudes and political will needed to strengthen our resolve to empower the poor. Harvard political scientist Michael Sandel argues that "the institutions of civil society draw us out of our private, self-interested concerns and get us in the habit of attending to the common good."[8] Too many affluent citizens are ready to retreat to gated communities, rationalize the growing gap between rich and poor, and ignore the growing danger to democratic society. Renewing civil society should help the rich transcend their self-indulgence.

The church's prophetic role in this is critical. Faithful Christians not only care for the poor and call them to forsake sinful choices and destructive behavior, Christians also ask why people are poor—and advocate change. A faithful church will issue a ringing summons to the middle class and rich to transcend their self-centered materialism and change what is unjust. A faithful church knows that great imbalances of power foster injustice and, therefore, acts to strengthen honest unions and encourage grassroots community organizing. A revitalized Christian church—truly understanding that God measures societies by how they treat the poor and that the Bible demands economic justice for all—could provide the critical leadership necessary to dramatically reduce poverty.

The breakdown of the two-parent family demonstrates negatively the importance of strong institutions of civil society such as the family. Most obvious is the connection between single parenthood and poverty. Forty-four percent of all female-headed families are poor, whereas only 9 percent of married-couple families are poor. Study after study by social scientists have demonstrated that kids in single-parent families are more likely to have lower SAT scores, drop out of high school, experience divorce, have children out of wedlock, use illicit drugs, and commit crimes—and all of these behaviors or circumstances are correlated with higher rates of poverty.[9] As Sylvia Ann Hewlett and Cornel West argue so powerfully in their new book, *The War against Parents,* unless we can renew the family, we simply cannot succeed in the battle against poverty.[10]

It is silly, of course, to think that government can restore the family and the moral values necessary for strong families. Therefore, it is puzzling that Lawrence Mead, at the end of his (substantially correct) argument that considerable poverty today results from wrong values and behaviors that cannot be corrected by economic incentives, proposes a "new paternalism" by a "custodial democracy" as his basic solution. If, as he argues, many poor people are "maimed in body and spirit," then surely government by itself can never solve their problems. In fact, Mead casts doubt on his own solution. He admits that even the most rigid government institutions (prisons, for example) "produce little *inner* change."[11] Since Mead does not know what else to propose beyond custodial democracy, he is profoundly pessimistic: "The Western tradition . . . has no solution for the passivity of today's poor."[12]

Mead's comment may be true of the Western *secular* tradition, but it certainly does not apply to the Judeo-Christian tradition. From the time of the prophets, biblical faith has taught that both inner spiritual conversion and external structural transformation are essential for societal wholeness—and also that they are possible.[13] Far more hope is realistic if the religious institutions play their proper role.

Religious Institutions

Religious institutions are—along with the family—the most influential components of civil society.[14] Fortunately, U.S. religious institutions have not declined the way the family has. In fact, in a typical week, attendance at U.S. churches and synagogues exceeds total attendance at all sports events by about thirteen to one![15] Studies show that church attendees are about twice (64 percent) as likely to volunteer time (*and* volunteer twice as much) as those who do not attend church.[16] Recent studies by social scientists underline the positive social impact of religious faith.[17] Harvard economist Richard B. Freeman discovered that the best predictor of whether young black inner-city males would escape the syndrome of drugs, crime, and prison was church attendance.[18]

Especially significant is some preliminary data that suggests that, sometimes at least, faith-based providers of social services are far more successful than secular programs. One study of Teen Challenge's Christ-centered drug rehabilitation program found a 95 percent success rate for heroin users and an 83 percent success rate for alcoholics.[19] A success rate of 5 to 10 percent is not uncommon in many secular programs. In conversation with a leader in the Salvation Army's drug and alcohol rehabilitation programs, I learned that they believe they achieve a success rate about ten times higher than that of secular programs.

We need extensive, sophisticated evaluations of a wide variety of secular and religious social service programs to evaluate these claims. But if careful studies by social scientists confirm that faith-based programs are more successful, it will not surprise believers. Jews and Christians know that persons are not just complex socioeconomic machines. They are also spiritual beings whose free decisions contribute to social problems. Therefore, dealing with whole persons rather than just the physical side of persons ought to produce better results. Especially in the case of persons caught in a destructive environment that makes misguided decisions about drugs, sex, school, and single parenthood extremely easy, religious conversion is important. An inward transformation of values and character produces a radical transformation of outward behavior.[20] While secular agencies and government programs cannot bring about such transformation, evidence clearly indicates that faith-based programs—especially those with a substantial religious content in their activities—can and do.[21]

Senator Daniel Moynihan is right to warn us not to expect too much from government. He knows that "restoration of individual character and moral instruction in everyday life" must be at the heart of a successful strategy. Both fiscal problems and the very nature of government prompt Moynihan to conclude: "It is time for small platoons."[22] That is an urgent plea for civil society in general and churches and other faith-based agencies in particular to play a much larger role.

Christians—and other religious people—should give much more generously to successful holistic faith-based programs. Our teachers and preachers must nurture far more generous citizens. But even if private religious donors doubled or tripled such giving, it would not be enough.

That is why the Charitable Choice provisions (section 104) in the 1996 welfare legislation are so important. These provisions insist that if state governments use nongovernment agencies for any of the services covered by the welfare bill, then state governments dare not discriminate against explicitly religious agencies. Such agencies may keep their religious symbols and hire staff that share their faith. No government funds dare be used for "sectarian worship, instruction, or proselytization," but the faith-based agency may raise private funds for such activities and include explicitly religious activities in their overall program.[23] It is absolutely crucial that government regulations allow faith-based providers to hire people who share their faith commitments. Not only does this allow faith-based agencies to assemble a united staff motivated by a common faith, it also makes it possible for all of that staff, not just a chaplain, to integrate concrete religious components into the overall program in a way that maximizes the positive impact of the religious component. Any "nondiscrimination" provision that would force a faith-based program seeking government funds to hire any technically qualified person, whether or not that person shared the agency's faith perspective, would fundamentally undermine precisely those parts of the program that make it so successful.

The Charitable Choice provisions offer a significant new opportunity to expand the role of civil society in solving our social problems. Many small, underfunded, faith-based programs work well and are often more effective than secular government programs. Fortunately, more politicians at the state and national level are demanding change. Texas Governor George W. Bush laments and is correcting the way that in the past "strong Bible-based programs like Teen Challenge (whose cure rates far surpass those of other programs) were crowded out by state regulations that embraced a strict medical model of addiction treatment."[24] In a major policy speech in June 1999, Vice President Gore embraced Charitable Choice, declaring his intention to "put the solutions that faith-based organizations are pioneering at the very heart of our national strategy for building a better, more just society." Expanding Charitable Choice beyond welfare to a broad range of government-funded programs would both strengthen civil society and be more cost effective.

Civil Society Is Not Enough

A greatly increased emphasis on the crucial role of civil society must be at the heart of any successful program to combat poverty. It would, however, be utterly wrong to suppose that civil society by itself can conquer poverty. If religious congregations were to replace the federal government's spending on just the four most basic programs for the poor, every one of the approximately 325,000[25] Christian, Jewish, and Muslim congregations in America would have to raise another $289,000 per year to assist the needy. And if these congregations also took over the federal government's share of Medicaid, the figure would be $612,000 per congregation each year.[26] That would be rather difficult since 50 percent of all U.S. congregations have less than one hundred regular participants and their total median annual budget is a mere $50,000 to $60,000.[27]

Without Social Security from the federal government, almost one out of two elderly Americans in 1997 would have lived in poverty. Thanks to Social Security, only about one in ten elderly Americans was poor.[28] Without government benefits, more than one-fifth of all Americans (21.6 percent) would have been poor in 1996. Government programs reduced the poverty level by almost 50 percent to 11.5 percent.[29] Unless jobs paying a family wage are available for everyone willing to work, poverty will prevail no matter how much individuals are spiritually renewed.

Let no one misunderstand my call for a greatly expanded role for faith-based agencies in civil society as a libertarian rejection of government's important role. We dare not allow politicians to use Charitable Choice to legitimize governmental abandonment of the poor. Furthermore, let no one suppose that if civil society and government get it right, then large private institutions like the media and business have no responsibilities. Civil society, business, the media, and government all have crucial roles to play if America is to dramatically reduce the scandal of widespread poverty in this land of abundance. We need a multi-sector strategy in which each group does what it does best.

Business

The twentieth century has taught us that market economies are more efficient than socialist economies. They also strengthen freedom. A biblical view of persons and sin also leads to the conclusion that market economies offer a better framework than present alternatives.[30]

Unacceptable levels of injustice and agony, however, are a part of the way today's market economy works in America. It is simply wrong that some people work full-time and still cannot escape poverty. It is immoral that over 43 million people lack health insurance. It is unacceptable that corporations treat labor as merely an economic input, undermine family life, and use advertising techniques that subtly, powerfully promote the lies that human fulfillment comes by means of more gadgets and joy comes through illicit sex. Business leaders can and must contribute to empowering the poor and renewing society.

Profits are essential, but elevating the maximization of profits above a concern for workers, the common good, and the environment is idolatry. Businesses have a moral responsibility to adopt policies that help make jobs available to everyone (especially the poor) and strengthen rather than undermine family life.

Businesses could consciously choose to offer family-friendly opportunities: "Flexible workplace arrangements, including tele-working, job sharing, compressed work weeks, career breaks, job protection and other benefits for short-term (up to six months) parental leave and job preferences and other benefits, such as graduated re-entry, for long-term (up to five years) parental leave."[31] Corporations that resolve to adopt policies that offer employees (including upper-level executives) more time for children and spouse will contribute enormously to social well-being.

Businesses have numerous opportunities to empower the poorer segments of society. Programs for profit sharing and employee ownership, generous on-the-job training for low-skill workers, and corporate giving focused on the poor would all help. It would also help for corporate leadership to urge the federal government to abolish most of the $125 billion in corporate welfare that private business now receives and spend those savings on effective programs to empower the poor.[32]

Fortunately, there is growing evidence that attention to all stakeholders in the long run also benefits shareholders. ServiceMaster is a fifty-year-old publicly traded, $4-billion-a-year corporation with a 24 percent annually compounded growth rate over the past twenty years. Most corporate executives define management as "getting work done through people." ServiceMaster, however, was consciously founded on biblical principles about persons and work. ServiceMaster views management as "developing people through work." This company has enjoyed widespread success in hiring low-skill, untrained employees, treating them as dignified persons, and offering them numerous opportunities for education and on-the-job learning. The result: widespread upward mobility into well-paying jobs. In North Carolina, the company is working with the state government and a religious nonprofit organization (Goodwill Industries) to hire former welfare recipients.[33]

After a careful study, Professor Joseph A. Maciariello at the Drucker Graduate School of Management at Claremont Graduate School concluded: "Clearly the pool of service employees that they draw from contains a large number of people caught in a vicious cycle of failure and low self-esteem. The implementation of ServiceMaster's commitment to developing people through training and motivational programs assists these 'least privileged' ones to break this cycle of failure and low self-esteem."[34] For ServiceMaster, placing an ethical concern for employees above short-term profit has contributed to stunning long-term profitability.

Unions

Strong unions also play an essential role in the fight against poverty. Biblical faith teaches what Lord Acton aptly summarized: In a fallen world, power tends to corrupt and absolute power tends to corrupt absolutely. Large corporations wield enormous power. By comparison, individual employees are mere ants. Top business executives are no less—or more— sinful than the rest of us, but their enormous power offers vast opportunity to use it for selfish advantage unless other power counterbalances corporate power. Wise government policy—e.g., antimonopoly legislation, antipollution laws, and occupational safety requirements—provides one counterweight to corporate power. Strong, honest, democratic unions offer another. Powerful unions, to be sure, have also misused power, forgetting the poorest and excluding minorities. But unions have often been effective tools, helping the poor to demand a living wage and minorities to find a place in economic life.

The Media

TV, movies, and the Internet are often the primary moral teachers for our children, and, tragically, what they teach concerning consumerism, sex, and violence is abominable. For both the poor, single mom struggling to raise her children alone and the busy middle-class parents preoccupied with economic success, however, the TV is often a welcome babysitter. Unless the media stop corrupting our children with destructive sexual and anti-family values, religious institutions will face an enormously difficult uphill battle to renew the family.

Lt. Col. David Grossman is one of the foremost experts on the psychology of killing.[35] In a stunning article on the impact of media violence, Grossman points out that the murder rate in America doubled between 1957 and 1992. Far more shocking is the attempted murder rate: In the same years, aggravated assault jumped from 60 per 100,000 to 440—an increase of more than 700 percent! Why? Grossman acknowledges many causes, but one clear culprit is TV. A careful study reported in the *Journal of the American Medical Association* comparing similar societies—except that one had TV and the other did not—concluded that when people started watching TV, the murder rate doubled within fifteen years. The article concluded: "The introduction of television in the 1950's caused a subsequent doubling of the homicide rate; i.e., long-term childhood exposure to television is a causal factor behind approximately one-half of all homicides committed in the United States, or approximately 10,000 homicides annually."[36]

Glorification of sexual permissiveness in movies and TV has undoubtedly had a similar effect on the breakdown of the family. Tragically, family decay and widespread violence are in direct correlation to the areas of most intense poverty.

Unfortunately, sex and violence attract viewers, who attract advertisers. Media executives and the large corporate owners of our media seem more concerned with their economic bottom line than the destructive impact media has on society. Former Senator Bill Bradley is right:

> We need a more civic minded media. . . . Too often T.V. producers and media executives and video game manufacturers feed young people a menu of violence without context and sex without attachment, and both with no consequences. . . . Too often those who trash government as an enemy of freedom and a destroyer of families are strangely silent about the market's corrosive effect on those very same values in civil society.[37]

What we need is clear: less sex and violence, and more positive stories about wholesome family life and successful social ministries that empower the poor. How to encourage—even demand—that the media change is less clear.

National TV-Turnoff Week, adoption of a voluntary television code and a "family hour" policy between 8:00 and 9:00 P.M. by the media industry, wise consumer boycotts, and limited government regulation (e.g., of hardcore pornography) can all help. Present media practice is on a collision course with the effort to renew morality and family life in America. Somehow, we must find a way to demand fundamental change.

Universities

The careful studies and analyses done in our great academic centers have played a crucial role in helping us understand poverty. That must continue.

One change, however, is essential. The widespread agnosticism described by Stephen Carter in *Culture of Disbelief* has misled academic researchers into a biased neglect of the role of religion. Formerly Princeton and now University of Pennsylvania political scientist Professor John J. DiIulio Jr. laments that "you can go through thousands and thousands of studies, and people don't even look at the religion variable."[38] Fortunately, that is beginning to change. The entire spring 1999 issue of the *Brookings Review,* published by perhaps the most prestigious Washington think tank, is devoted to the question, What's God got to do with the American experiment? Academic researchers do not have to become believers, but they ought to be objective enough to look at all the data. In fact, in those relatively few cases in which the "religion variable" was included, religious faith turned out to have an almost universally positive impact.[39]

If our society turns toward a greater appreciation of civil society and moves toward widespread adoption of policies such as Charitable Choice, then careful academic research and evaluation will become even more crucial. Are faith-based programs usually more successful than secular ones? Are Buddhist and New Age programs as effective at drug rehabilitation as Jewish or Christian ones? Are thoroughly faith-based programs more successful than nominally faith-related programs? What are the most significant components in faith-based programs? We need honest, objective answers to these and other questions.

Government policy, of course, must remain strictly neutral in its funding of all types of agencies that offer the public goods we need for the common good. All government needs to do is demand objective evaluation of results and then fund only the more cost-effective programs. Our universities must play a crucial role in providing everyone with solid, reliable program evaluation.

Government

I have argued that everyone would benefit if nongovernmental institutions, especially those in civil society, played a substantially larger role in combating poverty. When a social problem emerges, the first question should *not* be, What can government do? The first question should be, What institutions in society have primary responsibility for and are best able to correct this problem? Many times there will be overlapping responsibilities. In those cases, it is crucial that the several institutions support each other's respective roles. Frequently, nongovernmental institutions will be more effective at less cost. We must reject liberals' automatic preference for government solutions.

Libertarianism, however, is not the answer. To someone like John Stagliano, a major funder of the libertarian Cato Institute, "the less government the better" makes sense. After all, Stagliano is one of the leading publishers of pornography in America. He does not want government regulation to limit his profits. Biblical principles, church history, and realistic contemporary analysis, however, all lead us to reject libertarian approaches.

In chapter 2, we saw that God commanded the king to do justice and righteousness—and the Hebrew words here include economic justice. The king was to have a special concern to care for the poor and needy and restore productive assets to the impoverished. To be sure, the first responsibility lay not with the king but with the family. But there is not a shred of biblical support for those Christians who argue that individual believers and churches but not government should assist the poor. In fact, church history demonstrates that Christians over the centuries have supported the role of government in alleviating poverty.

It is totally unrealistic to suggest that churches and other voluntary agencies provide all the funds and staff to care for the poor in America. The task is too big. To be sure, if church members vastly expanded their giving and most of the money went to the poor, we could substantially reduce the need for welfare payments and food stamps. But the trend in church giving is down, not up. Church members have given to churches a smaller and smaller percent of their (growing) income virtually every year since 1969.[40] It is now less than 2.5 percent, and the vast bulk of what is given is spent on themselves in their own church programs, not the poor. Until radical revival produces sweeping growth in church giving and concern for the poor, any suggestion that churches replace governmental care for the poor is unrealistic.

Government must play a significant role in alleviating poverty, but not the only role, and in many cases, not even the primary role. Our society cannot long survive unless the family is renewed, and government can play only a modest, supportive role here. Religious institutions and the persons of high moral character whom they help shape have the primary responsibility for renewing family life.

When government does act, the first question should be, What institutions in society are best able to solve this problem? And second, How can government strengthen rather than weaken these institutions? Before legislatures enact any social policy, they should demand a careful "civil society impact" study just as we now demand "environmental impact" studies. Government policy must strengthen not weaken other societal institutions. That is why Charitable Choice is so promising. Charitable Choice recognizes that government funding and basic guidelines are essential, but it also understands that smaller nongovernmental agencies (many of which are faith-based) often do a better job than large state bureaucracies in providing the actual delivery systems for government-funded services. The resulting services can be more personal, more attentive to demanding individual responsibility, and far more able to bring the full strength of religious faith to bear on the problem. This new partnership between government and civil society is likely to be more effective, less expensive, and better able to strengthen civil society.

There are some things, however, that only the government can do. Even when the government uses nongovernmental providers for social services, the government must write the guidelines, demand, fund, and publicize careful evaluations, and provide much of the finances. Society needs marriage laws that apply to everyone. Even though the primary responsibility for renewing marriage and the family rests with churches and synagogues, governments should rewrite divorce laws to make them more family friendly. Government should act as a last resort when other institutions do not or cannot care for the poor. It is both morally right and in each person's long-term self-interest for the government to tax us all so it can provide funding for effective programs that empower and care for the needy. In the biblical perspective, poverty is a family affair. Therefore, using tax dollars to care for our needy brothers and sisters and restore them to dignity and community is right. It is also wise. None of us knows when drastic, permanent illness may swoop down on us, wiping out our savings and exhausting private insurance policies. When government serves as the insurer of last resorts, the risk for catastrophic events is shared by all citizens. Furthermore, effectively empowering the poor so they can become productive citizens (paying taxes instead of requiring public assistance or even police and prison) benefits everyone in society. Appropriately, therefore, everyone also contributes to make this happen.[41] Dramatic reduction of poverty in America demands a crucial role for government.

Conclusion

The following twelve principles summarize the biblical norms and holistic framework that I have outlined in chapters 2 and 3.

Twelve Principles for a Just Society

1. Made in the image of God, every person enjoys an inalienable dignity and worth that society must respect.
2. Persons are not just complex socioeconomic, materialistic machines; they are also spiritual beings enjoying God-given rights and responsibilities. Each person is a body-soul unity made for relationship with God, neighbor, and earth.
3. Because the trinitarian God created persons for mutual interdependence in community, society must be organized in ways that nurture the common good. Since persons reach their potential only in a multilayered community of diverse institutions (family, church, school, media, business, government), society must promote poli-

cies (consistent with religious freedom for all) that strengthen all institutions to play their full proper role.

4. Every policy, both public and private, must be measured by its impact on the poor and marginalized because biblical faith teaches that one of the central criterion by which God judges societies is how they treat the least advantaged.

5. Both because God wants all persons to be dignified participants in their communities and because centralized power is always dangerous, we must strengthen the economic and political power of the poor.

6. Renewing the family must be a central goal for both government and civil society. (A family is that set of persons related by marriage, blood, or adoption.) While recognizing that today's families come in many shapes (two-parent, single-parent, blended), all policies, both public and private, should promote the biblical norm of mother and father (united in lifelong marital covenant) with their children, surrounded by a larger extended family.

7. Every person and family should have the opportunity to acquire and use (without discrimination based on religion, race, or gender) the productive resources that, if used responsibly, will enable that person or family to earn a decent living and be a dignified participating member of the community.

8. Everyone able to work has an obligation to do so, and society, where possible, has the responsibility to make work opportunities available to all. Everyone who works responsibly should receive a living income.

9. Society should care—in a generous, compassionate way that strengthens dignity and respect—for those who cannot care for themselves.

10. Quality education must be available to all, regardless of family income.

11. Quality health care consistent with society's present knowledge and resources must be available to all, regardless of family income.

12. Every community must enjoy public safety. Communities should be places where people feel physically secure, violence is rare, and the police and courts function without bias for or against anyone.

The following chapters apply these principles to specific crucial areas in which substantial change must occur: wages, the family, health care, education, and welfare. In each case I will apply the holistic framework[42] outlined here and show what is best done by civil society, business, the media, the academy, and government.

We must, as the Call to Renewal covenant insists, stop making false choices "between good values and good jobs, between personal responsibility and social justice, between rebuilding families and rebuilding neighborhoods, between sexual restraint and educational opportunity, between good parenting and livable family wages, between individual moral choices and government responsibility. Every institution in society must do its share and each one must do what it does best."[43]

Widespread poverty in the richest nation on earth is unnecessary. Tolerating this tragedy contradicts biblical teaching. The right mix of social policies could produce dramatic change. If we move beyond the old impasse between liberals and conservatives, if we greatly strengthen the institutions of civil society without embracing libertarianism, if we unfetter faith-based social ministries without abandoning religious freedom for all, we can end the suffering for many of our poorest neighbors.

Part 3

Implementing
the Vision

4

If I Work, Can I Earn a Family Income?

> The Lord of heaven's armies says, "Then I will come to you and judge you . . . who cheat workers of their pay."
>
> Malachi 3:5 NCV

> People who work shouldn't be poor. Those who play by the rules should not lose the game.[1]

During the last two years of my doctoral studies, my wife, Arbutus, and I rented a third-floor apartment from a wonderful African American couple. Mr. Royster was a janitor at Yale, keeping the buildings clean for youth who looked forward to a lifetime of wealth and influence. But Yale did not pay its janitors enough to enable the Roysters to own their own home. So for years, Mr. Royster also held down a second full-time job. He worked sixteen hours a day year after year so his family could enjoy the kind of decent home most of us take for granted.

If a person works full-time all year, can that person earn enough so that his or her family can escape poverty? For millions of Americans today, the answer is no.

In 1998, a father or mother who worked forty hours a week for fifty weeks at minimum wage ($5.15 per hour) would earn only $10,300—less than two-thirds of the 1998 poverty level of $16,530 for a family of four. Even if the other parent also worked half-time at minimum wage, their combined earnings would still fall below the poverty level. And if you are a single mom with two kids trying to make it on your own, your full-time job at minimum wage falls $2,631 short of the poverty level of $12,931. Fortunately, as we shall see in a moment, government programs supplement earnings for working parents. But a minimum wage, by itself, does not even come close to enabling a family of three or four to escape poverty.

If we look at total income (earnings plus cash benefits from the government), we still see significant numbers of people working responsibly while living in poverty.[2] Twenty percent of all poor families have at least one person working full-time without escaping poverty.[3] Twenty-two percent of all black men work full-time all year round without their income reaching the poverty level.[4] 37.2 percent of all poor children in America live in a family in which at least one parent is working full-time. In fact, in the case of over 6 percent of those children, one parent is working full-time and the other parent at least half-time. And still they live below the poverty level.[5] Forty percent of all black and Latino single moms work full-time all year round without escaping poverty.[6]

Unfortunately, the situation has grown worse in the last couple decades. Even Michael Tanner of the conservative Cato Institute acknowledges that from 1974 to 1990 the percentage of full-time workers earning low wages (i.e., wages that would not lift them above the poverty level) rose dramatically.[7]

There is also a significant number of people who want to work full-time all year but cannot find jobs.[8] In 1999, in the midst of a booming economy, almost five million workers in the United States wanted full-time employment but could find only part-time work.[9]

Conservatives, however, rightly insist that we must face another set of facts. Lower-income people are working a lot less than those who are not poor. If 20 percent of all poor families have at least one person working full-time, 80 percent do not! In nonpoor families on the other hand, almost 80 percent have a full-time worker.[10] Furthermore, the poor are working much less than they used to. In 1960, two-thirds of all heads of households in the poorest fifth worked; by 1991, only one-third did.[11]

Why this dramatic drop in the work effort of poor people? Conservatives blame government welfare and the breakdown of the family. Liberals blame the economy. In fact, less-skilled men have suffered from high unemployment rates and falling wages. The unemployment rate (which counts only people *actively looking* for work) is five times higher for high school dropouts (15 percent) than college grads (3 percent).[12] As we saw in chapter 1, wages for low-skilled men (working full-time all year) have declined dramatically—22.5 percent from 1979 to 1993.[13] Even male high school graduates and those with some college (but not a four-year degree) lost ground.[14] Benefits (pension, health insurance, etc.) have also declined. Both male and female college graduates, on the other hand, saw their incomes increase substantially during this same period. It is not surprising that the work effort of low-skilled men has dropped as their wages have declined.[15] The close parallel between declining wages and declining work effort led Rebecca Blank to conclude that "over the 1980's, . . . the decline in less-skilled men's labor market behavior can be almost entirely explained by the decline in their wages."[16]

Others, such as Lawrence Mead, doubt that so much weight should be placed on structural economic factors. Moral choices and behavior are more important. After all, when things get tough, people can decide to work *more*. In the last couple decades, the middle class has chosen to work more, the poor less.[17]

In a fascinating chapter on why poverty rates remained so high in spite of the growing economy after the early 1980s, two scholars did a careful analysis to separate two different causes: changes in the economy and changes in family structure. Their study looks at the years 1949 to 1969 and 1973 to 1991. During the earlier period, most children lived in two-parent families. In the second period, the number of families headed by a single mom and the number of never-married women with children increased dramatically.

How much of poverty was due to changes in family structure, and how much was the result of changing economic factors?[18] The difference between the earlier and later period is striking. Between 1949 and 1969, the economy grew dramatically. Inequality declined slightly so the bottom fifth benefited a bit more than the top fifth from the strong economy. The result? A dramatic (25.7 percent) drop in the poverty rate,[19] due almost entirely to changes in the economy—i.e., economic growth combined with less inequality.

The years 1973 to 1991 were different. The economy did grow (albeit more slowly). But so did inequality, the poverty rates, and also the number of unmarried mothers and single-mom households. Was the growth in poverty during this period the result of economic changes? Or was it due to the decline of two-parent families? Both, according to this analysis. The economic changes (increasing inequality primarily due to declining wages for low-skilled workers) raised the poverty rate 2 percent. The shift away from married-couple families raised it 1.6 percent. These scholars (who prefer to emphasize the economic side) rightly conclude that the increase in female-headed households had a smaller effect than the economic changes.[20] Yet the growth in poverty that resulted from fewer two-parent families was not a lot less! Furthermore, these scholars also report that if

101

we focus only on the increase in poverty rates for children between 1973 to 1991, then two-thirds of the increase resulted from the changing family structure.[21]

The decay of stable two-parent families has clearly contributed to poverty. At the same time, we dare not forget that economic insecurity, lack of jobs, and poverty also contribute to family breakdown. We will explore this side more carefully in the next chapter. Conservatives who rightly deplore the decline of the family dare not ignore the economic causes of this tragedy.[22]

A crucial policy implication follows. Neither economic changes by themselves nor behavioral changes in family life by themselves can solve contemporary poverty. We must have both moral and spiritual renewal *and* economic change. In chapter 5, I discuss what we can do to renew family life. Here the focus is the economy.

What can we do to end the tragedy of people who work responsibly yet remain mired in poverty? Furthermore, would it not be desirable to increase economic incentives so the poor would work more? Biblical guidelines are clear. People who can work have a moral responsibility to do so. Society, where possible, must offer everyone the opportunity to work. All who work responsibly should receive an income that enables them to be healthy, dignified members of their community.

What can be done to implement these biblical principles? Obviously, additional quality education is the most significant long-term solution to declining wages for low-skilled people. That is one reason why chapter 7 on educational reform is so crucial. But we dare not leave today's poor entangled in poverty that we can help correct.[23]

As a nation we should resolve that federal, state, and city governments will implement policies so that any family in which parents collectively work at least forty hours a week receives after-tax compensation equal to 120 to 130 percent of the national poverty level.[24] (People with incomes 150 percent or less of the poverty level should also have access to adequate health insurance at a cost of no more than 5 to 10 percent of their income.[25]) That compensation should come from wages supplemented by a refundable Earned Income Tax Credit (EITC), food stamps, and refundable Dependent Care and Child Tax Credits. Economists should determine the complex technical question of which mix of an increased minimum wage, expanded EITC, and food stamps is most efficient. As citizens, we must demand that the business leaders and politicians make it happen.

Does that figure sound too generous? If it does, flip back to pages 19–20 and review what it means to live at the poverty level—no money for household appliances, vacations, toiletries, holidays, recreation, trips to the dentist, church donations, child care, and the list goes on and on. If our goal is 120 percent of the poverty level, that means $3,306 for all these things for a family of four. If we aim at 130 percent of the poverty level, it means an extra $4,959. How many four-person middle-class families are ready to volunteer to spend only $4,959 on the long list of items above that we all consider necessities?

Earned Income Tax Credit

Before signing the 1986 Tax Reform Act, which substantially expanded the Earned Income Tax Credit, President Reagan said, "The bill I'm signing today is the best anti-poverty bill, the best pro-family bill, the best job-creation program ever to come out of the Congress."[26] President Ford started the Earned Income Tax Credit and Presidents Reagan, Bush, and Clinton expanded it. Why do both liberals and conservatives, Democrats and Republicans like the EITC?[27] Because it helps the poor, rewards work, strengthens the family, and discourages welfare. Nobody gets a cent from the EITC unless they work. The more the poor work, the more they receive.

The basic principle is simple.[28] If persons (with children) work at low wages, then they receive a tax credit on federal income taxes. If their income is so low that they do not owe any taxes, the government sends them a check (that is what the word *refundable* means). Recipients can choose to receive the money either once a year when they file their tax forms or every month with their wages from their employer.

The amount of the EITC depends on the number of children in the family and the family's income. In 1998, the maximum benefit was $2,271 for a family with one child and $3,756 for a family with two or more children. For a family of four, the EITC adds an additional forty cents to every dollar earned through work up to an adjusted gross income of about $11,930. As family income continues to rise, the amount of the EITC slowly declines (see fig. 6).

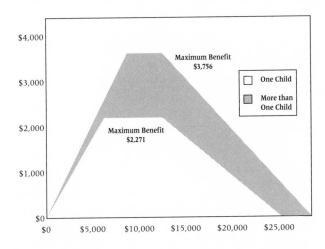

Fig. 6. The federal earned income tax credit in tax year 1998. *Source:* Kathryn Porter, Wendell Primus, Lynette Rawlings, and Esther Rosenbaum, *Strengths of the Safety Net* (Washington, D.C.: Center on Budget and Policy Priorities, 1998), 20.

Unlike some government programs, the EITC strengthens rather than weakens the family. Two-parent families get the same benefit at any earnings level as single-parent families. Since it makes no difference whether one parent earns all the money or both earn some, each family can decide who should work or stay home with young children. Parents who do not live with their children do not receive the family credit.

It is important to see how different the EITC is from the Guaranteed Annual Income that President Nixon proposed and Congress almost passed. The Guaranteed Annual Income would have provided a government check to every poor person whether or not they worked. Fortunately, the model was tested and its negative effects on both marriage and work became clear. Analysis of the experiment showed that people receiving the Guaranteed Annual Income worked less and abandoned their marriages more frequently.[29] In 1993, for the first time, the expansion of EITC granted a very small EITC to workers without children. But the maximum is only $332. All but 3 percent of all EITC benefits go to families with children.

The EITC is a highly successful government program. First, it dramatically reduces poverty. The Census Bureau reports that in 1996 the EITC raised the income of 4.6 million persons in low-income working families so that they were not poor. 2.4 million of those persons were children. The EITC now moves more children out of poverty than any other government program.[30]

Second, recent studies show that the expansions of EITC have significantly increased the work effort of single mothers. In fact, "these expansions explain more than half of the substantial increase in employment rates among single mothers over the 1984–1996 period."[31]

Third, the EITC has some other aspects that economists in particular like. Economists study the "efficiency costs" of redistributing money to the poor via taxation—and the EITC turns out to be especially efficient.[32] The EITC also has many of the advantages of raising the minimum wage without its disadvantages.[33]

In spite of its success, the EITC is not free of problems. Its error rate has been too high. An IRS report released and widely discussed in 1997 estimated that 20.7 percent of EITC benefits in 1994 were paid in error. House Speaker Newt Gingrich suggested that Congress could finance a tax cut by correcting these errors. Further analysis, however, has shown that this study overstated the problem. The same study reported a 1.7 percent *under*-payment, revealing that some people received less EITC than they should have. And in one-fifth of the errors, a child was simply claimed by the wrong person (e.g., a parent instead of a grandparent). These two corrections bring the error rate below 15 percent—which is the average error rate for all income tax filers! In 1997, Congress passed substantial measures to correct these errors.[34] Continuing problems demand correction, but they certainly do not call for cutting or abolishing the EITC.

In fact, we ought to expand it significantly. Even with the full $3,756 from the EITC, a family of four with one person working full-time at minimum wage would still be $356 below the poverty level.[35] But our goal is to provide every family in which parents collectively work full-time with compensation 120 to 130 percent above the poverty level. Therefore, we must increase the EITC *or* raise the minimum wage substantially *or* significantly expand food stamps for the poor. I am glad to let expert economists decide which approach will most effectively and efficiently get us to the goal. From what I have read, however, a substantial expansion of the EITC should be a primary part of the package. I propose increasing the EITC by $1,000 for a person who works forty hours a week.

After a lecture at the Kennedy School of Government in the fall of 1998, I asked Professor Richard Parker a question that I have frequently asked economists recently: "If one brackets the question of whether it is politically possible, is there any significant economic argument against an additional substantial increase in the EITC?" The answer is no.[36]

One problem with the federal EITC (based on a national poverty level) is that living costs differ greatly in different regions. A modest middle-class income adequate in rural Kansas is not enough for a decent life in New York City. State and city EITC's would be a good way to take regional differences into account. Through some combination of wages plus EITC and food stamps, the federal government could bring each family with children up to 120 to 130 percent of the national poverty level. State and city EITC's could supplement that where necessary to raise families to at least 130 percent of the regional poverty level. Every state is trying to encourage more people to move from welfare to work. One effective incentive is to make work more economically advantageous than welfare. An EITC does that.

There is another reason for state EITC's. Most states raise a great deal of their income from sales taxes. Unfortunately, sales taxes hit the poor with a disproportionate burden. A state EITC can correct that.[37]

In 1997, nine states already had a state EITC. At the same time, half of the states with state income taxes taxed people below the poverty line.[38] Those who care about the poor should urge their state politicians to do two things. First, raise the threshold at which the payment of state income taxes begins so that those below the poverty line pay no state income taxes. Second, adopt an appropriate state EITC.

There is a strong moral argument for substantially expanding the EITC. It rewards work, strengthens families, and reduces welfare. Economists say it is possible and effective. More important still, it is just. God wants people who work responsibly to enjoy a family livelihood. The richest society in human history can easily afford it.

Two things are needed: dissemination of information and lobbying. Many people eligible for the EITC do not use it—either because they do not know about it or because they do not understand how to get it. Businesses can encourage eligible employees and make it easy for them to receive regular payments in their paychecks. Churches and other faith-based organizations can help spread the word.[39] Second, we need to lobby Congress so that it expands the program. Do the well-to-do and politically powerful care enough to make it happen?

Food Stamps

Food stamps are a basic part of how low-income people survive. Persons with incomes up to 130 percent of the poverty level can receive food stamps from the government so they can buy food. In 1997, 30 million people benefited from food stamps at a cost of $26 billion.[40]

The federal government spends roughly equal amounts ($22 to $25 billion in 1998) on the EITC, food stamps, and direct cash welfare (TANF).[41] The federal government guarantees food stamp coupons as an entitlement to every poor person (childless adults as well as families with children). The amount of the food stamps depends on the person's other cash income as well as other assets.

Over the past two decades, hunger activists, especially Bread for the World, have fought repeated battles to maintain and strengthen the food stamp program. Sometimes they have won; sometimes they have lost.[42]

Several improvements are needed today. All legal immigrants should be eligible. (Because of the cutbacks in the 1996 Welfare Bill, 600,000 legal immigrants still cannot receive food stamps). The cap on the value of a car owned by a person eligible for food stamps is much too low. Currently, that cap is $4,650 and has risen only $150 since 1977. Lower-income workers needing a reliable car to get to work are precisely the kind of people we should support with food stamps. This cap should be raised.[43] The shelter cap should also be either raised or abolished.

Minimum Wage

Democrats and Republicans frequently battle over whether to raise the minimum wage. As of 1998, it stands at $5.15 per hour, but President Clinton has proposed raising it by the year 2000 to $6.15 per hour. Would that help the poor? The answer is complex.

Macroeconomists—a big label for economists who study the big picture—remind us that when the cost of labor increases, employers hire fewer workers. So when we raise the minimum wage, a few more people do not have a job at all while those who work at minimum wage earn more. Unfortunately, those most likely not to have a job are low-skilled persons, especially minority young adults.[44]

Interestingly, the vast majority of minimum-wage workers are not poor; only one-fifth live in poor families. Most are second- or third-wage earners (e.g., students or spouses) in middle-income families.[45] On the other hand, Labor Secretary Robert Reich pointed out in 1996 that 40 percent of all minimum-wage workers are sole breadwinners.[46] Studies of recent raises in the minimum wage show that these raises have caused very little loss of jobs.[47] In 1996, Nobel Prize–winning economist Robert Solow reported a near consensus among economists that "the employment effect of a moderate increase in the minimum wage would be very, very small."[48]

It is crucial to see how the minimum wage and the EITC are mutually supportive. It would be a mistake, as some have urged, to leave the minimum wage low and depend only on a greatly expanded EITC. That would place all the burden on the government without requiring employers to carry their share of the burden. The result would be greatly expanded government costs and higher taxes.[49] On the other hand, raising the minimum wage too much would cause significant loss of jobs.

The conclusion? A modest increase in the minimum wage and an expansion of the EITC would probably both be wise. The minimum wage at least needs to keep pace with inflation—it should probably be tied to the inflation rate. Economists can determine exactly what mix is most effective in reducing poverty. Christian citizens, however, need to know that ongoing modest increases in the minimum wage are not problematic and are necessary for justice. An increase to $5.50 an hour in 1999 would still mean that in inflation-adjusted dollars, it was lower than thirty years ago.[50] We need to let our politicians know we understand and demand that an appropriate minimum wage and an expanded EITC are essential if we are to have justice for the people at the bottom of the economic ladder.

Refundable Dependent Care Tax Credit

The cost of child care discourages some single moms and second-wage earners in two-parent, low-income families from working.[51] If one works at minimum wage ($5.15 an hour), child care and transportation costs can quickly consume as much as half of one's earnings. For many single moms, welfare is a wiser economic decision than work.

Many people want to solve this problem by expanding the current child-care subsidies. They come in two forms. A small number (18 percent) of working poor women have their children in child-care programs subsidized by state and federal governments.[52] One problem with this, as Senator Moynihan observes, is that it creates two classes of working moms. A minority get free (or subsidized) government-provided child care. The rest have to pay for it.[53] One solution, of course, would be to provide free child care for all poor working moms. But that would be highly unfair to poor two-parent families and even discourage marriage. We could solve that by providing free child care to all poor parents who work—single moms and two-parent families. But that would mean discriminating against two-parent families who treasure parenting so much that they choose to live on less money so one parent can be at home with the children. Five to seven million of our children are latchkey kids who go home to empty houses because dad and/or mom are away working.[54] The economic incentives from government policy should encourage, not discourage, parents to spend more time with their children.

The more common way we currently help with child care is through the Dependent Care Tax Credit. Low-income parents with incomes below $10,000 who work outside the home can claim a maximum tax credit of $1,440 for two children. People earning more than $20,000 receive a $960 credit for two children. But this tax credit is *not* refundable.[55] That means that if you owe no federal income taxes, you get no dependent care tax credit. As a result, poor people gain very little. In fact, most of the $3 billion credit claimed in 1994 went to middle-income and high-income families![56]

The obvious solution is to reduce the credit to high-income families and make this tax credit refundable so that poor people who owe no income taxes benefit at least as much as the middle class. That should be done immediately. Many advocates for the poor urge that we should not only make the dependent care credit refundable but also substantially expand it.[57] That is not a good idea for one very important reason: Two-parent families get it only if both work. That means that two-parent families who choose to have one parent at home to care for young children lose out completely. In fact, they get taxed to subsidize two-parent families in which both parents work. That is hardly a pro-family policy.

A better solution would be to offer a $1,000 to $1,500 refundable dependent care tax credit ($2,000 to $3,000 for two or more children under thirteen) to every parent (single moms or two-parent families) who works at least forty hours a week. (A proportionately smaller credit should go to those who work only part-time.) As in the case of the EITC, this credit must be available to the worker at least monthly with his or her paycheck. To hold down costs, this credit could be phased out gradually with no credit for those with adjusted gross incomes of over $25,000 or $30,000.[58]

This approach still encourages work. Only those who work are eligible. But it does not discriminate against two-parent families who want one parent at home part-time or full-time. Because it is refundable, it helps the poor.

Ironically, some conservative pro-family advocates support a dependent care tax credit but do not insist that it be refundable. Surely the kind of refundable dependent care tax credit proposed here encourages work, empowers the poor, and strengthens the family. Every pro-family person should endorse it.

Child Tax Credit

The Dependent Care Tax Credit just discussed should not be confused with the new Child Tax Credit, which became available for the first time in 1998. Starting in 1999, parents with children under seventeen may deduct $500 per child from federal income taxes they owe. This is a wonderful pro-family move, and it probably should be expanded to $1,000 per child over the next five years. There is one ghastly problem, however. This tax credit is *not* refundable. Therefore, it is absolutely useless to the poor who owe no taxes.[59] On the other hand, tax payers with incomes up to $75,000 ($110,000 for married parents) get the full tax credit. How can pro-family organizations celebrate tax breaks for middle-class families that offer no help at all for the families most in need of assistance?

A Job for Everyone Able to Work

It is a violation of biblical justice for a wealthy society to fail to offer a job to everyone willing and able to work. But that is exactly what we do. Even at the peak of one of the strongest periods of economic growth in our history, many low-skilled persons search in vain for a job.

The unemployment rate (and that includes only those *actively looking* for a job) is five times as high (15 percent) for high school dropouts as it is for college graduates (3 percent). Over 20 percent of black high school dropouts are searching for a job but cannot find one.[60] Remember that these people are all *actively looking* for work. These figures do not include the people who have given up for a variety of reasons, including unsuccessful job searches. In 1993, 43 percent of all adult black men were not working.[61]

In January 1999, the unemployment rate was at 4.3 percent, which is an extremely low figure for the United States. Even then, however, 5,950,000 people were looking for work.[62] Not all of those people, of course, were in financial trouble. Typically, almost half of the unemployed find work in five weeks or less; 75 percent within fifteen weeks. But 26 percent of the unemployed look in vain for more than six months.[63]

What should be done about the high level of unemployment for low-skilled workers? Long term, of course, our schools need to work better and private businesses need to create new jobs. In the short run, job training programs (see the next section) can help. The same is true for some of the proposals to overcome the mismatch between available suburban jobs and unemployed city residents.[64] Experiments with permanent relocation and better transportation arrangements offer some promise.[65]

The basic problem, however, remains. For a variety of reasons, including economic globalization and technological change, unemployment rates are high for low-skilled workers. There are significant numbers of poor people who could and would work if they had a job—but they cannot find one. We have only a few choices in the short run. We can turn our backs on their poverty and despair, we can write welfare checks and let the poor sit idle, or we can demand that the government offer a job to anyone who cannot find a job in the private sector. As Franklin Roosevelt understood during the depression, a job is better than the dole.

It is true that some people deny that there are many people unable to find low-skill jobs.[66] The truth is we do not know for sure. The government collects careful data on unemployment rates but not on the availability of jobs.[67] City mayors, however, think there is a lack of low-skill jobs. In a 1997 survey conducted by the U.S. Conference of Mayors, 92 percent said they would not have enough low-skill jobs to comply with the new welfare law's work requirements.[68]

Surely the just, sensible approach is to offer guaranteed jobs and find out if they are needed! We could offer government-funded jobs—the technical term is public service employment (PSE)—paying 10 to 15 percent below the minimum wage to anyone who cannot find a private job. Those with dependents should also be eligible for the EITC and Dependent Care Tax Credit. The lower pay would make sure that normal jobs remained preferable. If there is little need for such PSE, then few people will apply and the cost will be modest. If there are large numbers glad to work at such jobs, a just society will surely not condemn willing workers to grinding poverty and eventual despair.

Interestingly, polls have shown that 80 percent of the American people would support a program in which the government provides such jobs. Eighty percent also want the government to cut able-bodied persons from the welfare rolls.[69] We can do both at the same time by implementing the common wisdom that people should have the dignity that comes from earning one's own way.

There are compelling reasons for PSE. Providing subsidized jobs is better for people's self-respect and character than welfare payments. Some people have little work experience (which private employers want), so well-designed PSE can prepare people for future jobs in the private sector. Since many employers tend to be hesitant to hire certain kinds of people (e.g., long-term welfare recipients, persons with a criminal record, or young, inner-city men), PSE can provide a track record demonstrating that the person shows up on time and works responsibly.

Although wisely designed programs in PSE can prepare people for eventual jobs in the private sector, it is crucial not to forget their first and most important purpose: the justice and dignity that come from people being able to avoid poverty by their own work and be a dignified participant in the community. Whether or not any private employer will hire them, poor unemployed persons seeking work deserve a job. Why? Because work is essential to human dignity.

Unfortunately, the popular perception is that we have tried PSE and it has failed. That judgment is much too simplistic.[70] President Roosevelt's depression-era Works Progress Administration (WPA) provided millions of jobs for desperate, unemployed Americans. They built 617,000 miles of new roads, 124,000 bridges, and 35,000 buildings—including landmarks such as the Philadelphia Art Museum in my hometown.[71] The widely respected Center on Budget and Policy Priorities recently issued a summary of studies analyzing ten past and present public job-creation programs. They concluded that public job creation can be successful and effective, and they recommended a new generation of PSE experiments building on the careful analysis of previous programs.[72]

The fact that government guarantees a job for everyone does not mean that government agencies should operate all or even most of the programs. A wide variety of partnerships with businesses, community organizations, and nonprofit organizations should be tested. Especially promising may be partnerships with faith-based groups such as Jobs Partnership and Good Samaritan Ministries (see pp. 113–15, 186–88) using a Charitable Choice arrangement. There also ought to be an economic incentive for nongovernmental providers, not only to move people from government-funded jobs to private sector employment, but also to design effective programs that result in people succeeding over the long haul in the private sector.

A new PSE initiative could have two parts.[73] First, let's expand the summer job program for inner-city youth. From 1978 to 1981, the Youth Incentive Entitlement Pilot Project offered minimum-wage jobs (full-time during the summer and part-time the rest of the year) to inner-city youth who stayed in school. The organization was flooded with applicants. Two-thirds of all eligible persons participated—disproving the claim that ghetto youth will not work at minimum-wage jobs.[74] Careful analysis revealed that this program "virtually eliminated large gaps in employment rates between white and black youth." After they left the program, black participants enjoyed earnings that were 40 percent higher than comparable youth who did not participate.[75] This program offers a realistic way to reduce both unemployment and high school dropout rates for black youth.

Second, we should aim to reach a point at which we offer a public service job to anyone who shows that he or she has searched unsuccessfully for a regular job.[76] Since such a job would pay 10 to 15 percent below the minimum wage, participants would always have a clear incentive to move on to regular employment. That wage alone would bring a childless adult above the poverty level.[77] Wages plus EITC plus food stamps plus the refundable Dependent Care Tax Credit and Child Tax Credit would also lift any single-mom or two-parent family with one or two children above the poverty level.[78] Single moms would need to work only thirty hours a week to escape poverty.

Peter Gottschalk and Sheldon Danziger—two public policy scholars who favor this approach—suggest that we should start with a test. Since the federal government has not run such a program for almost two decades, a cautious beginning offering 250,000 to 500,000 such jobs might be prudent.[79]

A carefully designed program of this sort would settle the debate over whether it is needed. If not, great. But if it is, we should expand PSE jobs so that every American who wants to work can do so. The cost could be high but easily manageable for our wealthy society. The price of refusing to provide such jobs is ruined lives and wasted neighborhoods—not to mention blatant violation of justice.

Perhaps there is a different, a better way. To any reader who objects to this proposal for a public service job, I say, "Okay, show me a better approach." I have no commitment to a government-funded jobs program. What I—and I think all biblical people—must insist upon is guaranteeing that there is a job available to every person able and willing to work.

Job Training Programs

Many people who could and want work do not have the networks to learn about job openings, lack the skills necessary for a successful job application process, or need a little remedial education. Good job training programs can help them succeed.

The only federal job training program for disadvantaged workers is the Job Training Partnership Act (JTPA). JTPA is a public/private partnership. The federal government provides the funds; local business leaders and government (and increasingly also faith-based agencies) design programs to help unemployed people (who have usually been out of work for a considerable time) find a job. The funding is far too small to include all people who need help, but JTPA annually serves about a million people.[80]

Does it work? According to the evaluations, not too well, at least for men. Programs vary from state to state and some have positive results, but overall the results are disappointing, although further experimentation is warranted. As economist Rebecca Blank observes, "If all of this sounds discouraging for those who want to solve the labor market problems, it is."[81]

Adding a faith-based mentoring component might improve JTPA. Jobs Partnership is a private Christian job training program started in 1996 by a white businessman and a black pastor. By 1998, Jobs Partnership was working in twenty-two cities. Skip Long, the black Mennonite pastor who serves as national director, expected forty new groups to start in 1998.[82]

Jobs Partnership began in 1996, when a Christian businessman, Chris Mangum, met inner-city pastor Rev. Donald McCoy. The businessman needed workers and the pastor needed jobs. Together they launched what has quickly become a highly successful job training program.

The curriculum has two parts. The first part of the training program is an unabashedly biblical, twelve-week course on "The Keys to Personal and Professional Success." It deals with workplace skills, ethics, responding to authority, resolving conflict, stewardship of time and money, living with integrity, and striving for excellence. The textbook is the Bible. At the same time, participants take a course on job-finding and job-keeping skills (filling out applications, preparing resumes, succeeding at interviews) taught and funded by the local community college.

Probably the most important component, however, is the mentoring. A local church sponsors each student in Jobs Partnership. Through a personal mentor assigned by the church, the congregation provides transportation, child care, even housing—and more important, love, encouragement, affirmation, and accountability. Church members walk with the participants for up to two years as they complete training and begin a job.

Local businesses provide the jobs. Because of the training and ongoing church sponsorship for students, businesses eagerly list their openings with Jobs Partnership and hire their graduates. The employer also provides employee benefits and an on-the-job mentor.[83]

Just a few years ago, Leslie Brown was a single mom with three children and a live-in boyfriend. She barely scraped by on welfare and public housing. Fortunately, Leslie heard the gospel and became an active Christian. Her boyfriend, Tony, also started attending church and soon became a Christian. Spiritual transformation, however, did not improve their awful financial situation.

Joining Jobs Partnership made the difference. Two churches surrounded Leslie and Tony as they started the classes. Even before Tony completed the training, he found a job at a Pepsi company. Leslie also found part-time work. Tony and Leslie have been off welfare and out of public housing for over two years and are now married. Promoted four times, Tony is a foreman.[84]

It is too early for any extensive evaluation of Jobs Partnership, but 250 of the 280 people who finished the twelve-week training program in 1996 had full-time jobs two years later. This kind of partnership between business and faith-based agencies allows programs to minister to the whole person rather than treat them as mere economic actors. We could add government to this partnership by applying Charitable Choice policy to the job training program. If subsequent evaluation demonstrates that programs such as Jobs Partnership are far more effective than typical JTPA programs, the government should encourage greatly expanded participation by faith-based programs in federally funded job training programs.

Health and Unemployment Insurance

Both health insurance and unemployment insurance are fundamental to this chapter's call for an income that is fair to all and nurtures wholesome families. Universal health care (see chapter 6) would greatly reduce the anxiety that unemployment—even the fear of unemployment—inevitably brings. Generous unemployment insurance is also essential. Many people lose their jobs each year through no fault of their own. Large numbers of people have very little savings to tide them over, and it often takes time to locate a new job. Generous unemployment insurance provides temporary help so they and their families do not go hungry or lose their homes.

Implementing Just Compensation

I have proposed a set of policy changes in this chapter. If we raised the EITC by $1,000, added a *refundable* Dependent Care Tax Credit and Child Tax Credit, continued food stamps, and raised the minimum wage to $5.50, any family of four with at least one person working full-time at minimum wage would have compensation of about 128 percent of the poverty level. Table 3 compares current compensation with that proposed. Even a single mom working only thirty hours a week would rise to about 117 percent above the poverty level.

Table 3

Actual (1998)	Two-parent family of four (parent[s] working forty hrs)	Single parent with one child (parent working thirty hrs)	Proposed	Two-parent family of four (parent[s] working forty hrs)	Single parent with one child (parent working thirty hrs)
Minimum wage 5.15	10,300	7,725	Minimum wage 5.50	11,000	8,250
EITC*	3,756	2,271		4,410	2,814
Food stamps	2,906	1,316		2,738	1,190
Dependent Care Tax Credit (currently non-refundable	0		Refundable and expanded to $1500 per child for first two children	3,000	1,125
Child Tax Credit (currently non-refundable)	0		Refundable	800	400
Minus Social Security tax (7.65 percent)	788	590		842	631
Total	16,174	10,722		21,106	13,148
Poverty level	16,530	11,235		16,530	11,235

*My proposal adds an extra $1000 maximum for forty hours of work per week.

How do we get there? What needs to be done to awaken this rich society to do justice to the people on the bottom?

Government certainly cannot do it all. Churches and other shapers of the culture must rouse us with a new vision. Businesses can initiate better compensation packages no matter what government does. Unions can press businesses for better wage packages. Community organizing efforts can mobilize effective grassroots movements. All of us can renew our passion for a politics of justice for all, especially the least among us.

Churches must embrace the prophetic courage and zeal of Amos, Isaiah, and Jesus. In the past, the ringing call of modern prophets such as Martin Luther King Jr., Dorothy Day, and Cesar Chavez have roused us to renewed efforts for justice. Pastors, Sunday school teachers, and seminary professors must dare to condemn our neglect of the poor as vigorously and insistently as Jeremiah and Jesus.

Other cultural leaders should join with religious voices to nurture a broad cultural consensus for justice. Who will write the novels that will stir us as did *Uncle Tom's Cabin* or *The Jungle*? Who will compose and sing the popular songs that moved us as did Dylan's "The Times They Are A-Changin'"? Who will join with contemporary songwriters such as U2's Bono, Lauryn Hill, Bill Mallonee of the Vigilantes of Love, rappers Burning Spear, or Bruce Cockburn in crafting music that speaks for the poor and neglected? Who will direct the movies and the TV specials? Novelists, playwrights, songwriters and singers, artists, and TV and movie producers could all help tug the majority away from materialistic self-centeredness to growing generosity.

Business leaders need not wait for government. Business executives can choose to provide generous wages and benefits for full-time workers, proportionate benefits (health insurance, pension, etc.) to part-time workers; treat workers with respect; implement profit sharing—in short, create within their own businesses places where workers can work with dignity and earn a family wage.

Is that really possible, however, in today's cutthroat competitive corporate world? In a fascinating study of several highly successful billion-dollar-plus corporations, Joseph A. Maciariello, professor of management at the Peter F. Drucker Graduate School of Management in California, proves that the answer is clearly yes.[85]

The four corporations Maciariello studied were all founded by Christians determined to apply biblical principles to the business world. ServiceMaster ("In the Service of the Master") is now a $4-billion-a-year publicly traded corporation with a variety of well-known service products including Terminix and Merry Maids. Lincoln Electric (the leading manufacturer of welding products) had sales of $1.1 billion in 1996. Herman Miller (office furniture) passed the $1.5 billion mark in 1997. Donnelly Corporation (glass products for cars) was at $671 million in 1997. In purely economic terms, each of these companies is a stunning success.

More important, each works with a radically different definition of management. Most corporations define management as "getting work done through people." People are tools for making money. Maciariello's four corporations define management as "developing people through work."[86] ServiceMaster is very clear about its objectives. The first two are "honor God" and "help people develop." "To grow profitably" comes last—but they have enjoyed a 24 percent annually compounded growth in earnings per share for twenty years!

The companies are not all the same, but they all emphasize servant leadership and respectful, financially generous treatment of employees. Lincoln has above average salaries and employee stock ownership. Herman Miller stresses participative management, profit sharing, and starting salaries above the minimum wage so employees can support a family. Service-Master is especially successful at offering "first jobs" to poor people including welfare recipients (see p. 88). These low-skilled employees who work at the company's many service industries start at low wages, but Service-Master works hard to provide opportunity for upward mobility in the company. It also trains its managers to have a special concern for the "lowest employee."

A story about Ken Wessner (a former chairman of the board) provides a striking example of the ethos that pervades ServiceMaster. One day, while Ken was in charge of ServiceMaster's hospital maintenance operations, he strolled down a hospital hall chatting with ServiceMaster's workers who were cleaning the floors and windows. When he came to a man named Ellis, he stopped because Ellis's manager had told Ken that Ellis worked too slowly. Ellis was holding his squeegee with both hands as he awkwardly tried to clean a window. Instead of scolding Ellis, Ken asked him about himself and soon learned that Ellis suffered from an old wrist injury. After a moment's reflection, Ken asked Ellis if he thought he could handle a self-propelled floor finisher—he would only need to point it in the right direction. Ellis beamed. Ken recommended him for the first training program for floor cleaners. In time, Ellis became a trainer himself—and one of the hospital's most valued maintenance workers.[87]

I have seen the same kind of concern at the bottom of ServiceMaster's structure. One of my former students, Brian Mast, manages a small ServiceMaster business with about thirty-five employees. One of his employees, Vern, used to use and sell drugs. After his dad threw him out of the house, vowing never to speak to him again, Vern took to the streets and often slept in abandoned cars. Christ and the Whosoever Gospel Missions' drug rehab program, however, slowly changed his life. As Vern completed the rehab program, he had hope for the first time in years. But Vern had no work history and was having a difficult time finding a job.

About that same time, my friend Brian started a ServiceMaster business in inner-city Philadelphia. He had recently landed a large contract and was in desperate need of help. Brian called the mission, and they recommended Vern. With some uneasiness, Brian decided to take a chance and hire Vern. Vern had some rough edges, but he was willing to work and eager to learn.

Vern soon moved into Brian's house with some other Christian men. He was eager to learn about the Bible and how to live as a Christian. Brian spent many hours training and discipling Vern at home and on the job. Brian struggled as he applied the first two ServiceMaster corporate objectives (to honor God and to help people develop) as he worked with Vern, but Vern learned fast.

Today Vern is Brian's second in command, helping to manage thirty-five employees. Vern has a real heart to help "the least of these," especially the homeless and crack addicts whom society has written off. Vern is now married and owns his own home. He has even been reconciled to his father, who has started to attend church.

The right kind of business leader can play a major role in helping people enjoy jobs that pay a family wage. Not surprisingly, the moral vision that guides companies such as ServiceMaster does not operate everywhere. In a fallen world, powerful people regularly use that power for selfish advantage. That is why unions are needed to pressure corporations to do the right thing.

Christians—especially Catholics—have played an important part in the growth of American unions. In 1906, a young priest named John A. Ryan wrote a doctoral dissertation titled *A Living Wage* and later helped draft the "Bishops' Program of Social Reconstruction," which called for child labor laws, unemployment insurance, and a minimum wage.[88] Again and again— whether one thinks of Cesar Chavez and the farm workers or Martin Luther King Jr.'s support for the garbage collectors' strike—one sees Christians playing a significant role in supporting unions struggling for just wages. Clergy and Laity United for Economic Justice (CLUE) provides an exciting current example.

In 1997, CLUE worked with unions to persuade the Los Angeles City Council to vote 12-0 in favor of a living wage ordinance. As a result, every city contractor must pay employees $7.25 an hour plus health insurance (or $8.50 without insurance).[89] In 1998, CLUE cooperated with unions trying to increase the wages of the most poorly paid workers in Los Angeles's hotels. The union won a contract with downtown LA hotels that greatly increased salary and benefits, but the posh westside hotels that charged $281 a night refused to do the same. Pastor James Lawson Jr., who had worked with Martin Luther King Jr., organized the clergy. Working closely with the union, the clergy organized a large procession with a clear religious flavor. A rabbi conducted a mini-Seder (marking the flight of the Jews from slavery in Egypt) in front of a hotel that refused to pay more than the minimum wage. The union got the contract.[90]

A similar drama developed in Baltimore. A large, church-based grassroots organization called BUILD was dismayed with the way workers often lost out when the city contracted out former city jobs to private businesses. Custodians working for a minimum wage of $4.25 with no benefits replaced— and did the same job as—city custodians who had earned $13.00 an hour plus benefits. This powerful, church-led grassroots organization pressured the city council to pass a living wage ordinance requiring all companies with contracts with the city to pay their employees $7.70 an hour plus benefits. Then, after the victory, BUILD worked closely with the American Federation of State, County and Municipal Workers' Union to organize a local union specifically for the workers of firms doing business with the city.[91]

There are living wage campaigns in a number of local communities across the country. We need a national movement.

In chapter 1, we saw that the power and membership of unions have declined dramatically in the last several decades—a development that has contributed significantly to the increasing inequality in men's earnings (see p. 38). In 1953, 26.9 percent of the labor force was in unions; today, only 13.9 percent is. Biblical principles predict what history confirms: Concentrated power leads to injustice. Today, therefore, one significant way to work for justice is to strengthen unions.

Unions, however, must also do their part. To a certain degree, some unions deserve the bad reputation they have. Too often they have been corrupt and undemocratic. Too often they have become wealthy and powerful, defending the interests of highly paid workers and excluding minorities while failing to speak for the truly disadvantaged. Overall, though, unions do more to equalize earnings than the opposite.[92] They must continue, however, to weed out corruption and excessive salaries. They also must put more effort and money into organizing low-paid workers. Fortunately, the new head of the AFL-CIO (John Sweeney, who is an active Catholic) is doing just that.

Today the AFL-CIO also welcomes greater partnership with the religious community. Kim Bobo, a Christian friend of mine who worked for years with Bread for the World, now leads its National Interfaith Committee for Worker Justice. Kim has organized a national network of religious people working to strengthen union efforts to organize low-wage workers. Currently, they are working to support two hundred thousand mostly black and Hispanic poorly paid poultry workers.

Baldemar Velasquez is an ordained minister. He is also the founder and president of the AFL-CIO's Farm Labor Organizing Committee (FLOC), which organizes migrant workers and demands decent pay and humane working conditions. After a seven-year struggle, Velasquez's workers received a contract from Campbell Soup. The next challenge is North Carolina's Mt. Olive Pickle Company, the largest pickle company in the South, which refuses to negotiate with FLOC. Velasquez believes something is wrong when migrant farm workers grace our tables with fresh vegetables and fruit but have to rely on private charity and government welfare to feed, clothe, and care for their families. A deeply committed Christian, Velasquez feels called by God to empower migrant workers. "As long as God keeps putting that in my heart, I'll keep speaking it. The day he wants me to shut up, I'll shut up."[93]

Low wages is a family issue that all Christian pro-family groups should seek to correct. If unions today are to recover enough influence to play their proper role in demanding a family wage, Christians must play a crucial role in prophetic proclamation of the validity and importance of honest, democratic, strong unions.[94]

Government must also play a crucial role in providing just compensation. Governments (federal, state, and local) will decide whether to cut or raise the EITC, to cut or maintain food stamps, to raise the minimum wage or allow its value to decline year by year, and to adopt a refundable Dependent Care Tax Credit and Child Tax Credit. Governments will also decide whether unions will continue to enjoy full freedom for labor organizing and collective bargaining. Only the federal government can insist that the World Trade Organization's crucial policies—that affect people everywhere in the world—seek to empower the poor, strengthen democratic unions, and protect the environment.[95] Who will do the vigilant, persistent work to make sure crucial government decisions help rather than hurt the poor?

A tiny minority of wealthy people provide most of the money for both parties. Furthermore, the rich are far more likely to vote than the poor. In 1994, 63 percent of the people with incomes of $75,000 or more voted; only 20 percent of those with incomes under $5,000 did. We all know individual wealthy people who care deeply about the poor, but most rich people vote their pocketbooks. We should demand genuine campaign finance reform to protect democracy. Churches, civic groups, block clubs, and other organizations can all join in the important effort to register far more low-income voters and draw them into active engagement in the political process.

There is little hope that government will change enough to do justice to the poor unless a powerful movement emerges in our churches and synagogues to demand that public policy reflect a new concern to empower the poor. In chapter 10, I sketch a vision of how that might happen.

Conclusion

The Creator of the galaxies became a carpenter, demonstrating the dignity of work. It is that divine worker who summons all who know him to lead this wealthy society to do justice to all who work.

5

Broken Families and Rising Poverty

The more single parents, the more poverty.

Dr. Sara McLanahan,
Princeton sociologist

What God has joined together, let no one separate.

Jesus

Why include a chapter on the family in a book about poverty in America? Because the best single predictor of whether a child will suffer the agony of poverty is whether Mom and Dad are married. Marital status is a better predictor of who will become poor than education, race, neighborhood, or family background.[1]

The data is stunningly clear.[2] Children in one-parent families are *eleven times* more likely to experience *persistent* poverty than children in two-parent families. Seventy-three percent of all children from one-parent families fall into poverty at some point in their childhood; only 20 percent of children in two-parent families ever experience that trauma.[3] Writing in *The New York Times,* David Popenoe concluded: "I know of few other bodies of data in which the evidence is so decisively on one side of the issue: on the whole for children, two-parent families are preferable. . . . If our prevailing views on family structure hinged solely on scholarly evidence, the current debate would never have arisen."[4]

One study compared two groups of children. The first group contained children whose mother finished high school, married, and did not have a child until she was at least twenty. The second group contained those whose mother did not do these three things. Only 8 percent of the first group live in poverty. Seventy-nine percent of the second group do.[5]

More than three decades ago, when the out-of-wedlock birth rate was 3 percent for whites and 23.6 percent for blacks, future Senator Daniel Moynihan warned:

> There is one unmistakable lesson in American history: A community that allows a large number of young men to grow up in broken families, dominated by women, never acquiring any stable relationship to male authority . . . asks for and gets chaos. . . . Crime, violence, unrest, unrestrained lashing out at the whole social structure—that is not only to be expected; it is very near to inevitable.[6]

Moynihan was worried in 1965! A little more than thirty years later, 33 percent of all our children are born to unmarried women.[7] The white illegitimacy rate is now 25 percent and the black rate 70 percent.[8] About 25 million children in the United States (36 percent) today do not live with their fathers. Forty percent of those children have not seen their father for at least a year. Fifty percent have never once stepped inside their dad's house.[9]

Moynihan thinks that the high birth rate to unmarried parents is "the best leading indicator for whatever it is that is going on."[10] Another former Harvard professor, Richard T. Gill, makes the same point: "If one had to select the single most important factor responsible for the disturbing condition of many of today's younger generation, . . . the breakdown of the intact biological-parent family would almost certainly be at or near the top of the list."[11]

A crucial conclusion for social policy follows. Not even the best mix of effective, essential, economic policy changes discussed in the previous chapter can *by themselves* solve the problem of poverty in America today. Unless we can heal our broken families, it is simply impossible to end poverty.

Before I look in more detail at escalating single parenthood, we need to define our terms. Some people seek to redefine "family" and "marriage," speaking about "open marriage," "gay marriage," and a wide variety of "families." By marriage, I mean what Judeo-Christian civilization has meant for several millennia: a man and a woman committed to each other for life.[12] The federal government's definition of family is largely adequate for policy purposes: "a group of two or more persons related by birth, marriage, or adoption and residing together in a household." We must respect and deal fairly with single-parent and blended families, helping them do a good job raising their children. We must respect the civil rights of gay Americans, reject gay bashing, and vigorously root out continuing violence against gays and lesbians.[13] At the same time, however, all segments of society, including government, business, the media, and the church, ought to promote the norm for a family assumed by virtually all civilizations for millennia: a mother and father united in lifelong marital covenant, with their children, surrounded by a larger extended family.

The importance of two-parent families by no means suggests that women should stay with husbands who physically abuse them. The story of Patrice illustrates a tragically widespread problem. One day before Patrice left her husband, he was battering her as she lay on the floor. To her horror, this battered woman's little two-year-old son imitated his abusive father. "I will never forget those new little white shoes, baby walkers, kicking me in the head."[14] Pro-family advocates must lead the struggle to overcome physical and sexual abuse in the home.

One final point: "Pro-family" does *not* mean "antifeminist." There are, of course, many kinds of feminists. Biblical people must oppose radical secular feminists who deplore marriage as oppression and embrace lesbianism. Biblical feminism, on the other hand—but not patriarchalism or radical feminism—is fully consistent with this chapter's call to restore the family. Mutual submission and mutual servanthood (Eph. 5:21–25) by husbands and wives is an essential component for building strong Christian families today.[15]

Single Parenthood: Facts, Causes, and Consequences

Facts

Before we try to figure out how to change things, we must understand more clearly why so many children today end up in single-parent families. There are, of course, three ways this happens: a child's parents never marry; they separate and/or divorce; or one of them dies. The first two situations are by far the most common—and the most destructive to children. A mere 4 percent of children living in single-mom families are there because of the death of the father.[16] Divorce, separation, or a failure to marry at all are the major culprits.

The percentage of children born to unmarried parents has skyrocketed in the last forty years. In 1960, unmarried moms gave birth to only 5 percent of all children born that year. In 1980, it was 18 percent. By 1994, it was 33 percent—almost one-third of all children. According to the Alan Guttmacher Institute, 65 percent of these pregnancies were *not* intentional.[17]

A breakdown by age, race, and place is useful. Women in their twenties (53 percent)—not teenagers (30 percent) as one might expect—have the largest number of out-of-wedlock births. In 1994, 25.4 percent of white births, 43.1 percent of Hispanic births, and 70.4 percent of black births were to unmarried mothers.[18] To keep the high out-of-wedlock birth rate in the black community in perspective, it is essential to remember that this tragedy is a recent development. In every census from 1890 to 1960, 80 percent of all black households were headed by a married husband and wife.[19] The white illegitimacy rate has grown rapidly in recent decades, especially among lower-income and less-educated groups. For white high school dropouts, the out-of-wedlock birth rate is already 48 percent.[20] Births to unmarried parents are especially high in larger cities. For the fifty largest cities, it is almost one half (48 percent) of all births. In St. Louis, it reaches 69 percent; Baltimore, 68 percent; New York, 52 percent; and Minneapolis, 50 percent.[21]

Cohabitation is one reason for nonmarital births. In 1997, over four million couples were living together without being married.[22] Four out of every ten such couples have children together. Four out of ten such couples also eventually marry, but their likelihood of divorce is 50 percent above the norm.[23]

The escalation of nonmarital birth rates is not a problem in the United States alone. Figure 7 shows that in 1992, Iceland, Sweden, Denmark, and France all had higher rates than the United States. Most wealthy countries have seen huge jumps. (Japan is a striking exception—its tiny 1 percent rate in 1960 did not budge at all through 1992.)

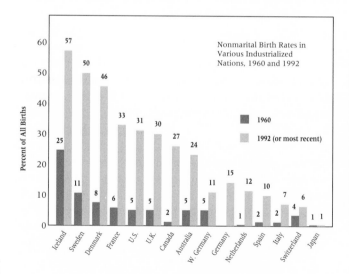

Fig. 7. The explosion in out-of-wedlock births occurred all across Northern Europe and Northern America. The Canadian ratio is just below the U.S. ratio, the French ratio just above. *Source:* Daniel Moynihan, *Miles to Go* (Cambridge: Harvard Univ. Press, 1996), 176.

The United States has a higher divorce rate than any other industrialized nation. In 1996, there were 2.34 million marriages and 1.15 million divorces. Over 40 percent of all first marriages today end in divorce—and 60 percent of all remarriages.

Since the early twentieth century, the American divorce rate has slowly risen. The huge jump came at the end of the sexual revolution in the sixties and just after the adoption of no-fault divorce laws. In a ten-year period from the late sixties to the late seventies, the divorce rate doubled!

A pincer movement composed of illegitimate births, cohabitation, and divorce is devastating the American family. Fully 32 percent of all families with children under eighteen today are single-parent families. Most of them are headed by a single mom.[24] Since at least 1990, the annual number of nonmarital births (1.165 million in 1990) has exceeded the number of children for whom divorce creates a single-parent home (1.075 million in 1990). The percentage of families headed by a single parent has tripled since 1960.

Two-thirds of all families with children under eighteen still have two parents living together, but that includes cohabiting and remarried couples. Less than half of all American children today live with their married, biological mom and dad for their entire childhood. One study, in fact, places the percent who experience this blessing at a mere 36 percent.[25]

Causes

It is much easier to describe what is happening than to explain why. The causes of escalating out-of-wedlock births, cohabitation, and divorce are complex and diverse. Conservatives are right in their charge that the sexual revolution of the sixties and the popularization of sexual permissiveness by movies, TV, popular heroes, and even high school textbooks has been a major factor.[26] The self-idolizing individualism articulated by academics and popularized by Hollywood has no room for the self-sacrifice required to care for children and make marriages work. As Sylvia Ann Hewlett and Cornel West say so pointedly, "The overwhelming message from progressive liberal folks in Hollywood is: *Who needs a husband to have a child?*"[27]

Unfortunately, conservatives often fail to see how economic factors, especially the inability of low-skilled men to earn enough to care for a family, have also played a role.[28] Thirty-two percent of all men between the ages of twenty-five and thirty-four do not earn enough to keep a family of four above the poverty level.[29] William Julius Wilson is almost certainly right that the low income of so many young black males contributes to less marriage and more single parenthood in the black community.[30] Especially for the middle and upper classes, growing materialism and the accompanying tendency to value making money more than family time has also contributed to family breakdown.[31] Complex economic changes have joined with widespread rejection of historic Judeo-Christian moral values to undermine the family.

One of the best features of Hewlett and West's important new book, *War against Parents,* is the balanced way they hold together the cultural and the economic causes of the decline in family life. They ruthlessly dissect the way Hollywood ridicules parents, belittles marriage, and glamorizes single parenthood. Equally important, however, is their critique of the way both business and government have undermined marriage and parenting in the last several decades.

Government policy was strikingly friendlier to families in the 1950s than it has been in the 1980s and 1990s. The $600 tax exemption per child adopted in the late 1940s would amount to $6,500 in 1996 dollars. (The 1998 deduction was only $2,700.) Married couples filing federal tax returns together received major advantages in the 1950s. Tax breaks and government regulations also favored home ownership by young married couples.[32] In the 1960s, things began to change. The personal exemption failed to keep pace with inflation. Married couples lost a major part of their tax breaks in joint returns. From 1969 to 1983, single people and couples without children saw no significant growth in their taxes, but couples with two children paid 43 percent more. Couples with four children saw a whopping 223 percent increase.[33]

The tax code's treatment of the interest deduction on home mortgages has also changed since the 1950s in a way that has become grossly unfair to lower-income families. Sixty-three million families in the United States own their own homes, but less than half (27 million) take an interest deduction for their mortgages on their federal tax forms. Why? Because itemizing deductions does not help lower-income persons. Furthermore, a tax deduction is far more beneficial to a rich person paying the top tax rate of 39.6 percent than a family in the 15 percent tax bracket.

All this may sound a bit complex, but the result is crystal clear. Fully one-half ($33 billion) of the total tax break of $66 billion that results from the mortgage interest deduction goes to households with incomes over $100,000! That $33-billion tax break for a small rich minority is four times what we spend on housing for low-income families. Ninety-four percent of all our children live in families with incomes below $100,000.[34] Is there any reason—other than who pays for political campaigns—why the richest 6 percent should get $33 billion in tax breaks for expensive houses when much poorer families who struggle to pay for a modest house of their own receive no such help?

Corporations fare no better than government in Hewlett and West's analysis. CEO's salaries have skyrocketed while many workers no longer earn a decent family wage. Downsizing by corporations has produced growing economic insecurity and greater pressure for salaried workers to put in longer hours—with negative effects on family stability. Meanwhile, most of the economic benefits go to a small executive elite.[35]

Society—cultural elites, government, and business—is undermining the family. The details may sound complex, but the consequences are clear—and horrendous.

Consequences

Single parenthood and divorce lead to more poverty, more crime, and more illegitimacy, resulting in a descending spiral of chaos and agony. Persistent poverty is eleven times more likely to plague children living in single-parent families. Persons living in mother-only families fall below the poverty level 59 percent of the time if the mother never married and 28.5 percent of the time if the mother has been divorced.[36] But the poverty rate for married-couple families is a mere 8.7 percent.[37] Princeton sociologist Sara McLanahan puts it bluntly: "The more single parents and the more out-of-wedlock single parents, the more poverty."[38] So many studies have confirmed this correlation between single parenthood and poverty that scholars now view it as one of the best established findings of "social scientific research."[39]

The links between single parenthood and poverty are rather obvious. Never-married mothers tend to have children at a younger age, which frequently interferes with their completing high school or college. Less educated, they find it more difficult to find decent-paying jobs. Child care problems make work more problematic and less financially rewarding. Divorced and separated mothers receive inadequate child support from absent fathers, and never-married mothers receive even less. In 1993, the Census Bureau reported that 87 percent of all mothers on welfare were either never married (48 percent), separated (17 percent), or divorced or widowed (23 percent).[40] In a widely cited book, Lenore Weitzman rightly denounced the economic injustice of divorced fathers failing to support their children. She claimed that divorced women with minor children suffered a 73 percent decline in living standards, while their divorced husbands' living standard jumped 42 percent. Probably more accurate are recent figures reported in the 1996 *American Sociological Review:* a 27 percent drop for divorced women and their children and a 10 percent increase for divorced men.[41] Whatever the precise figures, however, the basic picture is clear: Divorce has drastic, negative economic consequences for women and children. After their parents divorce, children are almost twice as likely to live in poverty.[42]

Tragically, the negative economic consequences often persist for a lifetime. Studies show that fewer children of divorced parents go to college (in large part for financial reasons) and fewer finish if they start.[43] Divorce is a major cause of both short-term and long-term economic inequality. In fact, as Dave Gushee says, it is "one of the most important economic justice issues of our time."[44]

Unfortunately, the most serious consequences for children in single-parent families are probably the emotional agony, inner devastation, and resulting dysfunction. Children in single-parent families and separated or divorced families are two to three times more likely than children in two-parent families to have emotional and behavioral problems. They are more likely to have academic trouble, drop out of high school, become pregnant as teenagers, abuse drugs, commit crimes, become mentally ill, or get into trouble with the law.[45]

Children of never-married mothers are 75 percent more likely to fail a grade in school and more than twice as likely to be expelled or suspended than children living with both biological parents.[46] White women raised in single-parent welfare homes are 164 percent more likely to become unwed mothers than those raised in two-parent families.[47] "Eighty percent of all adolescents in psychiatric hospitals come from broken homes. Three out of four teen suicides occur in single-parent homes. Seventy percent of the juveniles in state reform institutions grew up in fatherless homes."[48]

Some scholars have tried to argue that the heightened negative behavior associated with children of single and divorced parents is due not to inherent problems in single parenthood and divorce but to their poverty or to the stigma society has attached to their departure from the norm. According to these scholars, if we would just end poverty and be more tolerant and accepting of single parenthood and divorce, the negative behavior would disappear.[49] Careful studies, however, do not support this hypothesis.

In a thorough study, Douglas Smith and Roger Jarjoura discovered that the higher the single parenthood rate in a neighborhood, the higher the crime rate. In fact, single parenthood was a better predictor of criminal activity than low income. They concluded: "The relationship is so strong [between single parenthood rates and crime rates] that controlling for family configuration erases the relationship between race and crime and between low income and crime. This conclusion shows up time and time again in the literature: poverty is far from the sole determinant of crime."[50] Another study discovered that black men raised in single-parent families were twice as likely to commit crimes as black men raised in two-parent families—even when the researchers held constant variables such as family income, neighborhood environment, urban residence, and parents' education.[51]

Especially decisive is a new study by two professors at Princeton and the University of Pennsylvania. They followed a nationally representative sample of six thousand teenage boys for over fifteen years. Thirteen percent of the boys living with a single mom at age fourteen landed in prison by their early thirties. For boys whose fathers were present, the figure was only 5 percent. Naturally, the researchers controlled for many different variables to see if the difference really came from race, income, parents' education, child support payments, neighborhoods with many single moms, and so on. None of those factors were nearly as important as the absence of a father. After accounting for all these variables, fatherless boys were still twice as likely to go to jail as boys living with two parents. In fact, "for each year spent in a non-intact family, the odds of incarceration rise five percent."[52]

Are stepfathers a good substitute? No. Boys with stepfathers are 2.9 times more likely to go to jail than boys living with both mom and dad. In fact, this and another recent study indicate that delinquency rates are lower for boys living with a single mom than for boys living with mom's boyfriend or new husband.[53]

A study by Deborah A. Dawson of the National Institute of Health disproves the argument that stigmatization is a major factor in delinquency rates. Dawson's study showed that the negative behavior associated with children from single-parent and divorced families is "not based on stigmatization but rather on inherent problems in alternative family structures."[54] "Alternative family structures" here means something other than two-parent families. In other words, there is something inherent in single parenthood and divorce that hurts children. In the words of President Clinton's domestic policy advisor, William A. Galston, "There is a mountain of scientific evidence showing that when families disintegrate, children often end up with intellectual, physical, and emotional scars that persist for life. . . . We talk about the drug crisis, the education crisis, and the problems of teen pregnancy and juvenile crime. But all these ills trace back predominantly to one source: broken families."[55]

In light of all the evidence, it is ironic that so many "liberal, progressive" champions of the poor—in universities, politics, and even in some churches—are not equally vocal defenders of the biological, two-parent family. The evidence is abundantly clear. Contemporary social science confirms biblical norms: Children need to grow up in stable families with both their mom and their dad. Single parenthood and divorce substantially increase poverty and also harm children in many other ways. One of the most important ways to promote economic justice today in industrialized nations is to be vigorously pro-family. One significant measure of the objectivity of liberal intellectuals will be whether they will emphasize the renewal of two-parent family life as vigorously as the masses of research data warrant.

How do we get from where we are to where we ought to be?

Renewing Sexual Integrity and Two-Parent Families

Honestly facing how bad the situation is offers the only realistic starting point. Popular moral values, the media, and the economy all undermine historic Judeo-Christian sexual and family values. In a recent year, the three largest TV networks broadcast sixty-five thousand sexual references—and the vast majority involved unmarried persons. Even some churches have endorsed the dominant sexual ethic "sex within loving relationships." As long as the people treat each other with love, it is alleged, any sexual activity, whether homosexual, heterosexual, or bisexual, whether between people who are married or unmarried, is permissible. Modern society has cut the historic link between marriage, sex, and children. "What for the whole of human history had been inextricably joined has now been sundered."[56] To reverse this catastrophic moral decay will require herculean struggle.

A sustained, successful, Christian response[57] must start in the Christian community itself with wholesome, joyful families and congregations modeling a countercultural alternative to today's agony. From that base, we can then seek to shape society's cultural institutions, including the media and the arts, and even effect modest change through public policy.

At the core of our effort must be a sustained, massive campaign that helps Christian families and congregations nurture persons of moral integrity who gladly reserve sex for marriage and keep their marriage covenants as long as both live. That means greatly expanded programs to equip Christian parents, to strengthen sex and family education in church youth ministries, to expand premarital and postmarital counseling—the list goes on and on. Every piece is crucial.

Society today is reeling from wrenching pain and agony in our families. If Christian families and congregations offer the world a model of joyful, wholesome marriages and families, this model will be powerfully attractive. If we fail to live a radical alternative to today's sad insanity, nothing we say will make a difference.

Reducing Out-of-Wedlock Births

Movements such as True Love Waits demonstrate the power of a church-based approach. In the past five years, hundreds of thousands of Christian youth in more than forty-five denominations and one hundred countries have taken the pledge: "Believing that true love waits, I make a commitment to God, myself, my family, my friends, my future mate, and my future children to be sexually abstinent from this day until the day I enter a biblical marriage relationship."[58] I know from personal experience that pledges help. Decades ago as a teenager dating my future wife, I placed in my wallet a handwritten promise to God not to have sex with Arbutus until we were married.

True Love Waits (TLW) started in Tulip Grove Baptist Church in Nashville, Tennessee, when two fourteen-year-old girls shared with Richard Ross, their youth group leader, their fear that they were the only virgins in their junior high school. Knowing there were more, Ross dreamed up the idea of an abstinence pledge to offer social support for sexual purity.

The campaign has spread far beyond Ross's wildest dreams. In 1994, TLW placed 211,000 chastity cards in the National Mall in Washington, D.C. In 1996 at a TLW convention, there were 340,000 pledge cards stacked from floor to ceiling in Atlanta's Georgia Dome. At a large high school in Spartanburg, South Carolina, Ann Hodges led a group of students who braved crude jokes and rude comments to display 350 signed pledge cards in the school lunchroom—at the end of Valentine's Day week.

Imagine the impact if even one-half of all the unmarried youth in our churches gladly, wholeheartedly signed this pledge. Ten million American teenagers are sexually active. Three million each year experience the pain of wrestling with a sexually transmitted disease. One million teenage girls get pregnant every year. Many of those teenagers are in our youth groups and churches. If even half of our Christian youth made and kept this pledge, American culture would change dramatically.

Changing the entertainment industry will be a more difficult task. We need brilliant writers and producers who articulate Judeo-Christian norms plus wise campaigns that effectively challenge the glorification of destructive sexual and family values in movies and TV. In such campaigns, it is difficult to combine a spirit of love, dialogue, and fairness with appropriate challenge and confrontation, but some organizations succeed in that.[59] Too often, our moral crusades backfire. Too often, we fail to combine the ethical clarity and gentleness that Jesus displayed with the woman taken in adultery (John 8:3–11). Unlike the self-righteous Pharisees, Jesus refused to stone her, but he gently told her not to sin anymore. This is the spirit we need in our campaigns to change the media.

Public policy can do far less to prevent out-of-wedlock births than families, churches and synagogues, and the media, but the little it can do should be done well. Most public schools include sex education programs. Parents and citizens should make sure that historic Judeo-Christian sexual and family norms are clearly and fairly presented as a central part of the program. In the schools and in government-run teenage pregnancy prevention programs, we must insist on the promotion of abstinence until marriage and the ideal of two-parent, married families. Congress should abolish federal regulations that now prevent local school districts from adopting measures to discourage teen pregnancies.[60] The 1996 welfare legislation requires states to sponsor programs to prevent teen pregnancy. We should make sure that states implement this mandate in a way that uses the Charitable Choice provisions (see chapter 3) of that bill so that effective faith-based programs have equal access to available funds.

Policy recommendations in other chapters are also highly relevant to this topic. Poor schools and low wages contribute to single parenthood; therefore, ensuring quality schools (chapter 7) and a family wage (chapter 4) would help reduce out-of-wedlock births.

Reducing Divorce

The religious community is the place to begin when addressing the issue of divorce. If the marriages are more joyous and wholesome and the divorce rates are much lower in our churches than in surrounding society, our actions will be powerful and our words will enjoy respect. Tragically, when it comes to Christian marriages, many reflect the surrounding society rather than Jesus' dawning kingdom. We have a momentous task ahead.

In his book *Marriage Savers* and the movement of the same name, Michael McManus presents a comprehensive agenda for strengthening Christian marriages.[61] He outlines programs for the dating years, engagement, premarital counseling, postmarital counseling, and marriage enrichment at all stages of marriage. One of his many helpful suggestions is that all churches in a community adopt a "community marriage policy." Under this policy, all churches promise to require at least a minimal amount of Christian premarital counseling before allowing a church wedding for a couple.

If we work hard and pray without ceasing, Christian marriages could attract the wounded refugees from society's broken homes the way a crackling fire in a cozy living room draws frozen wanderers stumbling through a wintry blizzard. Christian marriages full of joy, goodness, and mutual submission could be one of our best gifts to our confused contemporaries.

Public policy is less important when attempting to reduce the incidence of divorce, but it still plays a significant role. Sylvia Ann Hewlett and Cornel West are right that "government should get back into the business of fostering the value of marriage as a long-term commitment."[62] That means strengthening the economic stability of lower-income families. Government should increase the Child Tax Credit for poor and middle-income families and make it refundable so poor working families also benefit. The amount of the per-person exemption for federal taxes should also be increased. To encourage more adequate preparation for marriage, states should use a two-tier marriage license to offer a modest incentive for voluntary premarital counseling—e.g., a $50 fee with no waiting period for those who can demonstrate participation in premarital counseling and a $200 fee and a sixty-day waiting period for those who cannot. To discourage divorce, states should significantly modify no-fault divorce law, offer the option of covenant marriage (see below), and legislate different divorce requirements for couples with children under eighteen.

In the early seventies, no-fault divorce laws swept the country, allowing either spouse to initiate divorce for any reason at any time. If one party claims "irreconcilable differences" and waits for a brief time, the court dissolves the marriage no matter what the other spouse desires. States could modify no-fault divorce laws by enacting three "speed bumps" to slow down persons contemplating divorce: (1) require substantially longer waiting periods; (2) give substantial weight to mutual consent; and (3) mandate more counseling before granting a divorce.

Louisiana's Covenant Marriage Law passed in 1997 merits widespread imitation. When a couple seeks a marriage license, they must voluntarily choose either marriage lite or a covenant marriage. The first permits a no-fault divorce process at any time. The license for a covenant marriage requires evidence of premarital counseling and a formal declaration of intent to enter a covenant marriage. This declaration includes the requirement that the couple must seek counseling if their marriage becomes troubled. It also mandates a fault-based process for any separation or divorce procedure. Adultery, imprisonment for a felony, desertion, or physical or sexual abuse of child or spouse are the only grounds for divorce. Even then, there must be two years of continuous separation. Arizona passed similar legislation in 1998. Other states should do the same.

Where children are involved, states should legislate even tougher procedures along the lines proposed by William Galston.[63] In today's divorce culture, children suffer the most. The mounting evidence of their agony demands that we offer them more protection. When children are present, states should legislate: (1) a five-year waiting period before parents may divorce unless there is mutual consent, in which case they still must wait two to three years; (2) mandatory classes on the impact of divorce on children for couples considering divorce; and (3) judicial discretion to delay or disallow frivolous cases. When a divorce does occur, child support awards should be larger and their enforcement tougher. Our laws should reflect the moral truth that parents are called to reject the popular modern notion that they are isolated individuals rightly focused on personal self-fulfillment. Our laws should strengthen their desire to fulfill their responsibilities to others, especially the children they have chosen to bring into this world.

Home Ownership for Poor Families

Would not a house to call their own strengthen poor families? Few material things anchor a family more securely than home ownership. A house of one's own provides security, stability, and dignity, and it encourages responsibility, discourages transience,[64] and makes one a stakeholder in one's community.

Mary Martinez used to live with her daughter, Theresa, in public housing in the Bronx. The buildings were crowded, noisy, dirty, and dangerous, and drug dealers were moving in. Mary worked long hours as a legal secretary, and she longed for something better for her five-year-old child. "I wanted her to grow up safe. I wanted her to have a yard. I wanted her to have quiet. Is that too much?" But Mary's meager salary did not permit her to move.

Everything changed when the Nehemiah project of the South Bronx churches built several hundred houses and condominiums for lower-income working families. Mary and Theresa got their own house and yard. "Theresa and her little friends play in the yard," Mary proudly reports. "Nehemiah is the best thing that ever happened to my family. Now we are working to make the neighborhood even better."[65]

If more Christians volunteered to work with Habitat for Humanity and other such organizations, we could help many more poorer families enjoy home ownership. We also need government policies that promote the same goal.

A refundable Home Ownership Tax Credit (HOTC) could offer significant economic incentive and hope for lower-income families to purchase a home of their own. Such a tax credit (worth $1,000 to $1,500 a year) could be modeled on the EITC.[66] Only homeowners working at least twenty hours a week would be eligible. We already give homeowners with incomes over $100,000 a year a $33-billion tax break on their mortgage interest. If we reduced that by one-half, we would have some of the necessary funds for the Home Ownership Tax Credit for those who truly need government help to enjoy a house of their own. That reallocation of present government resources would not undermine rich families; it would, however, significantly strengthen poor families.

Other Pro-Family Proposals

Reducing divorce and single parenthood and encouraging home ownership among the poor, of course, are not the only ways to strengthen two-parent families. Churches need to nurture persons who understand how creeping materialism undermines the family and learn to value parenting more than wealth and status. Media, business, and government could consciously choose to adopt more family-friendly policies.

If we work hard enough, we can pressure the broadcast industry to return to their earlier "family hour" policies and exclude inappropriate sex and violence during the times when the most children and teenagers watch TV. We could also demand that they adopt a "television code" to make all advertising and programming more family friendly.[67] Still more helpful would be a television rating system designed and controlled by parents rather than the media.[68]

Businesses could voluntarily expand the opportunities for flexible working arrangements so that parents can more easily attend to family responsibilities. The possibilities are many: working at home using today's sophisticated computer and communication systems; job sharing; compressed work weeks (e.g., four ten-hour days); job protection and benefits for short-term parental leave; job preferences and graduated reentry for long-term parental leave. In the long run, we all benefit if parents spend more time with their children.[69]

Government policy should be designed to encourage strong, stable, two-parent families. That means repealing any part of the tax code that offers tax incentives for cohabitation, unwed childbearing, or divorce. Using the federal tax code, we could offer refundable education tax credits for parents who leave paid employment to care for young children.[70] We certainly should return to some of the more family-friendly tax provisions of the 1950s that substantially reduced federal taxes for lower-income families raising children. We could do so by substantially increasing either the standard deduction for dependent children or the child tax credit.

Congress should amend the Fair Labor Standards Act (FLSA) to allow more family-friendly flex time in private businesses. Currently, federal employees can take overtime pay either as cash or paid time off. But federal law (the FLSA) prevents workers in private business from doing the same thing! This federal law—and similar state laws—should change. Congress should also change the FLSA to allow workers to choose to work extra hours one week and then "bank" those hours, saving them for paid time off later when extra time is needed for family responsibilities.[71]

One frequently suggested proposal we should *not* adopt is Assured Child Support for single parents. Since many fathers fail to pay child support, some scholars and politicians have proposed that government guarantee a certain level of child support to single moms and then collect that money when possible from the fathers using strengthened collection procedures.[72] The single moms, however, would receive the money whether or not the state collected from the father. There are strong arguments in favor of this

135

proposal, including the fact that it would strengthen the financial security of single moms,[73] but there are also major problems. For one thing, this proposal would make the government the direct link between absent dads and their children. Even when the courts must force fathers to pay by seizing some of their wages, it would probably be better for father-child relationships to establish special accounts so that money from fathers goes directly to their children. Furthermore, as Gary Bauer rightly points out, assured child support schemes "limit benefits solely to unmarried parents [and therefore] they essentially transfer wealth from married-couple families to single-parent families. In so doing, guaranteed support plans reward illegitimacy and divorce and penalize marriage and marital permanence."[74]

It is hardly a pro-family approach to guarantee cash child support benefits to single moms that we do not offer to equally poor two-parent families. We can accomplish the desired result by expanding the Earned Income Tax Credit and making the Dependent Care Tax Credit refundable and available to two-parent families even when only one parent works outside the home (see p. 108).

We should also get much tougher on delinquent dads. We should vigorously implement the recent legislation that strengthened the national child support clearinghouse to track child support awards, as well as the location and employment of absent fathers.[75] We should establish paternity for every child at birth, but we need to reconsider the wisdom of suspending driver's and professional licenses of fathers and mothers who do not pay court-ordered child support since that reduces their ability to earn money to support their children.[76]

At the same time, we need to recognize that poor fathers not living with their children are often among the most needy persons in our midst. Possessing few skills, frequently discouraged, often alone in the world, sometimes plagued by alcohol abuse, drug addiction, and criminal records, they have little opportunity to be responsible fathers. We should guarantee them a job (see chapter 4) as we toughen our demand that they support their children. Using the opportunities provided by Charitable Choice legislation, we should also encourage faith-based programs to offer them the same kind of holistic support in job training and personal growth that are now proving so successful for single moms (see pp. 187–88).[77]

Conclusion

All of the above will help restore wholesome family life. Without the crucial economic changes outlined in the previous chapter, without quality education (chapter 7), and without health insurance for everyone (chapter 6), however, our poorer families will still struggle with intolerable burdens. And unless, by God's help, our preachers, pastors, priests, and prophets renew people of moral integrity who keep their promises to their children and spouses, all other efforts will fail. Everything is interrelated. Our only hope is a holistic, comprehensive approach.

Somehow, by some blessed combination of faithful churches and synagogues, socially responsible businesses and media, wise public policy, and divine grace, we must strengthen two-parent families in the next couple decades. If we do not, more and more poor neighborhoods will descend even deeper into an agonizing abyss of social dysfunction, deadly despair, and violent death. In fact, more and more middle-class neighborhoods that now seem safe and stable will also spiral downward into the same agony.

Based on a fair-minded reading of the research, it is obvious that restoring stable, wholesome two-parent families must be at the heart of any effective policy to overcome poverty in the United States. Being pro-family is not a conservative agenda; it is a crucial component of any rational search for justice for the poor.

6

Does Justice Include Health Care for the Poor?

I was sick and you took care of me.

Matthew 25:36 NRSV

Nearly forty-three and a half million Americans lack health insurance.

Bob George is a dear friend and fellow elder in the small city church I attend. Bob also has a $100,000 medical bill he and his family can never repay. For three decades, Bob and his wife, Maggie, worked responsibly, raised their two sons, and generously shared their love, time, and money with needy neighbors.

For most of the last twenty years, the George family received medical coverage through Bob's work—most recently through Bob's small drug and alcohol treatment agency, which had a contract with the Allegheny University Hospital System. About a year ago, newspaper headlines reported that due to mismanagement by highly paid executives, the Allegheny system was collapsing and not paying its debts, including large payments owed to Bob's agency. His small company went under even though Allegheny executives continued to collect huge salaries. Bob lost his job and his medical insurance.

Then cancer struck. Doctors informed Bob that his cancer was life threatening. Within ten weeks, Bob owed over $100,000 in medical bills, and they keep climbing. Our small congregation helps with prayers, meals, love, and transportation, but repaying $100,000 in medical bills is simply impossible for Bob, his family, or his congregation.

Nearly forty-three and a half million Americans risk the same catastrophe that overwhelmed the George family. In 1997, 43.4 million people in the United States lived for at least one month with absolutely no health insurance. That is 16.1 percent of the total population.[1] Some people without health insurance manage to find coverage after some months, but about 22 million have to endure the worry and danger of no insurance for an entire year or more.[2]

The poor and minorities face the worst situation. Thirty-one percent of all people below the poverty line are uninsured, and half of all poor people *working full-time* are uninsured.[3] Over 22 percent of all African Americans and 35 percent of all Hispanics lack health insurance.[4] Unfortunately, the percentage of those uninsured steadily increases year by year.[5]

Why do 43.4 million people in the richest nation on earth run the risk of living without health insurance? Because they cannot afford it. Less than 10 percent are uninsured by choice. Poor and lower-middle-class people simply cannot afford the high cost of private health insurance, which today costs between $5,000 and $6,000 a year for a family of four.

The percentage of people covered by health insurance through their employment is dropping steadily—almost a 9 percent drop from 1979 to 1995.[6] Even full-time workers are less likely to receive health insurance as an employee benefit. Part-time workers fare much worse. Only a mere 38 percent of part-time workers twenty-five years old or older are even eligible for employer-funded health insurance, and only 22 percent receive it.[7] The high cost of health insurance means that millions of hardworking, low-income parents simply have to choose between providing food and clothing for their families or having health insurance.

What happens when people lack insurance? Some people calmly assure us that there is no real problem because emergency rooms in public hospitals and clinics are supposed to care for anyone, regardless of whether the person has insurance. The facts tell a different story: (1) the uninsured are four times as likely as the insured to report that they needed medical care but did not get it; (2) they are three times more likely to report problems in paying medical bills; (3) and the uninsured get substantially poorer medical care even when they do see a doctor. Studies show that the uninsured enter hospitals sicker than the insured, receive fewer tests, and leave the hospital sooner.[8] The 3.5 million people who go to the hospital every year without insurance face a terrible burden. This $7-billion bill places heavy financial and emotional burdens on poor families already struggling. Tragically, one result may be that they become uninsurable for years.[9]

Inferior access and treatment are especially common for minorities. Many studies show that African Americans are discharged "quicker and sicker" from hospitals and do not receive the same treatment white people do for similar problems—even when insured! Indeed, even when they have exactly the same coverage under Medicare as whites, they still receive inferior care.[10] Hispanics and Native Americans face similar problems.

Erica Aguilar is a hardworking single mom from Denver.[11] She has three children, but Erica somehow finds time to work twenty-six hours a week as a sales clerk. Medicaid covers her children, but at $6.50 per hour, Erica makes too much to receive Medicaid for herself. Unfortunately, Montgomery Ward, the store where she works, does not offer medical coverage to part-time workers, so like more than one-third of all Latinos in the United States, she has no health insurance. She uses home remedies for minor problems and hopes desperately that no major medical problem develops.

Poverty and poor health go hand in hand. Studies show that the poor experience more sickness than the nonpoor. They also die younger. Tragically, the health gap between the poor and the rest of us is widening.[12]

Unlike the United States, every other wealthy nation today guarantees health care to every citizen, no matter how poor. With 43.4 million people in the United States uninsured, our health care system offers "the highest cost and the worst access in the modern world."[13] The United States spends far more per person on health care than any other developed country, but the percent paid by the government is the lowest.[14] The wealthiest nation in the world is the only developed country with large numbers of people without health insurance.

How should biblical people respond to the way our society neglects the health care needs of the poor?

A Biblical Framework

Good health is God's will for every person created in his image. About that the Bible leaves absolutely no doubt. Physical wholeness was part of the original creation. Sickness and death resulted from human sin (Rom. 5:12–14). God the redeemer, however, rolled back the satanic devastation of the good creation when God entered history as the messianic healer and promised at Christ's return to complete the victory over sickness and disease, indeed, even death itself (1 Cor. 15:26).

In both the Old and New Testaments, the words for salvation include physical wholeness. (They also, of course, refer to forgiveness of sins and personal sanctification.[15]) Frequently, the Gospels use the word *save (sozo)* to describe physical healing. Jesus "saved" (i.e., healed) the Samaritan leper (Luke 17:19), blind Bartimaeus (Mark 10:52), and the man with the withered hand (Mark 3:4–5). Obviously, these people also needed Jesus to forgive their sins and transform their character, but physical healing was part of the salvation Jesus brought. Jesus' healings were a sign that the messianic kingdom was breaking into history.

At Christ's return, God will complete the victory over sickness. In Revelation 21, the Bible promises that the returning Christ "will wipe every tear from their eyes. . . . Mourning and crying and pain will be no more" (v. 4 NRSV). Isaiah's vision of God's ultimate design, echoed in Revelation 21, is equally explicit: "No more shall there be . . . an infant that lives but a few days, or an old person who does not live out a lifetime" (Isa. 65:20 NRSV).

That God desires health for persons created in God's very image is hardly surprising. God wants persons to be co-workers in shaping history, and God wants persons to be dignified participating members of their community. Poor health, sickness, and disease undermine these divine goals and eat away at human dignity like a cancer. Good health is one important part of the "abundant life" (John 10:10) that God desires for all.

Since God longs for health for everyone, his people are called to be instruments of healing. Jesus instructed his disciples to heal as he did (Matt. 10:1–8), and the early Christians followed Jesus' example (Acts 3:1–10; 5:15; James 5:14–15).

The biblical teaching on God's special concern for the poor and weak (see chapter 2) applies directly to those suffering poor health. Sick and injured persons are particularly vulnerable, especially children and the elderly who are ill, persons with severe physical or mental disabilities, and those with stigmatized diseases such as AIDS. Jesus' attitude toward the lepers should be our model.

Jesus' call to visit the sick must be our command, especially since he so identifies with the sick that ministering to them is like caring for him: "I was sick and you took care of me" (Matt. 25:36 NRSV). When we care for "the least of these" (v. 40) who are ill, we somehow nurse the wounds of the incarnate God. If we believe Jesus' words, how can his followers in a rich society rest until every member of their community is guaranteed access to quality health care?

In chapter 2, I discussed the biblical teaching on restorative justice. Restoring the weak to community and making sure all have access to productive resources so they can be dignified participants in society are central to the biblical understanding of justice. A healthy body is surely every person's most basic productive asset. Guaranteeing medical care so that even the poorest can regain health, return to their families, and enjoy the dignity of productive work is one of the crucial ways that we can "make them strong" again (Lev. 25:35–36).[16]

In chapter 2, we also saw that according to the Bible, distributive justice means we should guarantee the basic needs necessary for life in community.[17] Distribution according to need is sometimes a biblical imperative. That is not to deny that we properly distribute many things according to other criteria—e.g., grades according to merit, and sports awards to the most skillful. Some things should be distributed according to need and some should not. Need is a poor principle for allocating grades but a good one for allocating emergency food—and basic health services.

In the United States today, however, the market rather than need largely determines who gets health care. That is why 43.4 million largely poor people lack health insurance. They do not have the money to buy it. Biblical truth demands that this injustice end.

That is not to argue that a government-operated, single-payer system is the only one compatible with biblical justice. Individuals, churches, and employers all have responsibilities. Furthermore, just because the government guarantees health care to everyone does not mean that the government must operate the delivery systems. (The government, for example, guarantees food stamps to all who need them, but private businesses operating in a market economy deliver the food.) What biblical justice demands is access to good quality essential services in health care for every person.[18] The moral imperative is insurance that guarantees good, quality, basic services for all.

Health insurance for everyone is a pro-family issue. When an uninsured poor family such as the Georges rack up huge medical bills, they experience terrible pressures in their family. Health insurance for all so that even the poorest mom and dad can rest confident that their children will get decent health care when they need it is one important way to strengthen the family.

For those who begin with biblical norms, one thing is abundantly clear: Good health care for everyone—*especially* for the poor and marginalized—is a moral imperative. By tolerating a situation in which over 43 million people lack health insurance, this society stands in blatant defiance of God's will. This moral outrage must end—now.

To understand clearly how this can be done, we need to look briefly at the way most people today obtain access to health care.

The Situation Today

Job-Related Insurance

The majority of Americans under sixty-five receive health insurance through the job of a wage earner in the family. In 1995, 152 million people (65 percent) fell into this category.[19] Often, the employer offers health insurance as a non-salary benefit for which the employee pays nothing, not even taxes. (Increasingly, as we all know, some employees must pay part of the insurance premium.)

A significant, seldom-noted inequity results from this arrangement. It is the middle class and above who are most likely to enjoy this kind of job-related health insurance.[20] The comfortable pay absolutely no taxes—federal, state, or local—on employer-provided health insurance and thus receive a tax savings of approximately $600 per family for a total of $60 billion a year.[21] That $60 billion is more than the poor receive in both cash benefits (TANF) and food stamps. Who gets left out? Not the very poor who receive government-funded Medicaid (see below). It is the working poor without health insurance who are hit twice: They do not get free Medicaid and they cannot benefit from the tax subsidy on job-related insurance. One study found that tax-free health insurance provides an average annual benefit of $1,560 to each family in the richest fifth; the poorest fifth receive a meager $270 per family.[22]

Medicare

Almost all persons over sixty-five receive a major part of their health insurance from a government program called Medicare.[23] Part A of Medicare covers hospital expenses (after significant deductibles), and we all pay for it through a 1.45 percent payroll tax on our salaries. Part B of Medicare covers doctors' bills, outpatient hospital services, and so on (but not drugs) for all those who choose to pay a low monthly premium ($45.50 in 1999). It is so cheap that 98 percent of the elderly sign up. The premiums, however, cover only 25 percent of the cost, which means 75 percent of Part B expenses comes from general tax revenues. Many elderly people also purchase additional private insurance to cover the deductibles and drugs not covered by Medicare.

Medicaid

This program (run by the states with the government paying more than half of the costs) is how the poor receive health care. The blind, disabled, and those on welfare who receive cash grants (TANF) automatically qualify. So do the elderly poor who have few remaining assets. Recent changes mean that by the year 2000, states must provide Medicaid coverage for all children in families below the poverty level. States may also choose to include children close to the poverty level with the federal government paying half the cost. Begun in 1965 as part of the War on Poverty, Medicaid has been expanded in recent years to include more of the poor, and it has contributed significantly to improved health among this group of people.[24] Unfortunately, although the situation varies from state to state, Medicaid covers only about one half of all persons below the poverty level.[25]

Medicaid covers hospitalization, doctors, and drugs (in some states). Unlike Medicare, Medicaid also pays for nursing home care—and consequently serves as a safety net for the elderly middle class who can count on this government program to pay for their long-term nursing care if their personal funds run out. Medicaid covered 35 million people in 1995, almost half of them poor children. Only 25 percent of Medicaid recipients are aged, blind, and disabled, but about 60 percent of all Medicaid costs go to this relatively small group. Far less is spent on poor moms and their children. Long-term care for the elderly and the very disabled takes about one-third of all Medicaid funds.

Job-related private insurance, Medicare, and Medicaid cover about 84 percent of all Americans. That leaves 16 percent—over 43 million persons—with no insurance at all.

Creating a Better Situation

What should we do to correct this situation? The first thing is to firmly reject the conventional wisdom that nothing fundamental can be done for another ten to twenty years. Approximately every twenty years since World War II, there has been a major effort to fundamentally reform health care. Each one has failed. After the last failure in 1993–94 with President Clinton's American Health Security Act, the conventional wisdom is that no basic reform that would extend health insurance to everyone is politically possible for "the next ten or more years."[26]

That may be politically true, but it is morally wrong. What is politically possible, of course, changes quickly when enough people demand action. Christians must lead the way. Our situation today presents a stark test of the biblical faithfulness of middle-class Christians. Will we harden our hearts to over 43 million uninsured poor neighbors as we enjoy the security of our health insurance? Or will we demand that our politicians promptly legislate health care reform that guarantees coverage to every American?

Three Health Insurance Options

There are three basic ways to offer coverage to everyone.

1. Single-payer plan. We could abolish Medicare, Medicaid, and private job-related insurance and replace them with a government-funded program operated by the states and/or the federal government. This is the much discussed "Canadian" model.

2. Mandate job-related insurance for all employees and expand the current system. We could keep Medicare for the elderly, mandate that all employers provide job-related health insurance for their employees and their dependents (with some sharing of the cost of premiums), and extend Medicaid to all the unemployed. Public subsidy of the premiums of low-wage workers would be essential. This option most easily builds on present policy.

3. Mandate that all workers purchase private insurance. We could keep Medicare for the elderly, expand Medicaid to include all the unemployed, and require that all employees purchase private insurance for themselves and their dependents. This plan would require subsidy for low-income workers and be difficult to administer.

Which should we choose? I do not pretend to know enough to answer that question. Each plan has advantages and disadvantages. As a person whose extended family lives in Canada, I know that a single-payer system is much better than U.S. citizens frequently admit. It also significantly reduces the anxiety connected with losing a job. But I do not have nearly enough knowledge to argue for that option. Specialists must carefully assess the relative merits of each and clarify the options for us.

The most critical responsibility, however, rests with every citizen. We dare not make poor, uninsured people in the richest nation on earth wait another ten or twenty years for basic health insurance. That is both morally unacceptable and politically unnecessary. We should all write our political leaders and demand that the president and Congress appoint a bipartisan commission to recommend a workable way to insure everyone—implemented within four years. As voters we must make it clear that this is a nonnegotiable demand for which we will hold every politician accountable at the polls.

What would happen if even 20 percent of the Christians in the United States did that? What would happen if 20 percent of our congregations organized writing campaigns, sending letters such as the one in the box? We would get action—fast! Do 20 percent of middle-class Christians care enough about the poor to do that?

Congressperson (or Senator)
House of Representatives (or U.S. Senate)
Washington, D.C.

Dear _____:
More than 43 million American citizens lack health insurance. Most of them are poor. This is a moral outrage that defies Judeo-Christian moral teaching and the best of our history.

I ask you to request that Congress and the president promptly appoint a commission to recommend a workable way to offer health insurance to every person in the United States. Delay and partisan bickering are intolerable. Legislation should be completed within three to four years.

I appreciate your past support for justice for all, but this is a request for which I will hold you accountable the next time there is an election.

Sincerely,

In the short run, some smaller steps should also be taken, as long as we do not neglect the larger goal of coverage for everyone. It would be a mistake to do nothing for three or four years while we await basic reform. Here I sketch a few of the most crucial steps.[27]

Children's Health Insurance Program

An important expansion of insurance for low-income children took place with the adoption of the Children's Health Insurance Program (CHIP) in 1997. A new five-year federal block grant of $20.3 billion to the states is expected to insure an additional 2 million poor children.[28] We ought to do more, extending coverage at least to all children living in families below 133 percent of the poverty level.

Greatly expanded outreach efforts to inform all eligible people are essential if CHIP and Medicaid coverage of children is to reach its potential. In the mid-1990s, 20 percent (2.7 million) of all eligible children were not enrolled due to many factors, including lack of publicity, language and cultural barriers, parental neglect, and complex bureaucratic procedures. Both better government programs and more private groups including churches are needed to inform everyone about their eligibility for CHIP and Medicaid.

Expanding Medicaid

The 1997 federal Balanced Budget Act attempted to enroll more persons and encourage more use of managed care programs by Medicaid recipients. Nonetheless, almost half of the persons below the poverty level are not covered. It would be good to cover the parents of Medicaid eligible children and poor workers between jobs. Even better would be to expand and guarantee Medicaid-type coverage to everyone below 150 percent of the poverty level.[29] There is more than one way to do that. Government could mandate that all jobs (whether full- or part-time) include insurance for the worker and dependents and then provide employers with appropriate subsidies for workers below 150 percent of the poverty level. Or government could offer Medicaid coverage to every worker and dependents with the worker paying a reasonable premium on a sliding scale. For workers at the poverty level, that premium should be no more than 5 percent of income for family coverage.[30] Above that, the premium could gradually rise to 10 percent.

More Minority Doctors and Nurses

Poor minority communities do not have enough doctors. Since studies show that minority health professionals are more likely than white professionals to return to poor minority communities to practice medicine, we need to find new ways to train more minority doctors and nurses.[31] Unfortunately, this is not easy to do. Because the schools that minorities attend are often inferior, many minority students are poorly prepared for graduate study. In addition, changes in affirmative action programs in recent years have dramatically cut the number of minority students in medical school in some places. However difficult, we must find ways to train more minority health care professionals.

Medical Savings Accounts

A medical savings account (MSA) works a lot like an IRA. A person can put up to a certain amount of money into a special MSA without paying federal income taxes on the original amount or subsequent earnings. If that money is spent on medical expenses not covered by insurance, one never pays income tax on the money. Any amount left over at year-end can accumulate in the account but cannot be used for anything other than medical expenses (unless one pays a large penalty) until the person reaches sixty-five. At that point, one may use the money for any reason with no penalty but must pay normal income taxes on the principal plus earnings unless it is used for allowable medical expenses.

This proposal has obvious advantages. It allows a person to buy much cheaper medical insurance with high deductibles. If one does get sick, the MSA covers the deductibles. If one does not, one has money left over—a great deal after twenty or forty years if one is lucky enough to stay unusually healthy. MSAs offer more freedom to individuals and encourage people not to use medical help unless they really need it.

What is wrong with this plan? A lot. First, it would siphon off younger, healthier people and leave a disproportionately larger number of sick and older people with conventional insurance. Insurance plans work by spreading the risk. In any year, most of us stay healthy and need far less for medical bills than our insurance premiums pay. The difference between the premiums healthy people pay and the bills they have covers the unfortunate people who do have high bills. If you remove many of the people with few bills, the remaining people will cost insurance companies a great deal more per person. Since insurance companies are not charities, they will simply hike the insurance premiums. In fact, careful studies have suggested that conventional insurance would more than double in price if MSAs became widespread. The American Academy of Actuaries predicts that a disproportionate number of people left in conventional insurance would be older employees and pregnant women.[32] MSAs, therefore, would benefit the young and healthy and hurt the old and sick. That is hardly following the biblical call for a special concern for the poor and weak.

Furthermore, depending on how the law is written, MSAs could be a huge tax shelter for the rich. Republican proposals in 1998 (e.g., Senate Bill 2330) would have allowed anyone at any income level to open an MSA—and deposit from $3,375 to $4,500 per family per year. Rich people with good health insurance would never need to spend much or any of this on medical expenses. The result? It would be a tax-free way to invest $4,500 per year. Not until persons began to withdraw the money at age sixty-five would they pay a cent on the principal or earnings. We could, of course, write the law for MSAs in the same way we did for Individual Retirement Accounts—i.e., high-income tax payers cannot use them. But that is not the way the Republicans wrote the proposed bills in 1998.

On balance, MSAs are probably a great idea for the rich but not for the majority—and certainly not for the poor who could not afford to set aside money in the first place.

The Role of Civil Society

Private institutions, especially churches and church-related nonprofit organizations, have long played a crucial role in providing health care for the poor. Such agencies can find and serve persons who slip through the cracks, are neglected by official structures, or who need personal attention to take advantage of available services. Christians today should expand their direct health care services to the poor even as they strengthen their prophetic call for major structural reform.

The story of Jake shows how Christians can make a difference. Jake was battered so severely at age five that he lay comatose in the hospital for two months. Permanent brain damage meant Jake was destined for a troubled life. Thanks to good foster parents, he managed to finish high school and hold down a job as a kitchen aide for about ten years. After that, however, his multiple problems prevented him from finding stable work. Following several unsuccessful attempts at job retraining, it became clear that Jake's disability would make it impossible for him ever to support himself again. Fortunately, Jake had worked long enough to qualify for Social Security Disability Insurance (SSDI). Jake would probably have eked out a modest living on SSDI for the rest of his life if President Reagan had not cut 500,000 people from the rolls in the early 1980s. Jake found himself hungry and homeless, sleeping in storage rooms and doorways. One night he walked four miles in subzero temperature through three feet of snow.

Mercifully, a church group came to Jake's aid. They offered food and temporary lodging. More important, they found a lawyer, a psychiatrist, and a social worker who fought to have Jake's SSDI benefits restored. It took two years, but eventually the courts not only reinstated the benefits Jake had earned but awarded him $8,000 in back payments. Today Jake lives independently and comfortably with the help of a Christian friend whom the court appointed as his fiduciary guardian.[33]

Illegal immigrants have especially difficult problems and need the help of civil society. It may be legitimate for nations to provide services to citizens that they withhold from strangers, but the biblical concern for the alien and stranger compels Christians and Jews to offer health care to the millions of illegal immigrants.

Millions of poor children and adults do not take advantage of health care for which they are eligible. Some of those people are in our churches or live just around the corner. Inner-city congregations and suburban partners can develop programs to inform, enroll, and translate for them. Congregation-based health care ministries targeted toward the poor in both inner cities and rural areas play a crucial role.

In his moving book, *Not All of Us Are Saints,* David Hilfiker, a Christian doctor in inner-city Washington, describes two wonderful ministries, both founded by Washington's Church of the Savior. Christ House is a medical recovery shelter for homeless, addicted men. Columbia Road Health Services serves thousands of Hispanic refugees, many of whom are ineligible for government-funded programs.[34] The national Christian Community Health Fellowship's annual conference and newsletter provide excellent ways to learn more about the thousands of Christians involved in Christian medical care for the very poor.[35]

Christian congregations and nonprofit organizations—indeed, the whole range of institutions in civil society—must play an expanded role if all the poor are to have adequate health care. Even so, the role of government is still crucial. Medicaid alone in 1997 cost $172.5 billion.[36] If the 325,000 religious congregations in the United States tried to shoulder that load, each local congregation would have to raise an extra $529,000 per year.

Conclusion

One of the central public policy questions for U.S. citizens today is whether the richest nation on earth will continue to allow millions of poor people to exist without health insurance. To do so violates biblical justice.

How can pro-family Christian political voices not demand health insurance for poor families? How can pro-life Christian political coalitions not insist on decent health care for poor babies after they are born? How can any Christian read what the Bible says about the poor and what Jesus says about the sick without hearing a divine call to demand that every person in this nation, starting with the poor, have access to health insurance?

7

Quality Education for Everyone

> One child is programmed for Yale, one programmed for jail.
>
> Rev. Jesse Jackson[1]

Raymond Abbott is a high school dropout from Camden, which is just across the Delaware River from Philadelphia.[2] Camden is one of the poorest cities in America with over 60 percent of its residents on welfare. The schools Raymond attended—indeed, virtually all the schools in Camden—were and are a disaster.

During Raymond's academic years, Camden's schools spent about one-half as much per student as did Princeton schools. According to *The Philadelphia Inquirer,* Camden schools could not afford science, art, music, or physical education teachers, or staff to detect learning disabilities. As a result, Raymond's learning disabilities went undiagnosed, and the system promoted him year by year even though he was learning very little. When he dropped out of high school, he could read only at the seventh-grade level.

Raymond Abbott's name appeared as lead plaintiff in a court case brought by Camden and several other poor school districts against the State of New Jersey, demanding that the state provide equal funding for all schools. Seven years later, the judge agreed with the poor districts, but it was too late for Raymond. By then he was a cocaine addict living in the Camden County Jail. His mother sadly reported that she seldom heard from Raymond, except for "an occasional letter written in a childish scrawl."[3]

"It took a judge seven years and 607 pages," *The Philadelphia Inquirer* reported, "to explain why children in New Jersey's poor cities deserve the same basic education as kids in the state's affluent suburbs." The judicial decision would have meant more to Raymond, the paper lamented, "if it had come . . . when there was still a chance to teach him something."[4]

Two years after that legal decision, Jonathan Kozol visited the Camden schools while writing *Savage Inequalities,* his powerful book on education. At Pyne Point Junior High—98 percent black and Latino—the typing teacher complained that she had only Olympia typewriters, the same ones used by the present students' parents when they were in school a generation earlier. Every office today where these students will look for work uses computers, but the school had no money for computers.[5]

At Woodrow Wilson High, the chemistry lab had no lab equipment. Woodrow Wilson had computers at one time, but the heating system had malfunctioned, destroying most of them. Three hundred fifty ninth graders could read only at the sixth-grade level. Fifty-eight percent of all Woodrow Wilson's students drop out before they graduate. "We spend about $4,000 yearly on each student," the principal noted, "but Princeton is past $8,000 now."[6] Far more students from Camden high schools go to jail than to Yale—or Princeton or any other good four-year college.

The court asked some pointed questions when it ruled in favor of the poor school districts. "Why should urban districts not have microscopes?" Why are classes "larger in urban elementary schools than in suburban schools?"[7] What would be the impact, the court asked the superintendent of affluent South Brunswick, if his schools had no more money than low-income Trenton? His answer: An "absolute disaster." Class size would increase 17 percent, the purchase of computers would stop, Latin and German would disappear. "Our kids," he noted, would "get shortchanged, as these kids in these cities are getting shortchanged."[8]

Some people argued that lack of money is not the problem in places like Camden, but the judge was not convinced. He cited the written explanation given by a wealthy district for its request to back out of a cross-busing plan with a poor district: The wealthy district did not want to integrate with the poor district because of the latter's "old and dilapidated buildings, lack of adequate equipment and materials, [and] lack of science programs."[9]

A black principal from Camden High is more blunt. When she is invited to speak at places like Princeton and people try to argue that it makes little difference that Camden spends $4,000 and Princeton $8,000 per student, she retorts, "'If you don't believe that money makes a difference, let your children go to school in Camden. *Trade* with our children.' When I say this, people will not meet my eyes. They stare down at the floor."[10]

The schools serving our poorest children, especially poor black and Latino children in our big cities, are simply not working.[11] Only 46 percent of urban students can read at what specialists define as a "basic level," and in urban *high poverty* areas, the number is 23 percent. On the other hand, 63 percent of all nonurban students can read at the basic level.

Half of all African American public school students (but only 20 percent of whites) attend urban schools.[12] In Chicago, Detroit, Houston, Los Angeles, and Washington, D.C., minorities make up 88 percent or more of all public school students. In Philadelphia, New York, Cleveland, and Boston the figure is 75 percent.[13]

Dropout rates in urban schools vary dramatically, but in the poorest neighborhoods, the rates are astronomical. Of the children who start at Chicago's Andersen Elementary School, 76 percent drop out before they finish high school. At McKinley School, it is 81 percent, and at Woodson Elementary, 86 percent.[14] That kind of dropout rate wastes an immeasurable amount of God-given potential. It is also costly. New York City's Department of Corrections has reported that 90 percent of all male inmates in city prisons are high school dropouts. The department added that it costs society $60,000 a year to keep them in prison.[15] Nationally, dropout rates for blacks and Latinos are substantially lower. A significant number of African Americans go to much better schools in the suburbs where one-third of all African Americans now live. But the rates are still unacceptable. Almost twice as many blacks and over four times as many Latinos as whites drop out of school before completing high school.[16]

Nationally, seventeen-year-old black and Latino students read at the same level as thirteen-year-old whites.[17] Not surprisingly, less than one-half as many blacks (13.6 percent) and Hispanics (13.3 percent) as whites (29.7 percent) complete four years of college.[18]

One especially tragic measure of the failure of U.S. schools is that the initial gap between beginning students from advantaged and disadvantaged homes widens steadily as they continue through school.[19] Fortunately, the French system demonstrates that this outcome is not inevitable. In France, the gap between advantaged French children and disadvantaged North African immigrants who receive two years of French preschool *decreases* with each school grade.[20]

We live in an information society. Knowledge is the most important capital today. Increasingly, low-skill, poorly educated persons earn less and less in comparison with well-trained persons. They also have much more trouble finding jobs. The unemployment rate for high school dropouts is 20 percent. Even for high school graduates, it is 11 percent. For college grads, on the other hand, it is a tiny 2 percent.[21] "Inferior education is today the primary cause of social and economic injustice."[22] Fortunately, studies have demonstrated two relevant findings. While poor schools have a greater *negative* impact on disadvantaged kids than other children, good schools have a stronger *positive* impact on disadvantaged kids.[23] Quality education is the best way to empower the poorest, most disadvantaged children. Educational opportunity is the new civil rights struggle.

A recent study of the difference in wages between blacks and whites underlines the importance of genuine educational opportunity. When both black and white men have the same years of schooling, whites still earn about 16 percent more. But when one takes into account the fact that African Americans often attend inferior schools and, therefore, have poorer skills in spite of equal years in school, most (all but 4.8 percent) of the wage differential disappears.[24] Equally good schools for minorities are essential to correct this injustice.

Reasons behind Inferior Education

Before we can correct the injustice of inferior schools, however, we must answer the following question: Why do poor and minority children receive an inferior education?

Many factors are important when attempting to answer this question. It is not only—or even primarily—a matter of unequal funding, although that is one problem. Lingering racism, unsafe drug-infested neighborhoods, dysfunctional families, malnutrition, oversized administrative bureaucracies, unresponsive teachers' unions, and peer pressure that mocks academic success all play a role.

First, we must be honest about the way a long history of white racism has produced inferior schools for African American children. "Separate but equal" schools were unequal. In northern cities, white families fled schools and neighborhoods when blacks moved in. Often, white politicians and school boards allocated more resources to white schools. Racism is one major culprit.

Children from unsafe neighborhoods and dysfunctional homes are often more difficult to teach. The police allow drug sales and prostitution in poor, minority communities. Children in these neighborhoods regularly watch drug dealers make sales not only to the many neighborhood addicts but also to white people who drive in from the suburbs. The drug wars, easy availability of guns (with the National Rifle Association fighting every proposed restriction), and robberies by desperate drug addicts produce a climate of violence that spills over into the schools. The U.S. Department of

Education reports that Hispanic seniors are more likely than white students to say they feel unsafe at school and report disruptions that interfered with their education. Hispanic seniors report gangs in their schools almost three times as often as whites.[25] Black students are twice as likely as whites to feel unsafe in their schools.[26]

Study after study demonstrates that on average children in single-parent families do more poorly in school than children from intact two-parent families. Children of never-married mothers are 75 percent more likely to fail a grade in school and more than twice as likely to be expelled or suspended from school than children living with both biological parents. Children living with single divorced moms are 40 percent more likely to fail a grade and 70 percent more likely to be expelled or suspended.[27] Over two-thirds of all African American children today are born to unmarried mothers. For Latinos, the figure is 43 percent.[28] In the poorest black and Latino neighborhoods, the figures are even higher. Many single moms work incredibly hard and do a wonderful job as parents, but overall, the statistics are painfully clear. Single parenthood hurts kids in lots of ways, including their prospects for a successful education. Long term, the schools cannot succeed unless the family is renewed.

For at least some poor children, malnutrition hinders learning. In 1998, the Tufts University School of Nutrition Science and Policy summarized findings on the link between malnutrition and children's ability to learn. "We have now learned that even moderate under-nutrition, the type seen most frequently in the U.S., can have lasting effects on the cognitive development of children . . . and their later productivity as adults." Anemia (a common form of malnutrition) affects "nearly one quarter of all low-income children in the United States."[29] Fortunately, the same report indicates that programs such as WIC, school breakfasts, and food stamps successfully reduce malnutrition among poor Americans.

Large, centralized bureaucracies, often with vastly more administrators than more successful private schools, are also part of the problem. Many analysts have pointed out that one reason for less success in urban schools is "the larger size and often burdensome centralized bureaucracy of urban schools."[30] In an influential book published by the Brookings Institution, John Chubb and Terry Moe argued that "the freer schools are from external control—the more autonomous, the less subject to bureaucratic constraint—the more likely they are to have effective organizations." Chubb and Moe estimate that high school students in effectively organized schools acquire an extra year's worth of learning![31] Decentralized, nonbureaucratic organization is precisely what urban schools serving disadvantaged students are least likely to experience.

One of the most striking examples of successful decentralization comes from one of the poorest sections of New York City. In 1973, district 4 (14,000 students in K–9) in East Harlem had the poorest math and reading scores in the city. Almost all students came from poor, minority families, and more than half lived with single moms. In 1974, the district launched a radical experiment. Teachers, parents, and principals received sweeping freedom to form all kinds of new schools, and restrictive rules from collective bargaining and centralized bureaucracies were waived or ignored. A wide variety of new schools sprouted and flourished, and parents could choose which school their children would attend.

The result? Stunning success. Teachers loved their new freedom to be creative, and students learned. In 1973, only 15.6 percent of the district's students read at or above their grade level. By 1987, 62.6 percent did so. Whereas formerly the district's students seldom were admitted to the city's most selective high schools, now their acceptance at such schools is well above the city-wide average.[32] A careful evaluation released in 1998 demonstrated that the district's math scores were still above those in the rest of the city with similar concentrations of poor students. The researchers also discovered that the competition from the more than twenty new schools created in the district also prompted the existing schools to improve. The most important factor, they reported, was the number of new schools— for every new school, test scores rose 1.5 percentage points.[33]

A loss of high expectations for students and a hesitation to measure success with standardized tests is especially harmful to poor and minority children. Due to what one author calls a "poisonous brew of humanitarianism and condescension,"[34] many educators have low academic expectations for minority and poor children. Too often programs focused on relevance and self-esteem replace rigorous academic demands. "Zero failure" so nobody feels unhappy has often been the pattern. "Happy but dumb" is hardly what the poor need.

Standardized tests are one of the best means for determining whether schools are succeeding. In the past, standardized tests probably did include white, middle-class bias, but extensive efforts over the past twenty-five years have largely eliminated those items. Standardized tests do "discriminate" between those who do and those who do not know how to read and calculate well, but if our schools fail to teach poor and minority children what middle-class kids have learned with the result that poor, minority children do poorly on standardized tests, we should blame the schools, not the tests. Standardized tests simply offer an objective measure of how badly we are failing to provide educational opportunity to the disadvantaged.[35]

Finally, there are striking instances of gross inequality of educational spending in rich and poor districts. Funding also differs substantially from state to state. Central to the problem, of course, is that the majority of funds for elementary and secondary public schools come from local property taxes.

In 1968, citizens in the Edgewater District of San Antonio, Texas, filed a class action suit in the name of Demetrio Rodriguez. Edgewater was 96 percent nonwhite and poor. Even with one of the highest property tax rates in the area, it spent less than one-half as much per pupil on education as rich, predominantly white Alamo Heights. Alamo Heights lay within San Antonio, but this white enclave had its own school district and a lower tax rate than Edgewater.[36]

Rodriguez and the citizens of Edgewater won the early court battles, but the U.S. Supreme Court eventually ruled against them, so little changed. Then in 1989 a similar legal case argued in Texas's state courts was successful. In a 9-0 decision, the Texas Supreme Court denounced "glaring disparities" between rich and poor public school districts in the state. The justices cited differences that ranged from $2,112 to $19,333 per student. The richest one hundred districts, the judges observed, had a property tax rate 50 percent less than the one hundred poorest districts. At the same time, the one hundred richest districts spent over $7,000 per student; the one hundred poorest, less than $3,000.[37] According to the 1997 *Report on the Condition of Education* by the U.S. Department of Education, the nation's richest school districts spend 36 percent more per pupil than the poorest.[38]

When one focuses on national averages instead of the extremes, the overall picture is less unequal. The U.S. Department of Education's July 1998 report, *Inequalities in Public School District Revenues,* compares spending in different school districts in terms of percent of children in poverty, percent of minority students, and so on. On average, across the nation, schools with less than 8 percent of their students below the poverty line spend $5,080 per student; those with the most poor students (25 percent or more) spend $4,554. That means $526 less per pupil in poor schools.[39]

When the variable is median household income, the difference is greater. Schools with the most students from households with the lowest income spend $4,677 per student; those with the highest income spend $5,321. That means the well-off have an extra $644 per student.[40]

Interestingly, the differentials between high and low minority and urban, suburban, and rural schools are not as great. Schools with less than 5 percent minorities spend $4,739 per student; those with over 50 percent spend $4,574. That is a difference of $165. Urban schools spend $4593; suburban schools, $4,730; and rural schools, $4,597.[41]

Overall, the funding inequities are not huge, but they are not irrelevant. $664 extra per student in a school with five hundred students from low-income households would mean an extra $332,000 per year. That much money could pay for five or six more teachers and thirty-two more computers every year. Schools with many poor and minority students have fewer supplies, more run-down buildings, and less-qualified teachers. Part of the explanation is surely less funds.

Studies demonstrate that schools in wealthy neighborhoods get better qualified teachers. The National Commission on Teaching and America's Future found that new teachers without proper certification "are usually assigned to teach the most disadvantaged students in low-income and high-minority schools." Four times as many new teachers without a license in their main teaching field begin in schools in which more than 50 percent of the students are from low-income families than in high-income schools. Schools with the most minority students have less than a 50 percent chance of having math or science teachers with a license and degree in their field.[42]

The 1997 *Report on the Condition of Education* by the U.S. Department of Education shows that in schools with a high concentration of low-income students, more than 70 percent of teachers lacked necessary class materials. Only 53 percent of these schools had Internet access; 88 percent of affluent schools did.[43]

In a moment, we shall see that careful studies demonstrate that lack of funds is not the primary problem with our inner-city schools, but it rings a bit hollow when the wealthy tell the poor not to worry about less money for their schools. If, as *The Wall Street Journal* frequently argues, more money does not produce better education and higher expenditures have diminishing returns, then why not cut back state funds to the richest suburban districts by $1000 per pupil and use that money to renovate dilapidated school buildings, purchase state-of-the-art technology, and hire more teachers for inner-city schools?

If we want to overcome the obvious disadvantages that kids from poor, single-parent homes bring to school, then we ought to spend more on them, not less. At the very least, justice demands spending as much per pupil on poor minority children as on suburban students. We could abandon the local property tax as the primary source of public educational funds, or states could provide more funds to poor districts. Experts can determine the best mechanism. Biblical people, however, should demand that school budgets demonstrate that we value poor black children as much as white suburban children.

By itself, though, no change in funding, however sweeping or good, will correct the disaster of inner-city schools. In 1993, Washington, D.C., spent an above-average amount ($9,300) per pupil and had the nation's lowest pupil/teacher ratio, but still ranked forty-ninth in SAT scores.[44] Studies show that social class and family background are far better predictors of student achievement than the money spent on their education.[45] A distinguished panel of scholars recently conducted an important study on funding of elementary and secondary schools for the National Research Council. They discovered "no reason to believe that increases in spending would on average be any more effective than past spending, particularly when they rely on the same people operating with the same basic incentives."[46]

Every poor inner-city child is made in God's image. Every high school dropout is immeasurably precious to the Creator. The God of the poor who longs for every person to acquire the resources to be a self-sufficient, dignified member of society weeps over the colossal waste and devastation in inner-city schools.

The abysmal failure of the schools serving America's poorest students is morally intolerable, but it can be corrected.

Goals and Direction for Fundamental Education Reform

In order to correct the problems in our nation's educational system, we need to experiment with fundamental reform. We must begin by answering the questions, What should be the basic goals for such reform, and What basic direction should that reform take?

Goals

1. *Demand equity.* Every child, regardless of his or her family's race, religion, or income, should have full access to quality education so that he or she has the opportunity to realize God-given abilities. At the very least, therefore, schools for poor and minority children should have as much funding per student, as many qualified teachers, and as good physical facilities as other schools.

2. *Allow families to choose.* Since primary authority and responsibility for nurturing children rests with the family, parents should be able to choose the kind of school they want for their children. Biblical principles require what the United Nations' Universal Declaration of Human Rights (1948) stipulates: "Parents have a prior right to choose the kind of education that shall be given to their children" (Art. 26, 3).

3. *Respect freedom and pluralism.* The educational system should be organized in a way that offers genuine freedom and treats every religious tradition fairly, neither discriminating against nor benefiting any unequally. The amazing diversity of moral, religious, and philosophical perspectives in contemporary society makes impossible any effort to teach only one perspective—whether secularism or historic Christianity—in all schools.

4. *Promote the common good.* To promote the common good, society must use government's powers of taxation to ensure that every child has access to the necessary funds for a quality education. Since equal access to quality education for all is both morally right and also in the long-term interest of everyone, we dare not privatize the funding of education as some conservative Christians (e.g., the publisher of *World* magazine) propose.[47]

Making each child's access to quality education dependent on his or her family's economic status condemns the poor to inferior education in blatant defiance of biblical norms.

Direction of Change

The following changes would move us in the right direction to meet the goals just outlined.

1. Decentralized governance and administration. To a much greater extent than at present, the governance and administration of our schools should reduce bureaucracy and administrative overhead and promote innovation, flexibility, and competition among schools.

2. Smaller schools. Smaller schools have proven to be more effective than larger schools, especially with poor children (e.g., district 4 in East Harlem).

3. Competition. Schools will improve if the system allows competition and closes schools that parents do not choose.

4. Common curriculum in the basics. It is especially important for poor and minority students that all schools effectively teach the basics in reading, math, English (oral and written), and science that are essential to succeed in society.

5. Diversity of schools. We need more experimentation with a wide range of teaching methods, patterns of governance, and underlying philosophical and religious foundations while still maintaining an overall framework in which all schools teach the basics.

6. High expectations. Teachers should place high demands on every student, and administrators should demand excellent teaching from every teacher.

7. Standardized tests. Parents, students, and society should require objective measures of academic success to make informed decisions.

8. Broad social, economic, and racial mix. One of the best established facts of educational research is that the educational background and aspirations of fellow students significantly determine what a student will achieve. This is especially important for low-income students who learn more in schools with relatively few rather than a majority of low-income students.[48]

9. More parental control. If parents have more power in shaping where and what their children study, they will be more involved in the educational progress.

10. More teacher incentives. We need more incentives for well-qualified teachers to make a long-term commitment to teach disadvantaged children.

11. Adequate funding. Every state should determine how much quality education costs and guarantee that every school—especially those serving poor and minority children—has at least that much money.

Two Options for Reform

Is there any concrete reform that would substantially move public education in the direction just sketched? Obviously, no one reform by itself is enough. Adequate funding, a common curriculum in the basics, and standardized tests would all help. More and more people today, however, believe that nothing short of sweeping reform that breaks up the monopoly of large, centralized, bureaucratic school systems will work. There is also a growing demand for educational vouchers.

Vouchers—sometimes called public scholarships—would offer parents an "educational check" that could be cashed at any eligible school, whether public or private. Twenty years ago only a conservative minority endorsed vouchers. Today a majority does.

Why the change? Partly the abysmal failure of inner-city public schools. Partly the fact that private Catholic schools do better with disadvantaged children at much less cost. Partly because limited tests of parental choice offer promising preliminary results. Partly because this one reform would dramatically implement many of the desired changes outlined above: more and smaller schools, less bureaucracy and administrative overhead, more competition, more parental control, more diversity of schools, and maybe even more racial integration.

Should we switch to a voucher system for American elementary and secondary education? No. We do not know enough to undertake such a sweeping change. Should we test the use of vouchers? Yes. Such a proposal, of course, is enormously controversial. People of goodwill argue both sides. Many think that the best thing to do is simply invest more resources in a cluster of interrelated changes within the present system. Others are convinced the problems are too deeply entrenched for that to work.

I believe the best way for us to proceed is to invest several billion dollars in a massive five-year test of both proposals.[49] Since the most severe problems are in inner-city schools, we should focus our efforts at reform there. Why not spend equal money on two parallel tests: (1) a test of vouchers in a dozen places; and (2) a test of the best "reform the public schools" proposals in a dozen other places. Careful research can then tell us which approach is more successful, and especially which approach is better for poor and minority children. Let's begin by examining the two reform options.

Reform the Public Schools

No widely endorsed package of comprehensive reforms exists. As John Mitchell of the American Federation of Teachers told me, every local situation is different, and therefore, no one reform package applies everywhere.[50]

Widely affirmed proposals include the restructure of low-performing schools, more emphasis on the basics, safer classrooms, more rigorous graduation standards, periodic measurement of progress through some kind of standardized tests, longer days and year-round schooling, decentralization into smaller learning communities and greater freedom for those smaller units, smaller classes, better qualified teachers and improved salaries, more parental input, and more equitable funding.

If a dozen different public school systems were to embark on a five-year experiment as part of a larger nationwide experiment encouraged by federal dollars, local teams of educators, parents, and community leaders would need to devise appropriate local models. They would also need to report to state and federal educational officials so that the methods and results of the different local public school reforms could be compared to each other and to voucher experiments.

Educational Vouchers

Educational vouchers are still relatively new to many Americans. Therefore, before I outline a concrete proposal, it is essential to spend more time carefully examining the pros and cons of vouchers.[51]

Pros

1. Black parents want vouchers. Recent polls consistently show that African Americans, especially poorer, inner-city people and those with school-age children, favor vouchers more than middle-class whites. In a recent nationwide survey, Professor Terry Moe found that 79 percent of inner-city poor people favored vouchers and 59 percent of whites in more advantaged communities endorsed vouchers. A vast majority of both inner-city poor and advantaged whites agreed that school choice would be "especially helpful to low-income kids, because their public schools tend to have the most problems."[52] Another poll in 1997 found that 72 percent of blacks and 48 percent of the general population favored vouchers.[53] Still a third national survey (1997) discovered not only that a strong majority of African Americans (57 percent) and Hispanics (65 percent) favored vouchers, but also that it was precisely the black age group most likely to have children in the public schools (those twenty-six to thirty-five) who supported vouchers most strongly (86.5 percent!).[54] We ought to listen carefully to those whose children suffer in the worst schools.

2. Vouchers would give the poor what everybody else already has. Most Americans now have school choice—it is called enough money to buy a private education or a house in a suburb with a good educational system. We all know that middle-class parents with young children leave the city to seek better schools. Seventy-two percent of all families with incomes over $50,000 have their children in private schools, public schools they specifically chose (e.g., magnet schools), or schools selected through a conscious choice about where to live.[55] The poor are simply requesting the parental choice that middle-class Americans already enjoy.

3. *Private schools are more successful—especially with disadvantaged children.* One study concluded: "The achievement growth rates of Catholic school attendance are especially strong for students who are in one way or another disadvantaged: lower socio-economic status, black, or Hispanic." The dropout rates are strikingly lower in Catholic schools than public schools, even in the case of those at special risk of dropping out.[56] And the reason does not seem to be different policies on admission or expulsion but the different atmosphere of Catholic schools.[57] A more recent study is even more striking: "The achievement of students in Catholic high schools was less dependent on family background and personal circumstances than was true in the public schools." In fact, "Catholic high schools seem to correct the tragedy where minority students fall further and further behind white students the longer they stay in school. This study found that "the achievement advantage of white over minority students . . . increases in public schools during the last two years of schooling, whereas the minority gap actually decreases in Catholic schools."[58]

Equally striking is the evidence surrounding college enrollment. Students from every racial group are more likely to attend college if they go to a Catholic school, but the positive impact is greatest for urban minorities. If an urban minority student goes to a Catholic high school, the probability of graduating from college jumps from 11 percent to 27 percent.[59]

Recent analysis of the widely followed voucher experiment in Milwaukee shows that low-income minority students who attended private schools scored substantially better in reading and math after four years than those who remained in public schools. And it cost less! In fact, the researchers report that "if similar success could be achieved for all minority students nationwide, it could close the gap between white and minority test scores by at least a third, possibly by more than half."[60]

4. *Everyone—teachers, parents, students—is more satisfied with private schools.* That is the clear finding of a recent report by the U.S. Department of Education's National Center for Education Statistics. In spite of much lower salaries ($12,000–$20,000 less per year!), teachers in private schools were more than three times as likely as public school teachers to say they are "highly satisfied" with their jobs.[61] Less than half (48.7 percent) of parents whose children were assigned to a public school were satisfied, but 82.5 percent of parents who chose a private school were.[62] "In their answers to

almost all questions, parents are more enthusiastic about choice schools, usually by large margins."[63] And the private school students feel more safe, are only a quarter as likely to be apathetic, and one-sixth as likely to treat their teachers with disrespect.[64]

5. *Private schools do more with less.* In 1993–94, the average tuition in Catholic schools was $1,600 at the elementary level and $3,600 for high school. Average public school expenditures per pupil for the same years were $5,900.[65]

New York's John Cardinal O'Connor has repeatedly volunteered to accept the lowest five percent of the city's public school students at Catholic schools—at about *one-third the cost.*[66]

6. *Public school teachers prefer private schools for their own children.* Public school teachers in central cities are far more likely than the average central city resident to send their own children to private schools.[67] In fact, when pushed to estimate the percentage of urban-area school teachers with school-age children in private schools, Keith Geiger, the president of the National Education Association, replied: "It's about 40 percent."[68] Why should we force poor parents to send their children to public schools that the teachers themselves do not trust with their own children?

7. *Competition forces change.* Many recent analysts argue that lack of competition is a central reason for the failure of inner-city schools.[69] Vouchers would enable a wide range of nongovernment schools to compete with the current government-operated educational monopoly. In a competitive market, you either satisfy customers or close.

8. *Pluralism and morals.* Moral foundations are essential for good education. In an increasingly pluralistic society, however, it becomes harder and harder to define a common morality that all can accept. It is not fair, for example, to compel a child being raised by a gay couple to attend a school in which the teachers say homosexual practice is sin. Nor is it fair to compel a child from a home that embraces historic Christian sexual norms to attend a school in which the teachers portray homosexual practice or open marriage as just one of many equally acceptable lifestyle options. With a voucher system, every group has full freedom to sponsor a school grounded in its own moral and religious beliefs. Such a system respects society's pluralism in a way that allows vigorous moral teaching in the schools.

An educational experience grounded in historic Judeo-Christian morality is even more important at a time when a weakened family structure increasingly fails more children. A large majority of inner-city children live in single-parent homes. Small, faith-based schools with religiously motivated teachers are more likely to offer the special attention, loving intimacy, and moral standards that an increasing number of dysfunctional homes cannot provide.[70]

9. Vouchers strengthen the family. By returning effective control of education to the family, vouchers would enormously strengthen this crucial institution in society. Parents rather than the state would again control one of
the most significant influences shaping their children. As a result, parents
would be able to pass on their moral commitments through schools of their
choice.

10. Most democracies permit parental choice. In all of the countries of the
European Union (except Greece and Italy) and in Australia, New Zealand,
Scandinavia, and Japan, parents can choose to send their children to nongovernment schools (usually including religious schools) and receive government tax dollars to pay for tuition. In most cases, tax revenues pay the
costs at private schools up to the expenditures per pupil in government-
operated schools.[71]

The Universal Declaration of Human Rights (1948) states that "parents
have a prior right to choose the kind of education that shall be given to
their children" (Art. 26, 3). Unlike the United States, most democracies
think this means that tax dollars should accompany every student whether
he or she attends government-operated or privately operated schools.

With such strong supportive arguments, why do many people still oppose
a major test of vouchers?

Cons

There are six important criticisms: balkanization, segregation, creaming,
ignorant parents, fanatics, and the Constitution.

1. Vouchers will undermine democratic society. Some argue that a democracy
needs public schools that all students attend so all learn shared values and
discover how to work together across class and racial lines. Those who hold
this view believe that if people from different religious groups attend separate schools, our society may fly apart as has that of the Balkans, where
Catholic Croatians, Orthodox Serbs, and Bosnian Muslims slaughter each
other.

There are two problems with this argument. First, this vision of common schools that all class and racial groups attend is a myth. Today, the
rich attend private schools and elite public schools in wealthy suburbs.
Efforts at effective desegregation of largely minority inner-city schools and
largely white suburban schools have failed. If the unity of society requires
that children from all different backgrounds go to school together, then we
must outlaw private schools and compel suburban children to go to the
same schools inner-city children attend. No major anti-voucher voice promotes that politically impossible suggestion.

Second, the data we have does not suggest more intolerance on the part
of private school students. Rather, evidence suggests that students in pri-

vate schools are at least as tolerant as those in public schools. A 1992 survey by the U.S. Department of Education discovered that private school students had more community spirit and were more likely to value helping others and to volunteer in community causes.[72] A very recent study discovered that families with children in private schools are also significantly more involved in the common civic life of the community (voting, visiting the local public library, volunteering).[73] In one study of a fundamentalist Protestant academy (Bethany Bible Academy), a Jewish intellectual found the Bethany students more tolerant on issues of race, religion, and freedom of speech and less concerned with making a lot of money than their public school peers.[74] Widespread attendance at religious schools in a number of Western democracies, including Britain, Australia, France, Germany, the Netherlands, and Canada, has not resulted in more religious intolerance.[75]

2. Vouchers will increase racial segregation. It is true that private academies for white students sprang up in the South after the historic Supreme Court decision *Brown vs. Board of Education* in 1954. Won't vouchers simply help whites flee to segregated schools?

In reality, as a recent article in the prestigious *Brookings Review* points out, private schools today are more integrated than the public schools! The U.S. Department of Education reports that in 1992, 37 percent of private school students but only 18 percent of public school students attended schools in which the number of minority students was close to the national average. Fifty-five percent of public school students are in schools in which over 90 percent of all students are white or minority. Only 41 percent of private school students attend such overwhelmingly segregated schools.[76]

The same study also found that in private schools students are more likely to form cross-racial friendships. Private school students, teachers, and administrators all report fewer racial problems than in public schools.

Nationally, in 1990–91, Catholic schools were 25.2 percent minority, and conservative Protestant schools were 18 percent minority.[77] While court-mandated school integration has largely failed, integration in private schools that parents freely choose surpasses public schools. It may be that parental choice via vouchers—especially if the voucher mechanism favors integration—offers the best hope today for increasing integration in our schools. As Harvard professor Paul E. Peterson notes, one "attraction of inner-city school choice is the possibility that a choice-based system could reduce the racial isolation within the central city."[78]

3. Choice programs cream off the best students, leaving the poor and marginalized behind. Sandra Feldman, the president of the American Federation of Teachers, complains that vouchers take "money away from inner-city schools so a few selected children can get vouchers to attend private schools, while the majority of equally deserving kids, who remain in the public schools, are ignored."[79]

"Creaming" already happens. Well-to-do children go to private schools or elite suburban public schools. In most big cities, magnet schools, gifted classes, and honors tracks siphon off the most gifted. The only question is whether we will grant the poor and disadvantaged the choice that the majority already enjoy.

How we structure a voucher plan is, of course, crucial. First of all, it should cover at least all students with family incomes below 150 to 200 percent of the poverty level. Voucher programs that affect only a fraction of students do leave others behind, but that is not an argument against vouchers; it is an argument in favor of a voucher plan that is comprehensive.

Weighted vouchers so that children with special needs receive extra funds are also essential. I would also favor adding 15 percent to the vouchers of students from families with incomes below the poverty level. Done right, a voucher model could correct some of the unfairness that present creaming produces.

4. Some parents will use their vouchers unwisely. Some dysfunctional parents will not even care enough to choose a school. Other poorly educated parents, lacking the time and knowledge to shop and compare, will choose badly.

Again, this is a valid concern. There will be a small percent of highly dysfunctional parents who will not take responsibility for selecting a school. This is a complicated, delicate issue, but some careful provision for others to select a school for these children will be necessary.

In a voucher plan, state educational authorities will define minimum requirements for schools eligible to receive vouchers. Competition will force the poorest schools to improve or close. Even if a parent chooses the poorest voucher school, it will very likely be better than today's worst inner-city schools. At the same time, it will be necessary for educational authorities to operate an excellent informational program to tell all parents about their options.

Much of the discussion about bad choices by poor, uneducated parents is simply elitist paternalism. The overwhelming majority of poor, struggling, inner-city parents—including single moms—that I have been privileged to know care deeply about their children. I trust them to make decisions for their children that are at least as good as those being made today by huge administrative bureaucracies and teachers' unions in our inner-city school systems.

5. Vouchers will allow fanatics to operate schools. Won't the Ku Klux Klan start running schools?

Eligibility standards for all schools can exclude schools that teach racism and hatred without preventing wide methodological and religious diversity. Only schools accepting anyone regardless of race or religion should be eligible for vouchers. Again, the wide experience of voucher-type arrangements in many other democracies offers no reason to fear that fanatics will be able to operate schools at taxpayers' expense.

6. *It is not constitutional.* Vouchers will mean that tax dollars finance sectarian religious beliefs in violation of the First Amendment. For decades, the Supreme Court has rejected government funding for religious elementary and secondary schools on the ground that "no tax in any amount, large or small, can be levied to support any religious activities or institutions" (Everson, 1947).

Certainly tax dollars dare not fund narrowly religious activities such as worship and evangelism. But the First Amendment does not, I believe, preclude government funds going to faith-based programs that offer public goods (e.g., health care, job training, or education) that the society wants the government to fund. In America today, there is a vast range of religious, secular, and government organizations providing a wide variety of social services. If government funds only secular agencies, it promotes a secular faith.[80]

The fairest solution is for government to fund all successful providers of desired public goods such as education and health care whether or not a particular provider is religious or not. In fact, we already do that in a number of areas—Pell grants for poor college students, child care vouchers, Section 8 housing. An educational voucher goes to the parent, not a religious institution, and the parent freely chooses a school that is secular, Buddhist, Baptist, and so on. Government is fair if it offers equal benefits to those of every and no religious belief.

There is strong reason to believe that the Supreme Court will in fact approve a wisely devised voucher plan that includes but in no way favors religious schools.[81]

The arguments favoring a test of educational vouchers far outweigh the criticisms. Present evidence suggests that a voucher plan would probably be better for poor and minority children, increase integration, strengthen the family, better respect societal pluralism, renew moral values, and cost less! That is why a number of prominent progressive church leaders recently signed "A Progressive Call for Public Scholarships." Signers include the heads of several denominations, including the Progressive National Baptist Convention, the Disciples of Christ, and the Reformed Church in America.[82]

"Devastating problems demand daring experiments," the declaration insisted. "Inner-city public schools are a disaster." Together these leaders—long identified with the struggle for racial and economic justice—demand a test of vouchers with one basic criterion in mind: "Do public scholarships help or hurt our poorest children and the children of ethnic minorities? If significant new tests demonstrate this approach harms these children, we will lead the battle against educational vouchers. But if the tests do indicate that such scholarships help, no ideological straitjacket will prevent us from demanding their widespread adoption."

It is tragic that teachers' unions fight every and all voucher experiments. As Harvard's Paul E. Peterson says, if they are right that vouchers would be harmful, then "a few experiments will put the choice idea firmly to rest."[83] Are they afraid a fair test might prove that vouchers work?

As columnist William Raspberry says, "It's time for some serious experimentation."[84] Alongside the best public school reform proposals outlined above, I think as a nation we should invest equal resources in testing a voucher plan similar to the one outlined below.

A Model Voucher Plan[85]

Two Options

One option would be to offer vouchers in several different localities to a certain percent (no more than 50 percent) of students (randomly selected) who come from families with incomes no more than 150 to 200 percent of the national poverty level. The rest of the students in the district would remain in the existing schools as a control group.

A second option would be to give vouchers to every child (regardless of family income) eligible for K–12 education in several large areas—at least an entire city and possibly a metropolitan area (city and suburbs) or an entire state.

Public Scholarship (Vouchers)

The parent of every child from kindergarten through grade 12 would receive a public scholarship from the Department of Education, and the parent(s) could choose to use that voucher at any accredited school, whether religious or secular, government-run or private.

Every child's voucher should be enough to purchase a quality education. In the case of states that have established a "foundational" amount per student, the voucher should equal that figure. Where this has not been done, it would be sufficient to arrive at the amount of the public scholarship by dividing the current total statewide (or metropolitan-wide) expenditure on K–12 by the total number of students eligible for vouchers (with appropriate adjustments for weighted scholarships and larger scholarships for high school students).

Students from families below the poverty level should receive an additional 15 percent beyond the regular voucher, and this bonus should be progressively phased out so that children from families with incomes above 125 percent of the poverty level receive only the normal voucher. Larger vouchers for children with special educational needs will be set according to careful analysis of the extra cost for their education.

Eligible Schools: Equal Benefits for All

The Department of Education will develop a *minimal* set of criteria for schools eligible to receive students with public scholarships in a way that encourages flexibility, innovation, and full respect for society's diversity. These minimal criteria should include basic safety standards, basic educational standards (e.g., expectations in reading, math, writing, science, American history), participation in standardized tests, and nondiscrimination on the basis of race or religion in the admission of students. The Department of Education, however, dare not discriminate in any way against religious or secular schools. Every school, of whatever religious, ethical, or philosophical perspective, that meets the basic criteria should be accepted as an eligible school.

Diversity of Eligible Schools

Every eligible school is free to integrate its basic values and beliefs into its curricular and extracurricular programs and to hire only teachers, administrators, and staff who share those beliefs. (The Charitable Choice provisions of the 1996 Federal Welfare Act offer a basic framework for implementing this provision.) All students who choose a particular school must participate in all required activities, but no student is required to pray, worship, or believe any theological dogmas. Every group of citizens, no matter what their religious or secular worldview, must be free to develop a school that receives public scholarships as long as they meet the basic criteria for eligible schools.

Admission Process

Each school shall fully disclose to prospective students and their families the school's curriculum, value orientation, and students' scores on standardized tests. Knowing that their child must participate in all required activities, parents must have full knowledge about the school.

No school that receives public scholarships dare admit or reject students on the basis of race, religion, or lack of proficiency in English.

If a school receives more applicants than it can accept, the school has two choices: (1) all students who receive the full public scholarship must be selected on a random basis from the total pool of applicants, or (2) if the school elects to select a portion or all of its voucher students on the basis of some legitimate criteria (e.g., perceived academic ability), then the school will receive only 50 percent of the normal public scholarship for such students, and they may charge parents tuition for such students if their family income is above 150 percent of the poverty level.

Additional Funds for Eligible Schools

Every eligible school must agree to accept the normal public scholarship as full payment for attendance at the school for children from families whose income is no more than 150 percent of the federal poverty level, and they must admit students according to the guidelines discussed in the previous section. A school may choose to charge an additional tuition fee to students from families above 150 percent of the poverty level, but for all students who pay additional fees, the public scholarship will be reduced by 50 percent.

Any school is free to raise funds from private sources as long as gifts from children's parents do not become a requirement.

Any school that receives any income from public scholarships must graduate at least 10 percent of its students from families whose income is below the poverty level and another 10 percent with income below 150 percent of the poverty level.

The Role of Government

The essential role of government is to guarantee equal public benefits to every child in its jurisdiction. Normally, two levels of government would be involved: a state department of education and a local district board of education. The following tasks must be done by one of these two agencies, depending on the particular setting and situation:

State Department of Education
1. Funding every child's public scholarship with tax revenues.
2. Defining basic criteria for eligible schools.
3. Developing, supervising, and widely publicizing the results of standardized tests so that every parent can quickly and easily compare the academic achievement of students in all schools.

District Board of Education

1. Disseminating information widely (through schools; media; religious, ethnic, and community organizations; social service agencies, etc.) to every parent of every eligible child so that all parents have easily accessible, reliable information about how the public scholarships work and the range of school choices available. This process must include information in languages other than English where appropriate.
2. Determining which students have special educational needs.
3. Choosing a school for a child in that very small number of cases in which a child's family simply refuses to do so.
4. Providing free transportation to all eligible schools for all children.
5. Continuing to operate existing district schools as long as parents continue to choose such schools. Obviously, in the first years of such a test, the vast majority of students would be in these existing schools.

Conclusion

Somehow, as quickly as possible, we must discover the most effective ways to end the scandalous failure of our inner-city schools. Public school advocates offer one possible solution; voucher proponents urge another. We simply do not know enough to try only one or the other. We should be open enough to test both. Quality education for our children, especially those with the least opportunity, as the Progressive Call insisted, "is not a Republican or a Democratic issue, not a conservative or liberal cause, not a pro-business or pro-union agenda. It is rather a matter of justice and equal opportunity for our children."

Delay is unacceptable. For millions of poor children, education is a matter of despair or hope. For far too many, it is literally an issue of life or death.

8

Could Welfare Empower the Poor?

> Do not be hard-hearted or tight-fisted toward your needy neighbor.
>
> Deuteronomy 15:7 NRSV

Janice Cardano remembers the shame and destruction of growing up on welfare. At four, she was a happy child living in a seemingly contented middle-class Italian-American family in suburban Long Island. Then her dad deserted the family for another woman. In the next few months, they lost their car, their utilities were cut off, and the bank repossessed the house. Her mom searched desperately for work, but a former homemaker with only a grade 10 education and no job history had little to offer. Part-time work as a maid was all she could find. It was simply not enough for survival. Welfare was the only thing left.

Guilty, disgraced, Janice's mom carried her little daughter on endless ten-hour trips to noisy, smelly welfare offices. Mom's hope died when the welfare people told her she could not go back to school to study nursing—it was not "cost effective." Defrauding the welfare system with on-going, off-the-books work as a maid was the only way she could scrape together enough money to supplement welfare's modest help.

The saddest part of this oft-repeated tragedy is the way the experience destroyed Janice's mother: "Through the years I watched my mother's metamorphosis from a happy, warm, and attractive women to someone who was virtually unrecognizable. Her constant preoccupation with our survival left her aged, exhausted, irritable, and eventually unapproachable. . . . No one escapes unscathed from the shame, guilt and degradation of being poor."[1]

In early 1997, 7.6 million people were on welfare.[2] No two stories are identical, and the causes are always complex. But far too many suffer wrenching, unnecessary tragedy. The Cardano story could have ended far differently if a better welfare system had been in place. This chapter seeks to develop an understanding of what that better system would look like.

What is welfare? Definitions vary. Some people stretch the definition to include all "means-tested" government programs—i.e., all programs that offer government grants and services based on the income of the recipients. But that broad definition includes many programs that include people well above the poverty level as well as those below.

The most useful definition is the one that most people assume when they speak of welfare. They mean the basic grant that used to be called Aid to Families with Dependent Children (AFDC) and is now called Temporary Assistance for Needy Families (TANF), and related benefits available to able-bodied adults (mostly single moms) and their children. TANF recipients also receive food stamps and health coverage via Medicaid and are eligible for various housing subsidies and training programs. Funding comes primarily from federal and state governments, and local social welfare offices administer the programs according to federal, state, and local guidelines. The welfare rolls have dropped dramatically, but over 7 million people are still on welfare.

It is important to realize how relatively modest is the total cost of these programs. On election night in 1994, a poll revealed that a majority of those questioned thought either welfare or foreign aid was the biggest item in the federal budget. Together, they add up to just 3 percent![3] And in 1994, all federal spending on cash AFDC and food stamps amounted to a mere 2.9 percent of the federal budget. Just over half of the food stamps went to AFDC recipients. The federal government spent another 5.6 percent of its budget on Medicaid for the poor, but 72 percent of that went to the disabled and elderly and only 16 percent to welfare (AFDC) families.[4] In 1996, the federal government spent over four times as much on Medicare for *non*poor elderly Americans as it did on AFDC and food stamps, and eight times as much on Social Security.[5] Our welfare programs have problems that demand correction, but it is dishonest to suggest that they are bankrupting the government.

In fact, *corporate* welfare—special government subsidies, tax breaks, etc., to large businesses—drains much more money from the public purse each year than do welfare payments to the poor. In late 1998, *Time* ran a long article reporting that the federal government alone pays out $125 billion in corporate welfare to big corporations every year.[6] That is more money than the federal government spent in 1998 on food stamps, TANF, EITC, and SSI combined![7] State and local governments add billions more in corporate welfare each year. The welfare system—both for individuals and corporations—demands change.

In spite of, and partly because of, radical changes in 1996, the welfare system is still not just or wise. To understand how to change it, we must take a look at how the system developed.[8]

A Brief History of Welfare

The federally funded welfare program began very modestly in 1935. President Franklin Roosevelt was vigorously opposed to cash grants to healthy adults. A cash dole, he argued in his 1935 State of the Union Address, is a "narcotic, a subtle destroyer of the human spirit."[9] Roosevelt's primary response to the depression's widespread unemployment and poverty was to provide jobs—publicly funded jobs under the Works Progress Administration.

Roosevelt did believe, however, that the poor wives of deceased, divorced, and disabled workers should receive assistance so that they and their children could survive. As a result, the government gave small cash grants to families in which the breadwinner was "dead, disabled, or *absent.*"[10] Initially, almost all recipients were widows and their children. At that time, nobody expected mothers with young children to work.

Then two things happened. Congress transferred the program for widows and wives of disabled workers to the more generous old age insurance program (now called Social Security). That left just mothers and children of *absent* fathers—i.e., single-parent families. And their numbers started to grow. By 1960, 64 percent of all the people on welfare (AFDC) fell in the "absent father" category.[11]

The turbulent sixties quickened the pace of change. The War on Poverty extended health care to some poor people. Medicaid (1965) covered welfare recipients. In 1963, 80 percent of all Americans affirmed sexual abstinence until marriage. Just eight years later, only 30 percent opposed premarital sexual activity.[12] Not surprisingly, the number of illegitimate births and single parents increased dramatically.[13]

A new attitude toward welfare also emerged. The Welfare Rights Organization reflected a widespread conviction that welfare was a right, not an embarrassment. Lawyers, social justice advocates, and even welfare department staff urged all eligible people to sign up for welfare. They did. In spite of a good economy, the percentage of eligible families that applied and received welfare jumped from about 33 percent in the early 1960s to over 90 percent by 1971.[14] From 1960 to 1976, the price tag for means-tested benefits for the nonelderly and nondisabled also escalated from a mere one-half of 1 percent ($16 billion) of national income to 1.6 percent ($54 billion).[15]

As the welfare rolls expanded, single parenthood skyrocketed, and the economy slowed down in the seventies, more and more people began to worry about both the cost and possible negative effects of welfare. Retrenchment occurred between 1976 and 1987. Thanks to cutbacks in the early Reagan years and the fact that welfare benefits were not indexed to inflation, the real value of welfare cash benefits (AFDC) dropped by 50 percent from 1970 to 1993. Benefits, of course, vary dramatically from state to state, but in 1970 the median AFDC benefit for a mother with three children was $792 per month; in 1993, only $435.[16] Welfare case workers lost their flexibility, focusing more and more on bureaucratic application of detailed eligibility rules.[17]

By the late 1980s, almost everyone wanted to transform the welfare system. Welfare payments were so low that virtually every welfare mother had to "cheat" and find unreported income simply to survive.[18] That made welfare moms angry. It also contributed to the popular image of "welfare cheats." The Family Support Act of 1988 tried to focus on long-term self-sufficiency as the central goal. Congress designed new incentives, training programs, and work requirements to encourage work. In the short run, however, effective job training programs cost about twice as much as merely writing a welfare check, and Congress declined to provide enough funds. A few of the new programs worked, but many of the training programs failed. Many welfare caseworkers found it difficult to switch from bureaucratically determining eligibility to emphasizing self-sufficiency, and the work requirements for welfare recipients did not work.[19] Meanwhile, the welfare rolls remained stubbornly high—in fact, an all-time high of 14.8 percent of all families with children in 1994.[20] And the divorce rates and out-of-wedlock births remained at devastatingly high levels as well.

For well over a decade now, there has been a scholarly debate over whether welfare benefits for unmarried and divorced mothers has been a significant cause of escalating divorce, illegitimacy, single parenthood, and low work effort by poor single moms. Liberals argue that "virtually every careful social science study . . . has found that the welfare system has had little effect on the structure of families."[21] Conservatives marshal a long list of studies that suggest, to use Robert Rector's heated rhetoric, that "the welfare system has all but destroyed family structure in low-income communities."[22] Whether or not welfare has *caused* a variety of destructive social outcomes, it has—as Senator Daniel Moynihan firmly insists—subsidized them. Moynihan quotes Nicholas Eberstadt to make this point: "AFDC can therefore be accurately described as a policy instrument for financing illegitimacy in the contemporary United States. . . . To observe that such programs underwrite out-of-wedlock or single-parent lifestyles is not to judge whether they create the syndromes they support, but simply to recognize what they do."[23] The fact that about 50 percent of all Americans—and an even larger percent of poor Americans—had come to think that poor women had babies to collect welfare,[24] means that whatever the empirical facts might be, the current welfare system was becoming politically indefensible.

By the early 1990s, almost everybody was fed up with the welfare system. In his first election campaign, future President Bill Clinton promised to "end welfare as we have come to know it."[25] As president, he promised major reform: a two-year time limit on welfare payments and a job (as a last resort, a government-funded job) for those losing welfare benefits. In 1996, the Republican majority in Congress accepted time limits but forgot about the promise of a job. Although many top advisors urged him to veto the bill, President Clinton signed it—and was reelected.

The 1996 welfare legislation, called the Personal Responsibility and Work Opportunity Reconciliation Act, enacted the most sweeping changes in welfare policy in fifty years, at an estimated "savings" of $54.6 billion over six years. The following are the most important changes:[26]

- *End of entitlement.* Although AFDC payments were never a strict entitlement, the general understanding was that they were nonetheless available to all who met the eligibility standards. That promise to the needy ended in 1996. The federal government will spend only $16.4 billion per year through 2001 on block grants to the states, who have no obligation to provide cash benefits (now called TANF) to all who are eligible.
- *Five-year time limit.* Adults (whether one-parent or two-parent) can receive federally funded cash benefits for only five years of their entire adult life, although states *may* exempt up to 20 percent of their welfare recipients from this limit for particularly troubled families.
- *Two-year work requirement.* After two years, welfare recipients must work at least twenty hours a week or lose their federally funded benefits, although states *may* exempt single parents with children under age one for up to twelve months. (Although strict, this requirement

is phased in gradually: 25 percent of all recipients in each state had to be working by 1997; 50 percent by 2002.)

- *Cuts in food stamps.* Tougher eligibility standards reduced the outlay for food stamps by almost $24 billion.[27] Legal immigrants and unemployed adults without children lost their food stamps. The elimination of several inflation adjusters meant a decline in the value of food stamps over time. The program, however, remained as an entitlement so that funds will be increased or decreased according to demand in order to cover every eligible person who applies.

- *Loss of eligibility for legal immigrants.* Most current legal immigrants are no longer eligible for food stamps and SSI until they become citizens. Future legal immigrants will have to wait five years. States may also choose to exclude legal immigrants from cash benefits and Medicaid.

- *Strengthened enforcement of child support policies.* Stricter requirements for establishing paternity and strengthened federal and state programs to locate and enforce child support payments by parents not living with their children should improve the support that children get from absent fathers (and, occasionally, mothers).

- *Programs to reduce out-of-wedlock births.* The law mandated programs to discourage teenage pregnancy and encourage abstinence until marriage. It also required that teen parents receiving cash benefits must live at home or with a responsible adult and go to school.

- *Charitable Choice.* In order to encourage faith-based agencies to become more involved in delivering social services, Section 104 offered important stipulations to protect both the religious identity of faith-based agencies and the religious freedom of participants (see p. 86).

In 1997, President Clinton managed to persuade Congress to spend $13 billion to "correct" what he considered the worst mistakes of the 1996 law. The 1997 changes restored some of the cuts in food stamps and made some legal immigrants eligible again for many of the things they had lost in 1996.[28]

In the broadest terms, the 1996 welfare legislation changed policy in three basic ways. First, it dramatically reduced the role of the federal government and strengthened that of states in shaping welfare policy. We now have fifty different welfare systems supported by a few basic federal guidelines and block grants. Second, the 1996 law switched the focus of welfare programs from providing cash benefits to encouraging personal independence and self-sufficiency. Hence, the new name for the cash benefits: Temporary Assistance for Needy Families (TANF). Third, the bill opened the door to substantially expanded partnerships with a wide range of other organizations in civil society.[29]

Was the 1996 law good or bad? Some of both. Supporters of the legislation like to cite the recent dramatic drop in the welfare rolls as proof that the 1996 reforms were a success. In fact, the welfare rolls dropped a stunning 46 percent from 1994 to early 1999—from 14.2 million to 7.6 million recipients.[30] Since the decline had already started before 1996, the new law is not the only cause.[31] All through these years we have enjoyed a booming economy and very low unemployment, which tend to lower the welfare rolls. And there are disturbing reports that many—if not most—of the people dropped from the rolls have not found long-term jobs and certainly have not escaped poverty.[32] Many church-based social ministries have also reported dramatic increases in requests for emergency food and housing, which, they believe, result from the changes in the welfare legislation.[33]

The 1996 law had a number of clearly good features. Giving states more freedom to experiment, opening the door to new partnerships with faith-based groups via Charitable Choice, encouraging work, forcing absent fathers to support their children, and discouraging illegitimacy are all things to applaud.

Problems continue to exist, however.[34] Most important, perhaps, is the fact that the legislation requires that people work but fails to provide the funds to support that demand. It contains limited funds for education and training so that welfare recipients can acquire the skills needed for a job paying a family income. Strict term limits cut people off welfare without any guarantee that they will be able to find a job at all. (President Clinton tied his time limit on benefits to a guaranteed job.) The law's preference for "work first" over education and training may provide a quick fix that "ends welfare" but dooms people to low-paying jobs that cannot end poverty. Ending the entitlement and giving each state a fixed block grant means that when the next recession hits, states (whose budgets must be balanced) will either have to find more money for welfare at a time when their income is shrinking or simply let needy people go hungry and homeless. While the legislation adds appropriate pressure on absent fathers to support their children, it does almost nothing to encourage and empower them to do so.[35] Welfare recipients who start working may keep their Medicaid health coverage for a year—but only a year.[36] That means, since a high percentage of the jobs they can find do not include health insurance, they and their families will join the other 43.4 million people without health insurance.

We are still far from a just welfare policy. What should be done?

Needed Changes

What should be our goals and how do we achieve them?[37]

Goals

A just welfare policy would have the following six goals:

1. end poverty, not just welfare
2. encourage work, and therefore, allocate overall support for the working poor and welfare recipients in such a way that work always is economically advantageous
3. strengthen stable, two-parent families—and consequently, seek to reduce divorce, single parenthood, and out-of-wedlock births; therefore, seldom if ever should we offer help to single parents that is not also offered to two-parent families
4. recognize each person's God-given dignity, and therefore, maximize growth toward long-term, dignified self-sufficiency and responsibility
5. guarantee a generous sufficiency with dignity for all—especially children—who truly cannot provide for themselves
6. strengthen the institutions in civil society that nurture moral renewal

Groups Needing Help

Unless we understand the different characteristics and situations of people who need assistance, we will never be able to target our aid effectively. There are at least five significantly different groups of poor people:[38]

1. the working poor
2. nonworking healthy[39] adults without children (i.e., not living with children whether or not they are parents)
3. nonworking healthy adults who have children and experience temporary problems
4. nonworking healthy adults who have children and experience complex, long-term problems
5. elderly poor and disabled (physically and mentally) who can never provide fully for themselves without outside support

Each of these groups demands a different response.

Working poor. Thirty-seven percent of all children living in families below the poverty level live with at least one parent who is working full-time. Another 26 percent live with at least one parent who is working part-time.[40] That means almost two-thirds of our children in poverty live with at least one parent who is working.

The working poor do not need—and often do not want—welfare. They want the dignity and justice of a family income for their labor. Tragically, as Harvard professor David Ellwood laments, "Full-time working poor families are actually the poorest of the poor after transfers."[41] That outrage must end. The solution is to make work pay, using the mix of policies outlined in chapter 4. The right combination of a guaranteed job, an expanded EITC and minimum wage, food stamps, a refundable Dependent Care Tax Credit and Child Tax Credit should enable any family with a parent(s) working at least forty hours a week to enjoy the dignity of earning their way out of poverty. They do not need welfare; they need justice.

Nonworking healthy adults without children. We should not offer these people welfare; we should offer them a job. Society has no obligation to provide more than very modest help for those who could work but refuse. As chapter 4 proposes, government should guarantee a job to everyone who cannot find normal employment and thereby encourage personal responsibility.

That is not to say that civil society and perhaps even government should do nothing for that significant number of absent fathers frequently troubled by a wide range of problems. I discuss that below. Such help, however, should start with a double premise: They must work responsibly, and they can count on a job.

Nonworking healthy adults who have children and experience temporary problems. Most welfare funds go to the adults (and children) who fall into this and the following category. Conservative critics of welfare tend to ignore the fact that fully one-half of all women who go on welfare (TANF, formerly AFDC) stay on welfare for no more than two years.[42] Such women need transitional help for a short time so they can make it on their own.

Who are these women? Some are like Janice Cardano's mother who was dumped by her husband and left without support, education, or job experience. Others have chosen to leave a marriage. Many are young unmarried women who have just had a baby out of wedlock. In fact, over 80 percent of all first-time welfare cases are due to single parenthood: 42.1 percent when a wife becomes a single parent (primarily because of divorce or separation); 38.8 percent because an unmarried woman without a child has a baby.[43] Eighty-three percent of all women who go on welfare have a child under age six, and almost two-thirds have one under three.[44]

The fact that most people first go on welfare because they have recently become single parents does not mean we should not help. A woman overwhelmed by abandonment or divorce or a single mom struggling with a very young child usually cannot immediately support herself and her children.

Transitional help for families with children—both two-parent and one-parent families—that empowers them to get back on their feet and care for themselves is money well spent. The fact that fully one-half of all people who ever receive welfare stay on the rolls a total of only two years or less should lead us to reject all sweeping attacks on welfare as a drug that traps all who take it.

Nonworking healthy adults who have children and experience complex, long-term problems. There is another fact about welfare recipients that liberals love to ignore. The lion's share (about two-thirds) of the funds for welfare cash benefits go to long-term welfare recipients.[45] The time limits enacted in 1996 will, of course, change things. But in the past, 81 percent of all women receiving welfare at any one time would eventually receive welfare for five or more years. And over half (56.6 percent) would be on welfare for ten or more years.[46] Only 22 percent of all who ever receive welfare stay on for ten or more years, but because they remain so long, that relatively small group of long-termers consumes well over half of the funds (57 percent).[47]

Who are the long-termers? They are poorly educated, single moms without work experience. A high school dropout is twice as likely to be on welfare for ten years as a high school graduate. One-third of all never-married women who start welfare will be on for ten or more years. On the other hand, only 12.5 percent of divorced women will stay that long. And if a woman in a two-parent family goes on welfare, her chances of staying on for ten years are a mere one-half of 1 percent. The never-married woman is sixty times more likely than the currently married woman to experience welfare for ten or more years.[48]

Within the category of long-termers, there is an important distinction: cyclers go on and off welfare several times; continuous long-term recipients stay on without a break.[49] Cyclers are a sizable group. Studies have shown that within one year after leaving welfare, 45 percent are back on welfare, within two years of leaving, 58 percent return, and within four years, 69 percent are back.[50] Cyclers repeatedly try to replace welfare with work. Unfortunately, a variety of problems—inadequate child care, low wages, a child's illness, personal failure—soon land them back on welfare. We need to focus much more attention on helping cyclers, strengthening their own desire to find work, helping them overcome the problems that hold them back. Since every situation is unique, voluntary agencies not bound by rigid bureaucratic rules will often be more effective, especially if they support the person's moral and spiritual growth as well as help with things such as an apartment, day care, and a job.

Continuous long-term recipients represent the hardest cases. Myriad interrelated difficulties overwhelm them. They have the least education and the least work experience, are the least likely to have ever been married, and are most likely to live in ghetto neighborhoods and struggle with drugs, alcohol, depression, mental illness, low self-esteem, and hopelessness.

Elderly poor and disabled. Some people are too old or too disabled (physically or mentally) to earn an income. We should provide them with a generous sufficiency so they can live dignified lives. The government program for this need is Supplemental Security Income (SSI). If they have little income, elderly people and persons who are medically certified as physically or mentally unable to work are eligible for SSI.[51] Far fewer people receive SSI than TANF, but it costs the federal government more money.[52] Fortunately, most people agree that we should support the old and the disabled if they lack the income to care for themselves. As a consequence, SSI enjoys far more widespread political support and is not widely perceived as part of the awful welfare system that must end. Abuses should be corrected, but SSI is an important, essential program that must be protected from politicians seeking funds for middle-class tax cuts.

A Proposal

Near the end of one of his widely cited books on poverty and welfare, Lawrence Mead says that any convincing new proposal must "rest on an account of poverty psychology" and "a convincing theory of human nature."[53] For too long we have relied too exclusively on economic incentives (or disincentives) and legal penalties to solve the problem of long-term welfare dependency.[54] Of course, those things are important. But if persons are more than rational economic decision makers, economic incentives are not enough. Character formation, spiritual renewal, and caring communities are also essential if the biblical view of human nature is correct. Persons are material/spiritual beings created for community. Both our own and others' immoral personal choices as well as unjust social structures twist our very souls in ways that produce socially destructive behavior that can only be corrected in a lasting way through spiritual renewal.

That is not to suggest for a minute that every welfare recipient is an immoral character responsible for all his or her problems. Many are wonderful people of faith struggling mightily to conquer daunting challenges including unfair economic structures. Many have been sinned against by powerful people who need to repent. If we are honest, however, we will admit that many have made wrong choices and developed bad habits that must be changed if they are to succeed. They need both better welfare policies and inner moral renewal.

A genuine solution to our welfare dilemma can come only from a partnership between private sector institutions, especially faith-based groups, and better public policy. In the short run, many adults will persist in destructive behavior no matter how we modify laws and benefits, unless they experience genuine friendship from another caring neighbor as well as personal spiritual renewal. In the long run, we cannot solve welfare dependency, especially in the areas in which it is most concentrated, unless society nurtures many more people of high moral character and personal responsibility. Government programs and welfare bureaucrats are notoriously unsuccessful at doing those things. On the other hand, faith-based agencies are sometimes dramatically successful at just this point.

That is why the Charitable Choice provisions of the 1996 welfare legislation offer such promise. If there are enough people of faith who truly care about poor welfare moms and their kids, Charitable Choice opens a door for a dramatic new partnership that could minister to the material and spiritual needs of welfare recipients at the same time.

Good Samaritan Ministries (GSM) in Holland, Michigan, offers a striking illustration.[55] In 1996, the State of Michigan's Family Independence Agency (the new name for the Department of Social Services) invited GSM to be a partner in their innovative pilot welfare program called Project Zero. The goal of everyone, including the former caseworkers (now called Family Independence Specialists), was to move every welfare recipient to a job and self-sufficiency. The state believed that Good Samaritan Ministries, which had a long track record of coordinating volunteers from 250 churches to serve the needy in Ottawa County, could provide volunteer church mentors ready to walk with welfare families as they made the complicated transition to work and independence.[56]

Good Samaritan Ministries does not try to be either the government welfare agency or the local church. Rather, it is the bridge between them, along with three other local nonprofit organizations, that provides job training, transportation services, and child care. The county's Family Independence Agency administers the welfare programs (TANF, food stamps, etc.). After interviewing applicants, they refer them to GSM's Relational Ministries. After an interview with one of their professional staff, GSM links the welfare family to a congregation-based Relational Ministry Team (five to seven people), which has been carefully trained by GSM in "transformational relationships," which includes a mixture of love, regular contact and emotional support, prayer, and individualized care that government agencies cannot provide. During training, they warn church volunteers: "You must be ready to change as much as you expect these families to change."[57]

The ministry team establishes a close friendship with the welfare family, providing physical, social, emotional, and spiritual support for up to a year. The team is careful not to make the family dependent on them, but they offer whatever assistance is needed—help in finding an apartment, untangling legal problems, fixing or finding a car, emergency food and clothing, finding a job, improving work skills. Most important, however, they provide friendship. GSM trains one member of each team in financial counseling in order to help each family with budgeting, getting out of debt, and financial planning. The church team is careful not to impose their beliefs, but they pray regularly for their new friends, and after earning the right by gentle caring, they freely share their faith and talk about the way that God can transform a person's values, character, and life.

Government contracts provide about one quarter of GSM's budget; the rest comes from private donations. Bill Raymond, GSM's former executive director, stresses the importance of maintaining their independence as a church-based agency:

> The effectiveness of the church is directly tied to its ability to speak to spiritual realities and the role God plays in an individual's life. . . . If the church is going to have an impact on families, [Christians] need to be allowed to interact with families on the basis of the strength that brought them to the relationship. . . . True change will not occur if all that happens is that the church is co-opted in the service of the state in a short-sighted effort to save a few tax dollars.[58]

It works! Ottawa County became the first county in America to put every able-bodied welfare recipient in a job. Governor John Engler says the church mentors have been a crucial component.[59] Bill Raymond now travels all around the United States advising state and local governments, businesses, churches, and faith-based nonprofit organizations on how to partner together to end welfare through self-sufficiency. Mentoring programs similar to those in GSM are springing up in many places. The story of Michele shows how they work.

Michele was frightened and alone. She was finishing a job training program and hoped to leave welfare soon, but she had just three more weeks before she had to leave the transitional housing program where she and her one-year-old son lived. Fortunately, she discovered Bridge of Hope, a church-based mentoring program for homeless mothers.

A team from Hinkletown Mennonite Church near Lancaster, Pennsylvania, helped her find an apartment, a day care center, and a car. They even took turns driving her to work until Michele was able to renew her expired driver's license. Michele credits her mentoring team for her improved parenting skills and encouraging her dream of owning her own home, which she recently purchased. Most important, though, they led her to personal faith. "My mentors have helped me grow spiritually simply by the way they loved me through Jesus," Michele says. "I have learned to trust in him because he is the only one who truly knows what is best for me. This is the one thing that has helped me succeed." Now Michele says, "I want to teach my son to know Jesus."

She feared she would lose these special friends when the official mentoring relationship ended after fourteen months. To her surprise, they remained close friends and welcomed her into their church.

Michele is just one of seventy-five homeless women that Bridge of Hope has empowered in its first ten years. When they enter the program, a majority of the mothers are not active in the church. Eighty to 85 percent of the mothers complete the program. By the end of the twelve- to fourteen-month mentoring relationship, well over half are committed Christians, actively engaged in the church of their choice. Five years later, that is still true, and they are still also financially independent. Bridge of Hope now has materials available for church groups who want to establish an affiliate Bridge of Hope in their community.[60]

Bridge of Hope and Good Samaritan Ministries are just two of a rapidly growing circle of faith-based ministries helping welfare recipients move to self-sufficiency. Many of them, like GSM, partner with and receive funds from government agencies, thanks in part to the Charitable Choice provisions of the 1996 welfare legislation.[61] Mississippi's Faith and Families, Minnesota's Hope Makers Jobs Partnerships, and Texas's Family Pathfinders have enjoyed widespread attention. This emerging partnership is still in its infancy, but it offers enormous promise. If the faith-based partners are careful not to dilute the forthright spiritual dimension that makes them unique and successful, they will be able to add a crucial dimension to today's agenda of ending welfare.[62] Enough people might be transformed—not just welfare recipients but also middle-class mentors now rapidly discovering what it means to be poor—that we might even end a great deal of poverty. A greatly expanded role for faith-based programs that understand that persons are more than mere material beings must be at the heart of any successful welfare policy.

Caution, however, is needed. Mentoring programs of the sort just described are fairly new and small. They are available today to only a fraction of those persons who could benefit from them. To expand these mentoring programs so that we can offer them to a higher percentage of eligible persons will require massive effort, large numbers of volunteers, and much-increased financial giving by faith communites. Do enough Christians and other people of faith really care?

It is clear that the churches dare not try to replace government.[63] As GSM's Bill Raymond insists, the government must continue to operate a good welfare system precisely as it expands its partnership with faith-based organizations. That means we must return to the question of how to improve current welfare policies. In light of the goals and groups of poor people outlined earlier, what changes would enable the welfare system truly to empower people?

The working poor. We will never make progress unless work pays better than welfare. As a result, the mix of programs outlined in chapter 4 designed to guarantee that any family with a person or persons working a total of at least forty hours will be from 120 percent to 130 percent above the poverty level are absolutely essential to a successful welfare policy. That is not to imply in any way that the working poor who benefit from the EITC and Dependent Care Tax Credit are on welfare. It is essential for their dignity and sense of self-worth that we understand and describe such programs as justice not welfare. But unless such programs are in place to make work more advantageous than welfare, we cannot solve welfare dependence, unless, of course, we simply cut the rolls without offering any real alternative and callously tolerate growing hunger and homelessness in this land of abundance.

Nonworking healthy adults without children. Our basic program for this group should be a guaranteed job (see pp. 109–12) paying 85 to 90 percent of the minimum wage plus the option of purchasing Medicaid-type health insurance for 5 percent of their income (see p. 148).

One large segment of this group, however, merits further attention. As we saw earlier, absent (noncustodial) fathers are a particularly tragic group. They are often poorly educated, never-married young men living unsettled lives, working sporadically, and often struggling with drugs, alcoholism, and crime. Their children receive little money and less quality time and fatherly care. Tough child support policies are necessary, but by themselves they will not solve the problem. To date, neither government nor the church has invested much effort to help absent fathers connect with their children. Studies demonstrate that these children long for fatherly attention and need their financial support.[64]

A few policy changes plus a new effort by faith-based organizations could help significantly. Improving job skills and earnings would make it possible for absent fathers to provide more child support. Changing welfare policy so the mothers could keep more than a tiny fraction of that support would increase a father's incentive to pay.

How can we do that? A guaranteed job is the place to start. Then we could change the rules on EITC and allow fathers not living with their children to receive the EITC up to one-half or two-thirds of the child support they pay. We should end the current rule that welfare mothers' TANF benefits are cut dollar for dollar (beyond the initial $50, which the states *may* choose to pass on) for any child support provided by absent fathers. Fathers would be more likely to send money to their children if their funds actually benefited their children rather than the government. We should adopt a sliding scale that allows a welfare mother to keep a significantly higher percentage of an absent father's support payments.

Government programs and caseworkers, however, cannot provide what many absent fathers most need: emotional support, stronger parent-child relationships, improved parenting skills, a better relationship with their children's mother, ongoing love and encouragement from a caring mentor, and moral and spiritual renewal. These are precisely the things, as we have just seen, that a host of faith-based agencies are now successfully providing to welfare mothers and families. Numerous ministries such as Bridge of Hope and Good Samaritan Ministries could run "becoming better fathers" programs aimed specifically at absent fathers.[65] Using Charitable Choice arrangements, federal and state governments could even encourage such efforts by funding several substantial experiments. Paying more attention to demoralized, absent fathers could be a significant way to strengthen the family and reduce poverty in single-mom families.

Nonworking healthy adults who have children and experience temporary problems. For two-parent families, a temporary problem is typically no job (and no more unemployment insurance) or short-term disability. For a single parent, the problem is most frequently divorce, separation, or a child born out of wedlock, although temporary disability or unemployment are also problems. Whatever help both government and civil society offers must be understood by everyone as transitional assistance designed to help families move quickly to self-sufficiency.

For those who are able to work, the first and most important offer should be a government-funded job, when a regular job cannot be found. At 85 to 90 percent of the minimum wage, such a job plus EITC plus food stamps plus a refundable dependent care and child tax credit will help those able to work get through their temporary problems. Caseworkers should have the power to waive the normal six- to twelve-week waiting period for this type of job.

Many of the people in this category, however—new mothers, disoriented, recently abandoned, or divorced mothers, temporarily disabled persons—cannot work immediately.[66] We need to offer enough cash benefits (TANF), food stamps, and medical insurance (Medicaid), so they and their children can afford adequate food, clothing, health care, and housing. But this aid must have clear time limits and require job training or education for fifteen to twenty hours per week. The regulations should also mandate that soon after welfare payments begin, the caseworker (a Family Independence Specialist is Michigan's marvelous title) and the recipient work out a concrete plan for moving toward financial independence. Improving skills through additional education should be a high priority. The 1996 law wisely demands that in order to receive welfare, teen parents must live with a responsible adult and complete high school. Generous job training, job preparation, and job search services—often delivered by faith-based nonprofit organizations funded via Charitable Choice—should be available.

What should be the time limit for TANF? Everything depends on whether society cares enough about justice to guarantee a job to anyone who needs it. *If* that provision is in place, then I favor time limits at least as strict as the 1996 bill: twenty-four months for any one spell on welfare and four to five years total for life. Much greater emphasis on improving skills and knowledge through job training and education is crucial. Case workers should have the authority to extend the time limits for up to two years for persons working faithfully and successfully to complete an educational program.

Time limits are morally acceptable only if there is a government-guaranteed job available for everyone who needs it. (In the rare cases in which the time limit is used up and a mother refuses a government-funded job, she should lose her own welfare benefits, but her children should receive theirs.) A working mother at a government job will, of course, have to purchase child care.

Other things being equal, I strongly prefer having parents care for their own children rather than sending them to a day care center. But single moms have made choices that inevitably lead to less than ideal consequences. Most mothers with young children today work some and many work full-time. Children of single parents often do better when their mothers have a job than when they are on welfare.[67] A job that includes EITC and a refundable Dependent Care Tax Credit will provide both more income and more dignity than long-term welfare.[68]

Nonworking healthy adults who have children and experience complex, long-term problems. Here the problems are much tougher. Some current long-term welfare recipients could work. But what about alcoholics or drug-addicted parents, or adults with borderline physical or mental disabilities who cannot be medically certified as eligible for SSI? I favor a fairly tough-minded approach that applies basically the same rules to this category as to the previous one. Many people who think they cannot work will discover there are jobs they can do. Those who are truly disabled should receive SSI. Mothers or fathers so addicted to drugs or alcohol that they cannot keep a job are likely unfit to care for their children. However painful at the beginning, adoption or foster care would probably be better for the children in the long run.

That still leaves a small number of people who cannot work or receive SSI. A careful process including strict review procedures should be able to classify a very small number of welfare recipients as eligible beyond the four- to five-year time limit. As Harvard's Mary Jo Bane and David Ellwood insist, however, they should be treated on a case-by-case basis. We certainly should not design the welfare system around their needs.[69]

The most concentrated poverty and the most concentrated long-term welfare caseloads exist in large, urban ghetto neighborhoods. Only 12 percent of the poor live there, but they represent the most daunting challenge.

David Ellwood paints a powerful, painful picture of ghetto poverty.[70] The schools are terrible, crime and drugs are widespread, good jobs have migrated along with the middle class, single parenthood has reached astronomical levels, and hope has fled. Even for poor Latinos and African Americans, only a small percent live in urban ghettos. Only 28 percent of all African Americans and 29 percent of all Hispanics are poor.[71] And only 25 percent of all poor African Americans and 20 percent of all poor Latinos live in urban ghettos.[72] But here is where the agony is most severe and the solutions most difficult.

Only an integrated combination of interventions can offer hope. The police must be as determined to stamp out crime in the ghetto as in the suburbs. The schools must work. Widespread dependence on welfare must end. A job and health insurance must be available to everyone. These and other structural changes are essential. Ellwood, however, is certainly right: "The notion that only jobs and opportunity are the issues rings false."[73] Behavior and values must also change.

Perhaps it is in the urban ghettos that faith-based solutions have the clearest opportunity to demonstrate their potential. Almost every policy expert finally confesses that he or she does not really know how to solve the agony of urban ghettos. If faith-based approaches can succeed in the toughest places, their power will be clear to all.

There is growing evidence of astonishing success. Holistic ministries such as Chicago's Lawndale Community Center and Circle Urban Ministries and their related congregations are transforming one of the city's toughest neighborhoods with their multifaceted programs in health care, housing, tutoring, job training, small-business development, and evangelism. Hundreds and hundreds of lives have been transformed.[74] Both ministries are leaders in the Christian Community Development Association, a national network of over six hundred similar holistic ministries.[75]

In Boston, Rev. Eugene Rivers is demonstrating the power of church-based programs in overcoming gang violence. Stories on Rivers have appeared in many magazines and newspapers.[76] On June 1, 1998, Rev. Rivers made the cover of *Newsweek* with the caption "God vs. Gangs." The story detailed the way Rivers's holistic combination of faith and action seems to be working where everything else had failed.

Policy experts are taking note. The role of faith-based organizations in solving urban problems has become one of the hottest topics at Harvard's Kennedy School of Government. Dr. John J. DiIulio Jr., formerly professor of politics and public affairs at Princeton University and now Fox Leadership Professor of Politics, Religion and Civil Society at the University of Pennsylvania, is arguing in lectures everywhere from elite policy think tanks such as the Brookings Institution to gatherings of academic policy specialists at Ivy League universities to Congress that faith-based programs are a key to renewing our inner cities. DiIulio believes that overlooking and failing to support the "outreach efforts of black churches and other inner-city faith communities is the single biggest mistake that can be made by anyone who cares about the future of the truly disadvantaged . . . who call the inner cities home."[77]

Nora had been on welfare for twelve years.[78] She and her two children somehow managed to exist in a small, dark, dank basement apartment. There was no light at the end of the tunnel.

Then she met Mary Nelson and her colleagues at Bethel New Life, a faith-based community development corporation on Chicago's west side. She joined Bethel's new program that trained welfare mothers to run day care centers in their own homes for neighborhood children. She was one of twenty-six welfare moms who not only finished the training but also received new or rehabbed houses. Locations for the houses were chosen so that every mother in the community would have a day care center within walking distance, and each prospective owner had to invest hours of sweat equity in their new houses. Empty garbage-strewn lots became places of ownership and pride. Each welfare-mom-turned-businesswoman cares for four to six children a day in her home and earns $17,000 to $24,000 a year. Bethel New Life continues to provide support for bulk purchasing, ongoing training, and advice on insurance and licensing.

Chicago's mayor was there the day Nora and her children celebrated their move into their new home and the opening of her child care business. Nora's son took the mayor by the hand and proudly showed him his very own bedroom. School teachers soon began to comment on the change they noticed in Nora's children.

Moving from welfare to work was not easy for Nora. She made it only because peers and Bethel staff offered a lot of encouragement and prayers. At the dedication, reporters asked about Nora's journey. "A miracle has been wrought in my life," she replied. "I've always wanted to work, but I didn't have child care or transportation, and I didn't feel good about myself." Nora's faith in God gave her hope even in the most depressing times and strengthened her in her struggle for a new life.

After ten years, twenty-four of the original twenty-six day care homes are still in business. That is a 92 percent success rate! In 1998, Bethel New Life received a large, multiyear contract from the U.S. Department of Labor to train forty additional welfare mothers a year to start and operate similar small child care businesses.

This program of helping welfare moms start day care businesses is only a small part of Bethel New Life's $10-million-a-year holistic ministry. Programs in employment, housing, job creation, supportive care for the elderly, community organizing, and policy advocacy are all part of the agenda. In the last ten years, Bethel New Life has helped place over five thousand people in jobs and created one thousand new jobs in the community.

At the heart of everything is Bethel Lutheran Church, Mary's home congregation, situated in the heart of the community. The church anchors the community center's integration of faith, prayer vigils to stop gang wars, and celebrative worship that offers hope and power to carry on even during the toughest times. At the center of everything is Mary, who over twenty tough, exhilarating years has paid the price (including the trauma of being raped) to help create a powerful sign of hope in one of Chicago's toughest ghetto neighborhoods.

Yet, Mary knows the church cannot do it alone. That is why she is active in local, state, and national public policy organizations. But she also knows that even the best policies will fail unless discouraged, broken people like Nora discover not only economic opportunity but also inner spiritual renewal. That combination could reduce welfare dependency and provide hope for our most broken ghettos.

Conclusion

The present welfare system is simply not adequate. This society can do better. Ending welfare is not our goal. Justice calls us to seek to end poverty. To do that, we must offer a generous sufficiency of assistance to those temporarily unable to work in a way that strengthens the family, nurtures responsibility, develops skills, and encourages additional education. Important parts of this task can be done only by new partnerships between governments and voluntary (especially faith-based) organizations. At the same time, governments must not only fund and operate wise welfare programs. Equally important, they must place the temporary help of welfare assistance in a larger framework in which everyone enjoys health insurance and everyone able and willing to work responsibly can earn a living wage.

9

Other Important Issues Affecting the Poor

> Make them strong again . . . that they may live beside you.
>
> Leviticus 25:35–36[1]

In this book, I have tried to develop a holistic approach to overcoming poverty in this country. That means, since everything is interrelated, that I should deal with everything! Unfortunately, that is impossible.

The best alternative is to explore very briefly in this next to last chapter a few of the most important issues that I have not discussed in previous chapters. Safe streets are a desperate need for the poor. Whatever we decide in the next few years about tax policy and Social Security will profoundly affect the people with the least power to shape the debates and the results. Even a question we seldom discuss—Is our system of metropolitan governance fair?—has major implications for the least powerful. Finally, what would happen if churches devoted major attention to organizing poor communities so that the powerless became strong?[2]

Thorough treatment of these complex issues is impossible in a brief chapter. Instead, I hope to sketch the central issues, underline relevant biblical norms, offer a few basic suggestions, and point you to sources for additional information.

Safe Neighborhoods

Safe streets should not be a luxury reserved for the middle class and rich. Poorer citizens also have a right to safe neighborhoods where their children and elderly can walk without fear and danger.

That is not true today. Violent crimes such as murder, rape, robbery, aggravated assault, and weapons offenses have long been concentrated in low-income neighborhoods in big cities. The police simply do not provide equal protection in all neighborhoods. Even more unfortunate, many African Americans have reason to fear the police as well as criminals. Also true and tragic is the fact that young males of color represent a disproportionately high number of the victims and perpetrators of crime. Black males between the ages of fourteen and twenty-four make up 1 percent of the population, but they make up 17 percent of the homicide victims and 30 percent of the offenders.[3] It is hardly surprising that urban people feel more threatened by crime than suburban and rural people and that urban African Americans feel more threatened than everyone else.[4]

There is a growing number of young teenage criminals whom former Princeton professor John J. DiIulio Jr. calls "superpredators." They are callous, almost totally without moral values, and ready to kill on an impulse. At best, they have lived for a time with one parent. They have suffered from poor schools, high-crime neighborhoods, a delinquent peer group, broken families, lack of adult love and discipline, and often physical and sexual abuse. Many careful studies have demonstrated that these situations are leading contributors to juvenile crime and delinquency.[5] The adults in the lives of "superpredators" have given neglect and abuse rather than love and discipline.

When he was just nine years old, Willie Bosket, who had been sexually abused by his grandfather, landed in the state reformatory. Willie's mom seldom visited, and he had never met his dad, who had been beaten by his own father and had also gone to the state reformatory at age nine. When Willie stole, assaulted people, and even choked a nurse at the reformatory, admiring peers praised him: "Man, you real bad." By the time he was fifteen, Willie frequently shot and robbed New York subway passengers. He killed two men in cold blood. By 1988, when he tried to murder a prison guard, Willie had committed two thousand crimes, including two hundred armed robberies, twenty-five stabbings, two murders, and many "for-fun-and-profit" shootings.[6]

Only a small fraction of youth in poor inner-city neighborhoods are like Willie Bosket, but their numbers are growing, and they are responsible for a large portion of the crime and fear in those neighborhoods.

What can be done? In order to protect all of us, especially poor inner-city residents, the police and courts need to be fair but tough with the Willie Boskets. Equally important, we need desperately to intervene in effective holistic ways that can prevent the next generation of Willie Boskets from repeating his tragic story.

The following changes are especially crucial.[7]

- redouble efforts to eliminate racial prejudice in all (especially urban) police departments
- humanely imprison properly convicted violent and chronic offenders, but work toward zero prison growth
- oppose all plans to imprison juvenile offenders in adult prisons
- strengthen community policing against open-air drug markets
- tighten gun control laws to reduce the number of guns available to criminals
- reduce dramatically the number of alcohol outlets in poor urban neighborhoods
- greatly increase the availability of effective community and prison-based treatment programs for substance abuse by juvenile and adult offenders
- invest far more time (mentors) and money on the hundreds of thousands of low-income children who have one or both parents in prison
- expand literacy programs for prisoners and ex-prisoners (about 70 percent are not fully literate)
- strengthen church-anchored and other neighborhood patrol and town-watch efforts
- invest more in inner-city youth and community anti-violence outreach ministries
- increase the summer and full-time job opportunities for inner-city youth
- replicate widely the police-probation-clergy-corporate partnership that has helped to reduce citywide homicide rates in Boston to levels not seen since the 1950s

Boston's TenPoint Coalition started when a local gang chased a boy into a church during a funeral, beating and stabbing him in front of the shocked mourners. Three local ministers—Rev. Eugene Rivers, Rev. Jeffrey Brown, and Dr. Ray Hammond—decided to walk the streets, get to know gang members, and cooperate closely with the juvenile justice system. The Boston police commissioner was glad to cooperate because he had come to realize that "we couldn't simply arrest our way out of the escalating bloodshed."[8]

The "TenPoint Plan" developed by these ministers includes "Adopt-a-Gang" programs to organize and evangelize gangs and commission inner-city "missionaries" to do one-on-one evangelism with the toughest young drug traffickers and gang members. They walk the streets at night, develop education and economic development programs, and work in close cooperation with grateful police officers, probation officers, judges, and school principals.[9] The police trust the ministers so much that they often drop kids off at their churches instead of locking them up. For one long twenty-nine-month stretch, there was not a single gun-related youth homicide in Boston.

The vision and strategy is spreading rapidly. Police commissioners, district attorneys, judges, and local clergy from Philadelphia and other cities have traveled to Boston to talk with their counterparts there and have returned enthusiastic about the possibility of adopting Boston's success in their own city. Dr. Dean Trulear, vice president of Public/Private Ventures in Philadelphia, heads up the national effort called the National Faith-Based Demonstration Project. They are already working at thirteen sites in ten cities.[10] One can only hope that this model of ministers walking the streets, partnering with the police and courts, and combining spiritual transformation, jobs, and education will succeed everywhere in reducing inner-city youth violence and the tragic destruction of thousands of young black men.

The focus in this section on dramatically reducing crime in inner-city neighborhoods does not mean that middle-class people have no responsibilities. Providing the mentors (and funds) to walk with all the at-risk inner-city youth will require vastly more volunteers—both black and white—living in the suburbs. Key policy changes (including tighter gun control laws and jobs for inner-city youth) can happen only if suburban and rural citizens demand that their politicians support the necessary legislation. Finally, the millions of suburbanites investing in private security systems and moving to gated communities in distant suburbs must ask themselves a tough question: Is the existence of two different communities that experience radically different levels of safety compatible with either a democratic society or biblical justice?

Taxes

Nobody likes to pay taxes (I am reminded of this fact as I start to write this section the very same week I must work on my federal taxes for this year!). Not only are taxes disliked, tax law and theory are enormously complex. Here in this short summary chapter, I will mention only a few central things that people who care about the poor should remember as they fill out their tax forms and lobby their politicians.

The most basic point is that paying taxes is one important way we love our neighbors and promote the common good. If government has some responsibility to care for the poorest, if we want government to guarantee a living wage to all who work responsibly and ensure that even the poorest enjoy health insurance, then we have to pay taxes. If, as the Bible tells us, poverty is a family tragedy because one brother or sister is allowing another brother or sister to suffer unnecessarily, then paying taxes for wise, effective programs to empower the poor represents family cooperation and caring.

Second, people in the United States pay *low* taxes in comparison with virtually all industrialized nations. All tax revenues represent 48 percent of Gross Domestic Product (GDP) in France, 44 percent in Germany, 36 percent in England, and 56 percent in Sweden. In the United States, taxes are only 32 percent of GDP.[11] In comparison with most other wealthy nations, we could easily afford a few more taxes to fund good programs for the poor.

Third, federal taxes for the average family are less in 1999 than at any time since 1977. A Congressional Budget Office study indicates that a median income family—a family right in the middle of the income distribution—will pay 18.9 percent of its income in federal taxes in 1999. In 1977, the figure was 19.5 percent.[12]

Fourth, not all tax proposals are created equal—i.e., not equally just. In early 1999, for example, the majority leadership in Congress proposed a 10 percent across-the-board income tax-rate cut. If passed, that proposal would have reduced federal revenues by $1 trillion over ten years and made it more difficult to make the kind of changes recommended in chapter 4. At first glance, a 10 percent cut for everybody may sound fair. But who would have benefited?[13] Sixty percent of all taxpayers (everybody making less than $38,000 a year) would have received an average annual tax cut of $99. Each taxpayer in the richest 10 percent would have enjoyed an average tax cut of $4,000 a year. And for the very rich (the top 1 percent), the tax cut would have been a whopping $21,000 annually!

In recent years, prominent people have offered dramatic proposals for sweeping changes in present tax law. People concerned about justice need to study these proposals carefully with a special eye on their impact on our poorer neighbors. Briefly, let's compare three of the most prominent proposals to reform the present federal income tax system. (Remember: The present income tax is "progressive"—i.e., the rate of the tax increases as income goes up so that lower-income people who owe taxes pay at a 15 percent rate whereas wealthier people pay at 28 percent, then 31 percent, then 36 percent, and finally 39.6 percent.)

The Value-Added Tax (VAT) would replace personal and corporate income taxes with a tax on the value added at each stage of production.[14] (For example, when a carpenter buys lumber for $100 and builds a cabinet that he sells for $300, he has added a value of $200.)

The Armey-Shelby Flat Tax would replace the present system with a flat tax on persons' wages and pension income and on businesses' value added.

Economist Joseph Pechman proposed modifying the current federal income tax with more generous family and child exemptions and an expanded EITC in order to reduce the tax burden on low-income families (Pechman Plan). He also eliminated some deductions to broaden the tax base and substituted a simpler two-bracket rate structure of 15 and 30 percent. Others have proposed cutting corporate tax breaks ("corporate welfare") by $50 to $100 billion.

How do these different tax proposals affect the poorer members of society? The VAT and most flat tax proposals are less progressive than the present system or Pechman's proposal. That means—as the careful comparison of a Brookings Institution study summarized in table 4 shows—that with the VAT or flat tax, poorer people would pay more and the rich would pay less. The top line, for example, shows that people close to the bottom (fifth to tenth percentile) pay just 2.7 percent presently but would pay 6.8 percent of their income with a VAT. In fact, the flat tax almost doubles and the VAT almost triples the taxes of the poorest but lowers the taxes of the richest by many tens of thousands of dollars.

Table 4

Different Tax Systems

(average taxes in dollars and average effective rates)

Family Income in Percentiles	Current Law	Flat Tax	VAT	Pechman Plan
5–10	$175 (2.7%)	$318 (4.9%)	$448 (6.8%)	$171 (2.6%)
10–20	$627 (6.1%)	$872 (8.5%)	$1,300 (12.7%)	$517 (5.1%)
30–40	$3,159 (14.8%)	$3,633 (17%)	$4,644 (21.7%)	$2,716 (12.7%)
50–60	$7,145 (20.5%)	$7,204 (20.7%)	$8,709 (25%)	$6,214 (17.9%)
70–80	$13,284 (24.4%)	$13,718 (25.2%)	$14,733 (27%)	$12,956 (23.8%)
90–95	$26,714 (29%)	$27,531 (29.8%)	$25,951 (28.1%)	$29,099 (31.5%)
99–100 (the richest 1%)	$223,953 (41.6%)	$186,045 (34.5%)	$141,535 (26.3%)	$219,109 (40.7%)

Source: Henry J. Aaron and William G. Gale, eds., *Economic Effects of Fundamental Tax Reforms* (Washington, D.C.: Brookings Institution, 1996), summarized in John E. Anderson, "Taxation and Economic Justice," in *Toward a Just and Caring Society: Christian Responses to Poverty in America*, ed. David P. Gushee (Grand Rapids: Baker, 1999).

The simplicity of the flat tax is not nearly as important as many claim. Under the present system, the majority of taxpayers do not itemize deductions and consequently use the short form (1040EZ). Nor is it complicated for those whose income falls into more than one tax bracket because the tax tables are very simple to use.

I do not mean to deny the possibility that there might be a version of the flat tax that merits careful consideration. The conservative Family Research Council's *Family Policy* magazine (November–December 1998) attempts to spell out "a flat tax that's good for families, not just for business." This issue of *Family Policy* criticizes the fact that "every Republican tax proposal presented since 1995 will cause the broad middle class to pay significantly *higher* federal taxes"; laments the fact that the federal tax burden on business income has *dropped* from 30 percent to 14 percent over the last several decades; and proposes scrapping many of the write-offs and credits ("corporate welfare") that businesses now enjoy. This issue of *Family Policy* certainly points to the intriguing possibility that pro-family conservatives may be open to coalitions with others to design and implement a tax code that is both more pro-family and more pro-poor. That would certainly mean making the Dependent Care Tax Credit and the Child Tax Credit *refundable* (see pp. 107–9) so poor families can benefit. It would also mean substantially expanding either the Child Tax Credit or the deduction for dependent children.

Justice calls us to keep the tax system progressive. That means rejecting any VAT, flat tax, or sales tax that does just the opposite. It is right for those who are wealthy to contribute to their neighbors via the tax code by paying not just a larger amount but at a higher rate.

As the debate about alternative tax proposals grows more intense in the coming years, biblical people must be a strong voice for the poor. That will mean applying a few basic principles of justice to the detailed proposals. For solid data and responsible analysis, one of the widely respected places to go is the Center on Budget and Policy Priorities.[15]

Who Needs Social Security?

Reforming Social Security is one of the hottest topics on the political agenda. The system has problems serious enough that some people want radical change. Others insist that reasonable corrections can fix a basically good system. The issues are far too complex for me to try to offer a comprehensive overview, much less a thorough solution, in this short section. But we must examine Social Security briefly, because it is important to the poor. Without Social Security and a few other federal programs, fully 50 percent of elderly people in this rich country would have been poor in 1996. Largely because of Social Security, less than 10 percent of our elderly neighbors were poor.[16] Social Security alone lifted 16 million people out of poverty in 1996.[17] Therefore, we must understand the basic problems, grasp the relevant principles of justice, and be aware of how to protect the interests of the least advantaged.

What exactly is the payroll tax for? (The payroll tax is 15.3 percent of salary with employees and employers each paying half.) A small part (2.9 percent of salary) pays some of the costs of Medicare for the elderly (see p. 144). Most of it (12.4 percent of salary) pays for what we popularly call Social Security. The proper name, however, is "Old-Age, Survivors, and Disability Insurance" (OASDI). That full name is important because Social Security is far more than a pension fund for the retired.[18]

Social Security is not an individual retirement investment program in which workers invest money in their personal pension funds and then receive whatever their personal investments have earned over the years as a retirement pension. Rather, Social Security is a social insurance program designed to guarantee at least a modest income for all former workers (and their spouses) throughout their retirement. In addition, Social Security is a kind of life insurance because it provides benefits to spouses and children of workers who die young. Further, Social Security is also a disability insurance for workers, providing an ongoing income for workers who have been disabled. At the end of 1997, in addition to the 31.9 million retired people receiving Social Security, there were 6.2 million receiving Social Security payments because they were disabled workers and another 5.9 million receiving Social Security payments as dependents (e.g., widows and their children). The importance of the disability and survivors benefits in Social Security becomes especially clear when one remembers that three out of every ten people age twenty today will become disabled, and one in six will die before retirement.[19]

One other crucial fact about Social Security is essential. It is largely a pay-as-you-go system. Your payroll taxes are not invested somewhere earning interest so that the money is there to pay you a Social Security pension when you retire. Your and my payroll taxes paid this year go largely to fund current payments to today's Social Security recipients.[20]

That is why there is a problem. Today, there are 3.4 workers paying payroll taxes for every one Social Security recipient. But when the baby boom generation retires, the proportion of workers to retirees will decline quickly. By the year 2030, there will be just two workers paying into the system for every one recipient earning benefits. That means that by about 2032, the system will be broke—unable to pay all Social Security obligations—unless we make some changes.[21]

Before summarizing the most important issues to watch in evaluating reform proposals, I want to underline three key biblical principles that will help us evaluate suggested changes: Social Security is one of the important ways this society acts out our commitment to the dignity of every person, the common good, and a special concern for the poor.

By guaranteeing at least a modestly adequate level of income to all workers, even in sickness, disability, or old age, we live out the biblical truth that "the elderly and the disabled do not forfeit their claim to basic human rights because they are old or disabled."[22]

Second, because we are social beings, we become the persons and experience the dignity the Creator intended only as we care for each other and thereby promote the common good across generations and economic classes. The fact that we need each other to be truly human is particularly clear to me right now as my eighty-six-year-old father nears death. Dad and Mom cared for this helpless baby boy, slowly nurturing me into adulthood. Now Dad is almost totally dependent on his children, a government pension, and the loving caregivers in a wonderful Mennonite retirement home. Created for mutual interdependence, we cannot be what we were designed to be unless we care for each other and thus promote the common good. Social Security is one of the ways that we care for our neighbors across generational and economic lines.

Third, biblical people have a special concern for the poor. It is important to realize the ways that the Social Security system—precisely because it is a social insurance program not a retirement investment program—works to the advantage of the poorer members of society. While it is true that the amount of retired persons' Social Security pensions varies somewhat depending on their previous salary (and therefore the payroll taxes they paid), the benefit formula is progressive. That means that low-wage workers receive higher benefits in proportion to their former salaries and payroll taxes than do formerly higher paid workers. (For a minimum-wage retiree, Social Security benefits are 71 percent of the person's final year's earnings; for a maximum wage earner, benefits are just 25 percent.[23])

Since women on average have lower taxable earnings, women also benefit from this feature of Social Security. Women pay only 38 percent of Social Security payroll taxes, but they receive 53 percent of all Social Security retirement and survivor benefits. A far higher percentage of elderly women than elderly men are poor, but Social Security cuts this poverty gap almost in half. Sixty percent of all elderly people lifted out of poverty by Social Security are women.[24]

Minorities also probably benefit more, on average, than do whites.[25] That is true in part because a substantially higher percent of African Americans than whites receive disability and survivor benefits.[26]

In addition, the present system, regardless of payroll taxes paid by the worker, provides more benefits to larger families and pays extra benefits to a retired couple in which one spouse (usually the wife) had low or no earnings. A purely personal retirement investment system could not respond to special needs in these ways.

Social Security is especially important for the poor. Social Security payments make up fully two-thirds of the total income of all elderly poor. In fact, for 66 percent of all retired people who receive Social Security, it is the major source of their income.[27]

How do these three principles—the dignity of every person, the common good, and the poor—help us evaluate current proposals to reform Social Security? Probably the proposal that demands the most careful evaluation—and the one that would involve the greatest change—is the call to privatize all or part of Social Security. All privatization proposals assume that somehow we would keep our promises made to people who have been paying Social Security taxes. But privatization plans propose that some or all of the payroll taxes that future workers would otherwise pay would go instead into personal retirement accounts that each person would manage. Some privatization plans suggest diverting only 1 or 2 percent of the current payroll tax of 12.4 percent. Others propose diverting much more. That would mean, of course, that the guaranteed benefits under Social Security would have to be cut more or less in proportion to the amount diverted to personal investment accounts.

Would privatization be good or bad for the poor?[28] They offer at least one possible advantage. Each person would have a greater sense of wealth and stake in society as they invest their pension money in stocks and bonds and watch their personal fund grow.[29] It might also encourage greater savings at a time when the overall savings rate in the United States is very low. Most tempting, of course, is the high investment returns of stocks—if they keep performing indefinitely the way they have in the 1990s!

At the same time, privatization brings not only large transition costs but also significant risks. There would no longer be a guaranteed amount that a retired worker could count on. Everything would depend on how wisely each person invested his or her funds and how well the economy and stock market were doing at the moment of retirement. Poorer workers would lack both the knowledge about and the money to buy the best market investment information. Furthermore, it is astonishingly optimistic to suppose the U.S. stock market will keep growing indefinitely at the dizzying pace of the 1990s. If the stock market drops 60 percent (as Japan's did from 1990 to 1995) just before one retires, then one simply has that much less for the golden years. Furthermore, it costs a lot more to administer 150 million individual investment accounts, and there is also a major fee charged for converting accumulated savings into a monthly annuity payment. Careful estimates suggest these two factors alone could reduce the value of personal retirement accounts by 30 to 50 percent.[30]

According to most privatization proposals, a portion of the present payroll tax would continue to fund some ongoing Social Security benefits. Those benefits would include reduced payments for retired workers and also present disability and survivor benefits. But that would produce a big problem. The disability and survivor payments would become a much larger percentage of the Social Security system. Since the funds diverted to personal retirement accounts would not bear any of this burden, they would pay much higher returns than Social Security. Over time, the political support for Social Security would likely disappear among the middle class, and it would be much harder to maintain decent benefits for low-income retirees, low-earning spouses, widows, the disabled, and the children of disabled and deceased workers.

Furthermore, a privatized system would not be pro-family in the way Social Security is today. In the present system, a women who *never* works outside the home and therefore *never* pays a cent in Social Security taxes still receives Social Security payments equal to 50 percent of her husband's benefits—and if he dies, she gets 100 percent of his benefits. Spouses and children of workers who die young also receive substantial survivor benefits. All these pro-family benefits would disappear in a privatized system. That is why Christian conservative leader Gary Bauer (president of the Family Research Council before he ran for president) opposed privatizing Social Security in a widely discussed op-ed piece in *The New York Times.* Speaking of the privatization plans, Bauer argued, "For more than 20 years, I have worked to defend average American families which time and time again get the short end of the stick. I fear they will be the chief victims again as Washington considers three plans to 'reform' Social Security."[31]

Unless these and other problems with privatization proposals can be solved, it would be more prudent to reform the present system. There are solid workable proposals for fixing the system that avoid the risks of privatization.[32]

Whatever changes are made, however, must improve, not weaken, our society's commitment to the least advantaged.

Capital for the Poor

If it is true that in the biblical perspective "private property is so good that everybody ought to have some" (see p. 65), then we have a problem. Wealth (property, stocks, bonds, bank accounts, etc.) is even more unequally divided than annual income. The bottom 20 percent have negative wealth! Their debts are greater than their assets. In 1997, the bottom 40 percent of all households had on average only $3,200 in net worth. The top 1 percent, on the other hand, had an average of $9,977,000 and owned 39 percent of all wealth.[33] Eighty-six percent of all stock market gains between 1989 and 1997 went to the top 10 percent of households.[34]

In the previous section, we saw that some conservatives think privatizing Social Security might be a way to create wealth among the poor. There is strong reason to doubt that this specific proposal would really benefit the poor, but many of the reasons conservatives give for creating wealth among the poor are right on target. If the poor had a much stronger economic stake in society, destructive behavior might decline and democracy could be strengthened. We have a long history in this country of using government policy to help a large number of citizens own wealth. From Thomas Jefferson's decision to have the public lands conveyed not to large absentee landowners but to the farmers who worked the land, to the G.I. bill subsidizing veterans' education, to today's student grants and loans and individual retirement accounts, government has acted to diversify the ownership of wealth. A broad middle class has benefited.

Why not do the same for the poor? That is what Individual Development Accounts (IDAs) propose to do. The details of proposals by various scholars differ,[35] but the basic suggestion is the same. At birth and/or at other points (e.g., each birthday until age sixteen, passing a grade, finishing high school), the government would deposit money in the IDA of every poor U.S. citizen, and the money would be invested in stocks and bonds. The person would also be encouraged (or required) to add additional contributions. A portion of the person's growing IDA could be used at certain points to create additional wealth—e.g., 50 percent of accumulated assets for a college education; 25 percent of accumulated assets after age thirty for a down payment on one's first house. At age sixty-five, the IDA would add to the person's retirement income.

There are many questions about size, administration, funding, and so on that are important but beyond the scope of this short section. The basic proposal, however, merits careful discussion. In fact, in 1998, Congress approved $125 million for a five-year pilot program. What would be the effect if every inner-city youth knew (with the schools providing in-depth teaching on IDAs) that he had a personal IDA that would provide tens of thousands of dollars for a college education and/or the purchase of a first home? Genuine hope for the future might encourage different behavior. This proposal deserves widespread public debate.

Metropolitan Governance and Justice

Metropolitan governance in the United States differs dramatically from that in most other countries. In most nations, as cities expanded outward, the city simply annexed ever new areas, thus including the entire metropolitan region under one city government. That happened in the United States in the last century and then largely stopped. In this century, suburban communities successfully resisted annexation, preferring to be politically autonomous. The result is the typical U.S. central city surrounded by several rings of politically independent suburbs.

Why is that important for our discussion of the poor? In a perceptive chapter, economist John Mason wrestles with this question.[36] He points out that the suburbs have acted in ways that have made it more difficult for the poor to live there and that federal policy has subsidized this arrangement. The result has been greater concentration of poverty in central cities and older inner-city suburbs.

Suburban zoning regulations requiring large lots for houses and preventing multiple housing units have prevented builders from constructing scattered-site lower-income housing in the suburbs. Federal policy also played a role as the FHA subsidized mortgages and thus house purchases primarily in *non*poor areas. Federal help for housing for the poor, on the other hand, for years took the form of public housing projects concentrated in poor neighborhoods.

In addition, government programs promoted transportation systems that contributed to suburban sprawl. The most subsidized rail and subway lines serve largely to enable suburbanites to travel quickly from the suburbs to center city and back. City residents have to live with less subsidized bus lines. Federally funded interstate highways and beltways largely benefit the more well-to-do car owners living in the suburbs.

In the last several decades, the poor have become more concentrated in high-poverty neighborhoods (where at least 40 percent of all residents are poor) located in our major cities.[37] To deal with the host of problems in these areas, including high-crime rates, poor schools, dilapidated housing, and dysfunctional families, urban governments need to spend extra money at a time when middle-class flight to the suburbs has lowered the urban tax base. Politically independent suburbs spend their money from their strong tax base on excellent schools, streets, and police departments for themselves. In principle, state and federal governments could correct the imbalance, but political power has also switched to the suburbs as central cities lost people and suburban areas gained more residents. Suburban politicians are far more inclined to vote for services for their suburban constituents than for restoring inner cities.

There is no easy solution. Switching to some form of metropolitan-wide governance like that in most nations would create a large tax base available to solve the problems of the entire region. Politically, however, that is impossible in the near future.

In his essay, John Mason expresses the hope that Christians and Jews will find resources in the biblical material on the city to strengthen a sense of metropolitan-wide moral responsibility and concern for each other. That is not a short-term solution, but it may offer a way to struggle with a complex, underlying problem that seems as unsolvable as it is important.

Faith-Based Community Organizing

The poor lack power. Poverty by definition means little economic power. It also involves far less political power and social respect.

Low voter turnout at the polls by the poor provides one striking illustration. The U.S. Bureau of the Census reports that in the 1994 elections, 64 percent of the people with incomes over $75,000 voted. On the other hand, a mere 20 percent of the people with incomes under $5000 bothered to vote as did only 24 percent of those with incomes between $5000 and $10,000.[38]

In the poorest neighborhoods, most of the institutions important for a thriving community—block clubs, local political clubs, local unions, schools, medical clinics, banks, strong families—are weak or absent. Their absence not only diminishes the external world of the poor but also gnaws away at their sense of worth and dignity, producing a pervasive sense of powerlessness.

Biblical faith—not some partial version but full-fledged biblical faith—can overcome this powerlessness. Biblical faith affirms the inestimable worth and dignity of all persons, no matter how poor, and invites them into a personal saving relationship with the Creator of the galaxies. Biblical faith teaches those marginalized by society that the Lord of history hates oppression, cares especially for the poor, and is active now seeking justice for them. Biblical faith insists that justice means restoration to community—i.e., to the economic and social power to be dignified participants in their community (see pp. 59–61).

As Martin Luther King Jr. and the other organizers of the civil rights movement understood so well, however, the poor acquire power and self-respect only as they come to realize that they themselves can organize and demand change. To an important degree, power cannot be given to the powerless. Leaders and movements demanding change must arise among the poor themselves.

Congregation-based community organizing is proving to be a powerful tool to enable the poor to end their sense of powerlessness. The church is often the one institution that offers opportunities for even the most marginalized to exercise leadership. Several national community organization networks now work with groups of local congregations around the United States helping them organize their local communities.[39] They help them identify key problems, define winnable battles, and organize to demand the changes they want—more police attention to drug trafficking, better neighborhood schools, affordable housing, an end to redlining by banks and insurance companies.

Rev. Johnnie Ray Youngblood is chairperson of one of the most successful of the congregation-based community organizing efforts, the East Brooklyn Congregations (EBC), which is an affiliate of the national Industrial Areas Foundation (IAF). Rev. Youngblood started with his own congregation, encouraging his poor black members to move beyond hopeless despair. The IAF's training program helped him see how to define winnable projects that could force politicians and bureaucracies to do what they were supposed to do. Their first campaign compelled the borough president to put up thirty-two thousand street signs. Sixteen years and many successful campaigns later, Youngblood's congregation-based EBC had built twenty-three hundred new, modestly priced, owner-occupied, single-family homes in a devastated section of their community. Almost half of the new homeowners moved directly from housing projects. They also forced the Board of Education to create two new high schools, demanded and received an agreement from five local banks to hire students from the two high schools, and increased police patrols in high-crime neighborhoods. Rev. Youngblood's congregation-based community organization is empowering the poor to transform their community.

Historically, mainline Protestant, Catholic, and African American churches have been most active in congregation-based community organizing. Recently, however, Marilyn Stranske has founded an evangelical network—Christians Supporting Community Organizing—that is articulating a biblical foundation for congregation-based community organizing.[40] Another leader in this new organization, Bishop George McKinney, pastor of St. Stephen's Church of God in Christ in San Diego, even reports that community organizing and evangelism can go hand in hand: "Because of the church's involvement in addressing certain social and justice issues, we have been able to present God to many who would never have come to church. Thus community-based organizing has been used by God as a tool of evangelism."[41]

Conclusion

Everything affects everything else. If poor youth could watch their individual investment accounts grow larger year by year, they would have more hope for the future and be less likely to act irresponsibly. If community organizing can help poor neighborhoods cast off paralyzing powerlessness and discover decisive ways to shape their future, the growing sense of hope will reduce violence, strengthen families, and encourage work. A family-friendly Social Security system can strengthen marriage and family. A progressive tax policy can produce adequate funds so that government is able to play its proper role in empowering the poor. All this and more is possible if enough people catch the biblical vision of generosity and justice.

Part 4

The Generous Christians Generation

10

We Can End the Scandal

> There should be no poor among you . . . if only you fully obey the LORD your God.
>
> Deuteronomy 15:4–5 NIV

Cornel West reports a painful encounter after a speech in Newark with a demoralized young man. The youth admired Dr. West's hard work and distinguished achievements, but he felt drawn to the streets. "I'm the smartest guy in my class," he told the famous Harvard professor, "but I can't find any motivation. . . . More and more I feel I belong on the streets, hustling, dealing, and hurting like everyone else."

The young man pressed West to tell him why he had worked so hard. West explained how his mom and dad disciplined and encouraged him and how his older brother helped with homework and his younger sisters cheered him on. Slowly, painfully, the young man replied, "I'm in this world by myself. My mother's strung out and tuned out. I have brothers, but I don't know them, and as for my father, where he is nobody knows. I sure have never seen him." Professor West was overwhelmed with helpless grief.[1]

I do not know how that story will end. But I want to tell you how it worked out for another young man facing a similar agony.

One cold wintry morning in 1986, Tee's mother kicked him out of her apartment in North Philadelphia, leaving the sixteen-year-old to face the world by himself. Dad had not been around for most of Tee's life. Mom had tried hard, but the death of a child and depression overwhelmed her. She was simply unable to care for Tee. That night, Tee slept in his mother's doorway.

Fortunately, Tee had started attending the youth group at Diamond Street Mennonite Church, a small active congregation a few blocks away. He had friends there from an earlier summer program, and he especially liked meeting girls. Tee poured out his heart to a close friend, Ernest, who then encouraged him to talk to the pastor, Rev. Charles Baynard. Embarrassed about his situation, Tee agreed only reluctantly. Leo and Sharon Gabriel, a couple in the church invited Tee into their home. For one and a half years, Tee lived with Leo and Sharon, enjoying and learning from his substitute mom and dad. They comforted and counseled, nurturing him into a strong personal faith and encouraging him in his studies. Many friends in the church provided an extended family. (Tee even lived in our home his senior year of college.)

Continuing a level of excellence that his mother taught him in spite of her troubles, Tee excelled. He was a city-wide cross-country champion his senior year of high school. After high school, he earned his bachelor's degree at Philadelphia's University of the Arts. Pell grants and other federal and state grants and loans helped substitute for the funds middle-class parents provide their kids for college. For the first two years, Tee received enough financial aid to cover his books, art supplies, and miscellaneous expenses associated with college. His last two years were more difficult financially because the Reagan Administration was cutting back on these programs. But by the grace of God and a lot of hard work—plus a supportive church community and significant government aid—Tee graduated with his degree in graphic design.

Today, Tee is a successful graphic artist. Happily married—to the former pastor's daughter—he is showering his little son with the fatherly love he missed as a boy. His active faith anchors his marriage and career.

Could that be the happy ending for the thousands of poor youth such as the tortured young man Cornel West met? In fact, it is happening. It is quite possible for Tee's story to be more than just an inspiring anecdote; it can be a decisive clue.

Success Stories

Lawndale Community Church (LCC) in Chicago shows that it is possible to duplicate Tee's story over and over again. Thirty years ago, Lawndale was a discouraged, broken community. It was one of the twenty poorest communities in the United States. Virtually nobody went to college from Lawndale's awful schools. The infant mortality rate approached third-world levels.

Over the last twenty years, however, Lawndale Community Church's social ministries have grown into a $10-million-a-year holistic program. The health clinic has twenty-two full-time doctors. The college prep program has assisted and enabled one hundred Lawndale youth to graduate from college. Fifty of them have returned to inner-city Lawndale to offer the same hope to their younger siblings and friends that LCC gave to them.

The health clinic is so successful (even though the doctors receive only one-third of a typical doctor's salary) that the infant mortality rate has dropped by 60 percent, making headlines in Chicago newspapers. The federal health officials in the Chicago region came to LCC to ask if they could fund some of LCC's enormously successful programs. Now the federal office requires all its regional staff to read the book about LCC's amazing success.[2]

Why is LCC so successful? There are many reasons: outstanding leadership, good funding, help from the Chicago Bears. The enthusiastic partnership of a few suburban churches has also made a big difference. Years ago, Dr. Art DeKruyter, prominent pastor of large, wealthy Christ Church of Oakbrook in Chicago's western suburbs, pulled on his blue jeans, climbed into an old, borrowed pickup, and delivered some donated appliances to Lawndale. His parishioners followed his example. Accountants, radiologists, architects, and lawyers in his church donated large amounts of pro bono work. A computer store owner has provided free computers, consultation, and servicing for Lawndale's learning center. A masonry businessman donated the materials and labor to build a six-thousand-square-foot addition to the health center and church.

Nor is it a one-way street. Mutual respect, trust, and lasting friendship have slowly developed between the people at Lawndale and their suburban partners. Dr. DeKruyter tells his Lawndale friends, "You're the ones who have changed our lives."

Lawndale's co-founder and pastor enthusiastically recommends this kind of partnership to others. "I strongly encourage urban and suburban churches all over this nation to reach out to each other."[3]

According to Wayne Gordon, the single most important reason for their success is faith. "None of this would work the way it does," Wayne says, "apart from the vibrant faith in Christ that motivates all our staff and the active relational evangelism that has led hundreds and hundreds of Lawndale residents to personal faith and transformed lives." Wayne is also quick to add, "We have over four thousand people around the world who pray for us regularly."

There is now a worshiping congregation of over one thousand people at the core of LCC's work. Most of the community center's 160 staff attend. LCC staff respect every person's integrity and freedom. They do not cram religion down people's throats. Rather, sensitively, carefully, the staff openly talk about the way faith in Christ transforms broken lives.

I asked Wayne how he has been able to assemble a large staff ready to work at ridiculously low pay and filled with a passion for both empowering the poor and sharing their faith. "The answer is simple," Wayne said. "I interviewed every staff candidate for years and only hired people who were both highly skilled and highly motivated to lead people to personal faith." When the federal government asked to fund some of their health programs, there was one condition: "We won't change our Christ-centered approach. That is why we are so successful."

Lawndale offers one inspiring story in one neighborhood. Can their success be duplicated nationally? We need to be cautious. It will take time, involve failure, and require much sacrifice. But again the answer is yes. Dr. John Perkins is the founder and Wayne Gordon is the president of the Christian Community Development Association, which now has over six hundred Lawndale-like holistic ministries in scores of towns and cities—and that is just one holistic network.[4]

The historic black church has been engaged in highly successful holistic ministry for centuries. The list of large African American churches that combine vast programs of socioeconomic empowerment with personal spiritual conversion and renewal would require an entire book. One thinks especially of former Congressman Floyd Flake's Allen African Methodist Episcopal Church in Queens and its $26-million annual social programs;[5] Rev. Johnny Ray Youngblood's St. Paul Community Baptist Church in New York;[6] Rev. J. Alfred Smith Sr.'s Allen Temple Baptist Church in Oakland;[7] or Dr. Cheryl Sanders's Third Church of God in Washington. The list goes on and on.

The Charitable Choice legislation offers a historic opportunity for faith-based ministries to vastly expand their successful programs through the use of government funds without losing the religious component that makes them so successful. As I have insisted elsewhere, this does not mean that Christians—or Muslims—dare use government money for specifically religious activities.[8] But it does mean that governments can fund that portion of faith-based programs of all beliefs including secularism that effectively produce public goods such as transformed addicts, healthy, well-educated children, and successful workers no longer needing welfare. If government offers equal benefits to social programs run by people of all religious beliefs (even those who claim to have none), we preserve our historic commitment to religious freedom for all. We also enable the churches to offer their full contribution to the healing of our most broken communities.[9]

A Changing Climate

There is, of course, another side to all this optimism. The skeptic will rightly insist that many churches care little about the poor. Very few enjoy the skilled leadership of former Congressman Floyd Flake. Many middle-class people—both black and white—with the skills needed to be effective mentors have moved to the suburbs. Will they return to volunteer and serve, or even relocate, in the areas of most desperate need? Can churches and other faith groups really make a major difference that could significantly reduce poverty? Major changes both inside and outside the Christian church in the United States offer substantial reasons for thinking they can. Internally, a century-old battle has ended, and widely diverse church traditions are beginning to work together on ending poverty. Externally, the end of the cold war has created a more favorable climate, and the secular policy world is open in an astonishing new way to the contribution of people of faith.

The bitter battle between conservative Christians who emphasize evangelism and liberal Christians who stress social action that weakened the church for much of this century has largely ended. Increasingly, most agree that Christians should combine the Good News with good works and imitate Jesus' special concern for the poor.[10] (In practice, of course, many local ministries are still lopsided. I hope all who read this book will check to see whether their congregation's social ministries also place major emphasis on the crucial dimension of spiritual transformation.)

The Call to Renewal is perhaps the most striking example of how Christians from a wide range of traditions are ready to work together around the agenda of overcoming poverty. Evangelicals and mainliners, blacks and whites, conservatives and liberals, Catholics and Protestants have all joined enthusiastically in Call to Renewal's Economic Round Table. Wes Granberg-Michaelson, a prominent leader in the National Council of Churches, says, "This has probably been the most religiously diverse gathering of the Christian community to address the issue of poverty, certainly in this decade."[11] In the words of Rich Cizik, Washington staffer for the National Association of Evangelicals: "The Cold War between religious groups over the poor is over!"[12] As Jim Wallis, founder of Call to Renewal, comments, "Wonderfully, the poor are bringing the churches back together."

The March for Jesus illustrates the same thing. This march has annually drawn hundreds of thousands of evangelicals together in scores of U.S. cities. Now March for Jesus is transforming itself into an annual Jesus Day with a central focus on the poor.[13] Perhaps new developments such as Jesus Day can persuade additional volunteers to join those in organizations such as Bread for the World and Evangelicals for Social Action who have been struggling faithfully for years to empower the poor. The result could be a swelling tide of Christians and other people of goodwill able to transform this nation.

Externally, too, the climate has changed. We enjoy a booming economy and—for the first time in decades—a budget surplus. Surely we ought to welcome the poorest members of our community into the circle of people who benefit from our unusually strong economy. Thanks to the end of the cold war, we spend less money on the military, and Christian social activists calling for justice for the poor are far less likely to be dismissed as communists. Even more important, the secular policy world of academic experts, journalists, and the legal community is in the midst of the most astonishing changes that I have experienced in my thirty years of advocacy for the poor. After decades of fairly hostile marginalization of religious voices,[14] the top levels of the public policy community have begun to warmly welcome and seriously explore the contribution that faith-based agencies can make to overcoming poverty, especially in our desperate inner cities.

Does all this enthusiasm about a much expanded role for religious institutions mean that we can forget about government? Absolutely not. That would be just as one-sided as the earlier illusion that good government programs by themselves could end poverty. I have stressed the expanded role that faith-based agencies can play because that part has been less well understood in the last few decades. But the libertarian dream of fully or largely privatizing society's obligations to the least among us is impractical, unrealistic, and wrong. It flatly contradicts both church history and a biblical understanding of the role of government.[15] Federal, state, and local governments must make the kind of structural changes outlined earlier. If the schools do not work and responsible workers cannot escape poverty, we will fail, no matter how many broken people the churches transform. Tee certainly needed the loving embrace of a Christian family and church and the personal faith they nurtured, but he also needed the government's Pell grants so he could afford to go to college.

Will a Holistic, Comprehensive Framework Work?

I have sketched a holistic, comprehensive framework in which all the different societal institutions—civil society (especially families and religious bodies), media, business, unions, and government—each play their proper, indispensable roles. It is time to get beyond the silly argument between liberals and conservatives about whether it takes a village or a family to raise a child. Hillary Clinton *and* Kay James are both right.[16] It takes both.

Pressing questions persist. Can we afford a comprehensive set of policies that offer a genuine possibility for dramatically reducing U.S. poverty? Will the long-divided Christian community really manage to work together on some common agenda? Most important, perhaps, do enough Christians really care about the poor?

Any serious effort to reduce poverty will be costly, not only for courageous practitioners such as Eugene Rivers and Mary Nelson, but also in terms of our time, our private donations, and our tax dollars.

We need more volunteers. Some will mentor one person, others will mentor a neighborhood or city. Don Williams is the chairman of Trammell Crow Company, one of the largest corporate realty companies in the United States. He is also a committed Christian who cares deeply about the poor. A couple years ago, he decided to reduce his responsibilities at Trammell Crow so he could devote approximately 50 percent of his time to helping with comprehensive renewal in South Dallas, one of the city's poorest neighborhoods. Because of his prominence as a leading Dallas business executive, Don can marshal major resources and call together all segments of the Dallas community.[17] But it takes a lot of time.

We also need more private donations. I know inner-city pastors working their hearts out to walk with broken people as Christ transforms their lives. Thousands upon thousands of them struggle with inadequate funding. The typical suburban church member could double—or even quadruple—his or her giving to charitable causes without coming close to poverty. Remember that the typical church member gives less than 2.5 percent of his or her income. It would be costly, but think of the urban-suburban partnerships that could be funded.

I have also proposed increasing the right kind of government programs that empower the poor. Can we afford it? Remember that we now spend well over $125 billion a year on largely unnecessary corporate welfare. We could cut much of the $33 billion in tax credits for mortgage interest that go to persons earning more than $100,000 a year. The middle and upper classes receive a $60-billion tax benefit because of their untaxed health benefits. I do not mean that all of the $218 billion tax breaks for the *non*poor should end, but substantial cuts would release large amounts to empower those who truly need help. In the long run, of course, we will save money if we can truly empower the poor to become working, contributing members of society. It is nonsense to claim that a successful, holistic campaign against poverty will bankrupt the government.

Can conservative and liberal Christians work together to reduce poverty? Only time will tell. But my recent experience provides renewed hope. I have recently helped draft documents in two groups. The one would be perceived as overwhelmingly conservative, the other largely liberal. But both groups adopted a pro-poor *and* a pro-family agenda. People such as

Charles Colson, James Dobson, Gary Bauer, Ralph Reed, and Richard John Neuhaus were the majority in the first;[18] persons such as Jim Wallis, Joan Campbell, Tony Campolo, Sharon Daly, Eugene Rivers, and James Forbes predominated in the second.[19] It will not be easy, but just maybe a broad coalition that brings together these diverse Christians will find a way to work together for the sake of the poorest.[20]

Will there be enough Christians to make a major impact? Recent research demonstrates that large numbers of Christians and Jews are already deeply engaged with the poor.[21]

I still wonder, however. Do enough Christians really care? This question troubles me the most. Suffocating materialism and narcissistic individualism have wormed their way into so many Christian hearts and congregations. Fearfully, I wonder if most Christians may not sleep through one of the most amazing opportunities in our history.

I am convinced that in the first five to ten years of the new millennium, Christians in the United States have a historic opportunity unparalleled in decades, perhaps in the twentieth century. Dismayed by repeated failures to reduce poverty, secular policy elites are astonishingly open to faith-based proposals and contributions. With some old fears and battles resolved, the widely divided Christian community shows increasing signs of readiness to work together to empower the poor. With more empirical evidence emerging every year, faith-based approaches look increasingly attractive. It is realistic to think that a biblically based, empirically grounded holistic vision and strategy could become widely influential and dramatically reduce poverty in the next decade.

American Christians stand at a historic crossroads. We face one of the greatest opportunities in our history. We have more material resources than ever before. Tragically, we are also more materialistic and more focused on individual self-fulfillment. Will we take the path of generosity and justice? Or will we slip slowly into ever greater self-gratification?

The path of self-indulgence defies God and threatens democracy. A large number of poor, angry, disenfranchised youth with no stake in society and no hope for the future live in the heart of all our great cities. Unless we end their agony, they will shatter our comfort.

That will happen, however, only if a large movement of Christians and other citizens join together around a common vision and agenda. That can happen only if we are ready to work hard and sacrifice narrow self-interest. That can happen only if God mysteriously blesses us with inner renewal and spiritual revival that transforms millions of comfortable Christian materialists into passionate champions of the poor.

Christians have every reason to pay the price. For starters, we—at least politically conservative Christians—asked government to cut programs for the poor with the promise that churches could do it better. It is now time to fulfill the promise and demonstrate the claim. Our society's public policy elites have offered us a wide-open door to show that faith-based programs combining strong spiritual components with the best of the medical and social sciences can succeed where others have failed. If much hard work, prayer, and money make good on that claim in the next decade, it will be a powerful witness for the gospel. Not only will many, many broken people twisted and demoralized by poverty be transformed by faith in Christ, but our secular intellectual community will take note.

Make no mistake. Policy experts in our best universities are seriously examining whether or not there is hard evidence to prove that faith-based programs succeed where others fail. They will not tolerate empty claims or poorly managed programs. But if repeated studies by careful scholars demonstrate that inner spiritual renewal significantly increases the positive impact of social programs empowering the poor, the impact will be striking. The dominant secularism in today's academic world will be on the defensive. Historic Christian faith will become a more credible intellectual option.

Still, however much Christians desire that result, it dare not be our primary motive. We have even better reasons to redouble our commitment to walk with the poor toward dignity and wholeness. Past heroes such as the evangelical British politician William Wilberforce, who ended the slave trade, American evangelist Charles Finney and his colleagues in the U.S. abolitionist movement, and Martin Luther King Jr. and his daring band of marching civil rights activists all remind us that empowering the least and poorest is at the heart of our Christian heritage.

Most important, God's Word demands renewed efforts to conquer poverty. Hundreds of biblical texts call faithful believers to share God's concern for the poor.[22] If today's Christians fail to respond, we not only miss a historic opportunity, we also blatantly defy the Lord we worship.

Think of the impact if several million Christians came to care as much about the poor as the Bible says God does. Are you willing to pledge to open your heart to God's call to care as much about the poor as Jesus did? Don't panic. Taking that pledge does not mean that you promise tomorrow to be as loving as Jesus. It only commits you to opening your heart to allow God to make you more like Jesus. How can any genuine Christian refuse to pray that prayer?

I invite you to take the following Generous Christians pledge:

I pledge to open my heart to God's call to care as much about the poor as the Bible does. I therefore commit:

> *daily*, to pray for the poor, beginning with the Generous Christians prayer: "Lord Jesus, teach my heart to share your love for the poor."

weekly, to minister at least one hour, helping, serving, sharing with, and, mostly, getting to know someone in need.

monthly, to study at least one story, book, article, or film about the plight of the poor and hungry and discuss it with others.

yearly, to retreat for a few hours to meditate on this one question in light of Scripture: "Is caring for the poor as important in my life as it is in the Bible?" and to examine my budget and priorities in light of it, asking God what changes he would like me to make in the use of my time, money, influence, and citizenship.

I encourage you to find a small group who takes the pledge together and helps each other implement it. If you want to add your name and join many others making this pledge or would like a retreat kit, see the listing of the Generous Christians Campaign in the list of organizations beginning on page 257.

Conclusion

If enough Christians and others of goodwill join together at this historic moment, we can end the tragedy of widespread poverty in the richest society on earth. Indeed, we could dramatically reduce poverty around the world. If that happens, future historians will call us the Generous Christians Generation. It is possible in the next two decades to move our world, even our most broken inner cities, a little closer to the messianic ideal pictured so powerfully in Isaiah 65.

> No more shall the sound of weeping be heard in it. . . . No more shall there be in it an infant that lives but a few days, or an old person who does not live out a lifetime. . . . They shall build houses and inhabit them; they shall plant vineyards and eat their fruit. They shall not build and another inhabit; they shall not plant and another eat.
>
> Isaiah 65:19–22 NRSV

That vision will become full reality only when our Lord returns. Surely, however, the God who promises that one day the broken kingdoms of this world will become the kingdom of our Lord is honored when faithful Christians enact little signs now of that coming wholeness.

Generous Christians and other people of goodwill can transform our country. We can end the scandal of widespread poverty in the richest nation in history.

Afterword

I first met Ron Sider thirty years ago when he was living and working in North Philadelphia. He knows from years of personal experiences in North Philadelphia and Germantown that we face a desperate situation. In fact, he probably understates the problem—at least for large numbers of urban black Americans.

Each day, 1,118 black teenagers are victims of violent crimes, 1,451 black children are arrested, and 907 teenage girls become pregnant. A generation of black males is drowning in its own blood in the prison camps we euphemistically call "inner cities." And things are likely to get much worse.

Some forty years after the beginning of the civil rights movement, many younger black Americans are growing up unqualified for gainful employment even as slaves. Consider the dimensions of this failure. A black boy has a 1 in 3,700 chance of getting a Ph.D. in mathematics, engineering, or the physical sciences; a 1 in 766 chance of becoming a lawyer; a 1 in 395 chance of becoming a physician; a 1 in 195 chance of becoming a teacher. But his chances are 1 in 2 of never attending college, even if he graduates from high school; 1 in 9 of using cocaine; 1 in 12 of having gonorrhea; and 1 in 20 of being imprisoned while in his twenties. Only the details are different for his sister.

For the last twenty years, the domestic policy wars have been directed against the urban black poor. For both Republicans and Democrats, poor blacks are a politically disposable population.

The result is growing desperation for millions of poor urban minority youth. If homicide among teenagers continues to increase at the rate at which is has for the past ten years, a huge increase in this cohort will create an unprecedented epidemic in violent crime. If the current political and structural economic trends persist (and there is little reason to assume they will not), we are looking at a future blood bath of violence that will make our present nightmare look pleasant.

What can be done?

In the spring of 1998, some of *Newsweek*'s top editors invited John J. DiIulio Jr. and myself to meet to talk about the possibility that faith-based programs might provide a solution that our society had not adequately explored. I presented the evidence from the church-based approach to reducing teenage homicide in Boston's TenPoint Coalition. We debated whether small, existing faith-based successes could be greatly expanded. The usual secular fears about destroying the separation of church and state surfaced.

In the end, I bluntly insisted that America's policy elites have two alternatives. They can continue down the present path until some spark ignites the boiling rage of poor black inner-city youth and white society responds to widespread violence with brutal repression. That way lies apartheid. Or they can greatly expand societal support for the one inner-city institution that has the ability to produce genuine peaceful change—the many faith-based social ministries related to churches and other religious groups. Secular policy elites must choose: either apartheid or faith.

Sider's book is vitally important because he understands the crucial, expanded role that faith-based programs must play if there is to be hope for the urban poor. At the same time, Sider refuses to fall into the libertarian trap that rejects any significant role for government. If black and white Americans could unite around the kind of comprehensive holistic strategy outlined in this book, we might be able to avoid the violent blood bath that otherwise seems ever more likely.

Eugene F. Rivers, 3rd, is the pastor of Azusa Christian Community in Boston, co-chair of the National TenPoint Leadership Foundation, and personal mentor for children and youth in the inner-city neighborhood where he lives with his family.

Notes

Foreword

1. Robert Rector, "America Has the World's Richest Poor People," *The Wall Street Journal*, 24 September 1998, p. A18.

2. Christopher DeMuth, quoted in "Attitude Adjustments: Affluence Has Given Compassion a New Spin," *The Philadelphia Inquirer Magazine* (20 September 1998): 21.

3. Diane Cohen and A. Robert Jaeger, reporting the results of research conducted by Ram A. Cnaan, *Sacred Places at Risk* (Philadelphia: Partners for Sacred Places, 1998), 19–20. Also see Jeremy White and Mary de Marcellus, "Faith-Based Outreach to At-Risk Youth," The Jeremiah Project Report 98-1, The Manhattan Institute, December 1998.

4. For an overview, see Rob Geen et al., "The Cost of Protecting Vulnerable Children," Occasional Paper 20, The Urban Institute, January 1999, 12.

5. Paul E. Barton, "Welfare: Indicators of Dependency," Policy Information Center, Educational Testing Service, August 1998, 14.

6. Frank Thompson and John J. DiIulio Jr., eds., *Medicaid and Devolution: A View from the States* (Washington, D.C.: The Brookings Institution, 1998), 280.

7. The Center for Public Justice and The Christian Legal Society, "A Guide to Charitable Choice: The Rules of Section 104 of the 1996 Federal Welfare Law," January 1997.

8. William Julius Wilson, *When Work Disappears: The World of the New Urban Poor* (New York: Knopf, 1996); Katherine S. Newman, *No Shame in My Game: The Working Poor in the Inner City* (New York: Knopf, 1999).

9. National Center for Policy Analysis (NCPA), summarizing data from a June 1998 report by the U.S. General Accounting Office, NCPA Executive Alert, November/December 1998, 5.

10. "The State of Welfare Caseloads in America's Cities: 1999," Center on Urban and Metropolitan Policy, The Brookings Institution, February 1999, 1.

11. Ibid.

12. Barbara Vobejda and Judith Havemann, "Untouched by Reform," *The Washington Post,* 11 January 1999, p. 29.

13. Barton, "Welfare," 16–17.

14. Ronald J. Sider, ed., *The Chicago Declaration* (Carol Stream, Ill.: Creation House, 1974), 17.

15. Ronald J. Sider, *Cup of Water, Bread of Life: Inspiring Stories about Overcoming Lopsided Christianity* (Grand Rapids: Zondervan, 1994), 178.

16. Ronald J. Sider, *Rich Christians in an Age of Hunger: Moving from Affluence to Generosity,* 4th ed. (Dallas: Word, 1997), 231.

17. Ronald J. Sider, *Good News and Good Works: A Theology for the Whole Gospel* (Grand Rapids: Baker, 1999), 18.

Introduction

1. I figure $600 for liability insurance, $500 for repairs, $400 for gas (10,000 miles per year), and $1,000 for car payments for an old car.

2. Daniel Moynihan, *Miles to Go: A Personal History of Social Policy* (Cambridge: Harvard Univ. Press, 1996), 225.

3. Michael Harrington, *The Other America: Poverty in the United States* (New York: Macmillan, 1962), 166–67.

4. Charles Murray, *Losing Ground: American Social Policy, 1950–1980* (New York: Basic Books, 1984).

5. Marvin Olasky, *The Tragedy of American Compassion* (Wheaton: Crossway, 1992).

Chapter 1: What Does Poverty Look Like?

1. 35.6 million (13.3 percent of the population) in 1997; Census Bureau, Current Population Reports, P-60-201, Poverty in the United States, 1997, v.

2. Christine Wicker, "A Celebration of Hope," *Dallas Morning News,* 16 September 1998, p. 27A. Some of the details come from personal conversations with Kathy Dudley and Mrs. Styles.

3. Poverty thresholds: 1998, U.S. Census Bureau, http://www.census.gov/ftp/pub/hhes/poverty/threshold/thresh98.html (3 February 1999). Family of three: $13,133; two: $11,235; one: $8,480.

4. Census Bureau, Current Population Reports, Series P-60-200, Money Income in the United States, 1997, B-8.

5. Committee on Ways and Means, *1998 Green Book* (Washington, D.C.: U.S. Government Printing Office, 1998), 1307; 11.3 percent of all U.S. families are in poverty; 4.5 percent of them have income under 50 percent of the poverty level.

6. When calculating a family's income to determine whether a family is poor, only cash income (e.g., earnings, Social Security payments, welfare, etc.) is counted, not noncash benefits (e.g., food stamps, Medicaid, etc.). On the other hand, taxes and necessary costs of employment (e.g., child care) are not deducted from income. More precise measures are needed and have been proposed. See Rebecca M. Blank, *It Takes a Nation: A New Agenda for Fighting Poverty* (Princeton: Princeton Univ. Press, 1997), 10–11, and almost the entire spring 1998 issue of *Focus* of the University of Wisconsin-Madison Institute for Research on Poverty (hereafter UW-MIRP). It is also important to note that the official poverty level does not reflect a general rise in the standard of living. In 1959, the poverty level for a non-farm family of four was 55 percent of the general society's median family income; in 1993, it was only 38 percent. Sheldon H. Danziger and Peter Gottschalk, *America Unequal* (Cambridge: Harvard Univ. Press, 1995), 181.

7. Kathryn Porter, Wendell Primus, Lynette Rawlings, and Esther Rosenbaum, *Strengths of the Safety Net* (Washington, D.C.: Center on Budget and Policy Priorities, 1998), v.

8. Unless otherwise indicated, I will use the official poverty level figures since almost all data and research on poverty in the last few decades use those figures.

9. Clarke E. Cochran, "Health Policy and the Poverty Trap," in *Toward a Just and Caring Society: Christian Responses to Poverty in America,* ed. David P. Gushee (Grand Rapids: Baker, 1999), chap. 8.

10. I have changed their names, but details of the story are accurate, and I have talked personally with the wife.

11. Fortunately for this family, the debt was recently written off by the hospital. Such an act, however, merely arbitrarily switches the cost to others and does not provide insurance for the future.

12. 1993 figures; see Blank's superb *It Takes a Nation,* 16–17.

13. Ibid., 31. In 1989, 9.2 percent of all persons and 16.2 percent of all family heads with income below the poverty level were working full-time for the entire year. Lawrence M. Mead, *The New Politics of Poverty* (New York: Basic Books, 1992), 50.

14. Daniel T. Lichter and Erica L. Gardner, "Welfare Reform and the Poor Children of Working Parents," *Focus* (UW-MIRP) 18, no. 2 (fall/winter 1996–97): 65. The figures are from 1990.

15. 1995 figures; Wendell Primus, "Who Are the Poor in America?" (unpublished paper).

16. *1998 Green Book,* 1299.

17. 1993 figures; Blank, *It Takes a Nation,* 27–29. The exact figures are: rural (24.6%); suburbs (32.6%); cities (42.8%).

18. Bob Herbert, "The Other America," *The New York Times,* 8 April 1999, p. A27.

19. 1996 figures; *1998 Green Book,* table H-1, 1299.

20. Blank, *It Takes a Nation,* 16.

21. *1998 Green Book,* table H-1, 1299.

22. Primus, "Who Are the Poor?" 5.

23. Blank, *It Takes a Nation,* 12.

24. Ibid., 23.

25. Robert Rector, "The Myth of Widespread American Poverty," *Backgrounder* 1221 (18 September 1998), The Heritage Foundation, Washington, D.C. Rector has been arguing this thesis since the early 1990s.

26. Robert Rector and William F. Lauber, *America's Failed $5.4 Trillion War on Poverty* (Washington, D.C.: The Heritage Foundation, 1995), especially 23–33.

27. Quoted in Sharon Parrott, "How Much Do We Spend on 'Welfare'?" Center on Budget and Policy Priorities, 4 August 1995, 8.

28. Ibid., 4–6.

29. Actually, more, because a major portion of the poor are not covered by Medicaid.

30. A study by the National Academy of Sciences has recently agreed that health care should be excluded from calculation of poverty guidelines. Constance F. Citro and Robert T. Michael, eds., *Measuring Poverty: A New Approach* (Washington, D.C.: National Academy Press, 1995), 2.

31. See the careful medical studies cited in Blank, *It Takes a Nation,* 162–64 (and 133ff.).

32. Center on Budget and Policy Priorities, 17 March 1998.

33. Blank, *It Takes a Nation,* 165.

34. See, for example, William Julius Wilson, *When Work Disappears: The World of the New Urban Poor* (New York: Knopf, 1996).

35. See, for example, Joe Klein's highly critical review of Wilson's *When Work Disappears* in "The True Disadvantage," *New Republic* (28 October 1996): 32–36.

36. "The Two Nations of Black America," *Brookings Review* (spring 1998): 7.

37. Glenn C. Loury, "Discrimination in the Post–Civil Rights Era," *Journal of Economic Perspectives* 12, no. 2 (spring 1998): 117ff.

38. Wilson, *When Work Disappears*, xiv.

39. Blank, *It Takes a Nation*, 153.

40. 1989 figures; Mead, *New Politics of Poverty*, 7.

41. Wilson, *When Work Disappears;* but Mead, *New Politics of Poverty*, cites data (chaps. 5 and 6) that demonstrate that Wilson's argument only explains part of the problem. Low-skill, *low-pay* jobs are still available; Blank, *It Takes a Nation*, 57.

42. Blank, *It Takes a Nation*, 61–62.

43. Ibid., 63.

44. Ibid., 54–56.

45. Ibid., 68–71. Again, Mead's data warns us against attributing the low work only to low pay; *New Politics of Poverty*, 67–69.

46. For this complex discussion, see J. David Richardson, "Income Inequality and Trade: How to Think, What to Conclude," *Journal of Economic Perspectives* 9, no. 3 (summer 1995): 33–35; J. David Richardson et al., "U.S. Performance and Trade Strategy in a Shifting Global Economy," in *Trade Strategies for a New Era*, ed. Geza Feketekuty and Bruce Stokes (New York: Council on Foreign Relations, 1998); Susan M. Collins, ed., *Imports, Exports, and the American Worker* (Washington, D.C.: Brookings Institution Press, 1998).

47. George N. Monsma, "Income Distribution in the United States," in *Toward a Just and Caring Society*, chap. 6.

48. *1998 Green Book*, cited in Monsma, "Income Distribution."

49. From the U.S. Bureau of Labor Statistics, which has collected data from the Current Population Survey from 1983–1998, and from labor unions from 1930–1980. The two sets of data are not fully comparable, but they are useful to show the overall trend.

50. Richard Freeman, "How Much Has De-Unionization Contributed to the Rise in Male Earnings Inequality?" in *Uneven Tides: Rising Inequality in America*, ed. Sheldon H. Danziger and Peter Gottschalk (New York: Russell Sage Foundation, 1993), 137, 153.

51. See Loury, "Discrimination," 117ff.; William A. Darity Jr. and Patrick L. Mason, "Evidence on Discrimination in Employment," *Journal of Economic Perspectives* 12, no. 2 (spring 1998): 63ff.; Ronald F. Ferguson, "Shifting Challenges: Fifty Years of Economic Change toward Black-White Earnings Equality," *Daedalus* 124 (winter 1995): 37–76.

52. Loury, "Discrimination."

53. Darity and Mason, "Evidence on Discrimination."

54. See Danziger and Gottschalk, *America Unequal*, 19–27, for the supporting data for this and the previous paragraph. The rising unemployment rate at this time also contributed to rising child poverty.

55. Primus, "Who Are the Poor?" 11.

56. *1998 Green Book*, 1299.

57. Blank, *It Takes a Nation*, 33–42.

58. Primus, "Who Are the Poor?" 9–10.

59. *The State of America's Children: Yearbook 1998* (Washington, D.C.: Children's Defense Fund, 1998), 94.

60. Primus, "Who Are the Poor?" 9–10.

61. Christopher Jencks, *Rethinking Social Policy, Race, Poverty and the Underclass* (New York: Harper Perennial, 1992), 132–35.

62. Primus, "Who Are the Poor?" 10.

63. Ibid., 7.

64. Ibid., 14. A recent study by the Justice Department found that women in prison were twice as likely as women in the general population to report that they had been physically or sexually abused as children; *The New York Times*, 12 April 1999, p. A19.

65. Quoted in Daniel Moynihan, *Miles to Go: A Personal History of Social Policy* (Cambridge: Harvard Univ. Press, 1996), 65.

66. The above table and the analysis works with pre-tax money income. A different analysis that deducts federal income and payroll taxes and adds the estimated value of food stamps and food lunches indicates slightly less inequality. But the bottom fifth still lost ground between 1979 and 1994. Monsma, "Income Distribution"; *1996 Green Book,* 1240.

67. Lawrence Mishel, Jared Bernstein, and John Schmitt, *The State of Working America, 1998–1999* (Ithaca, N.Y.: Cornell Univ. Press, 1999), 49.

68. *1998 Green Book,* cited in Monsma, "Income Distribution," 36.

69. Isaac Shapiro and Robert Greenstein, "Trends in the Distribution of After-Tax Income," Center on Budget and Policy Priorities, 14 August 1997, 6. If in-kind benefits including Medicaid and Medicare are included, the bottom fifth's share only increases by 0.7 percentage points.

70. For definitions, see Edward N. Wolff, *Top Heavy* (New York: Twentieth Century Fund, 1995), 1. See also Gary Burtless, "Growing American Inequality: Sources and Remedies," *Brookings Review* (winter 1999): 31–35.

71. John Weicher, *The Distribution of Wealth* (Washington, D.C.: AEI Press, 1996), 13; Monsma, "Income Distribution."

72. Mishel, Bernstein, and Schmitt, *Working America, 1998–1999,* 258, 262.

73. Ibid., 260, 267, 271.

74. Wolff, *Top Heavy,* 2.

75. See the Luxemburg study on income inequality in Bread for the World Institute, *Hunger 1997* (Silver Spring, Md.: Bread for the World Institute, 1997), 12–14.

76. Timothy M. Smeeding and Peter Gottschalk, "Cross-National Income Inequality," *Focus* (UW-MIRP) 19, no. 3 (summer/fall 1998): 16–18.

77. Peter Gottschalk and Sheldon H. Danziger, "Family Income Mobility," *Focus* (UW-MIRP) 19, no. 3 (summer/fall 1998): 20–23.

78. Blank, *It Takes a Nation,* 140.

79. *Business Week,* 21 April 1997.

80. *Executive Pay Watch,* 24 July 1998, 1.

81. Peter Gottschalk and Timothy Smeeding, "Cross-National Comparisons of Earnings and Income Inequality," *Journal of Economic Literature* 35 (June 1997): 661; Monsma, "Income Distribution."

82. 1992 data (latest year for which there is complete data); "A Brief History of Money in Politics," home page, Center for Responsive Politics, www.crp.org.

Chapter 2: A Biblical Foundation

1. See Robert Wuthnow, *The Crisis in the Churches* (New York: Oxford, 1997).

2. The remainder of this chapter is a shortened version of Stephen Charles Mott and Ronald J. Sider, "Economic Justice: A Biblical Paradigm," in *Toward a Just and Caring Society: Christian Responses to Poverty in America,* ed. David P. Gushee (Grand Rapids: Baker, 1999), chap. 1. See that chapter for detailed documentation and biblical references.

3. *Economic Justice for All: Pastoral Letter on Catholic Social Teaching and the U.S. Economy* (Washington, D.C.: National Conference of Catholic Bishops, 1986), 34 (sect. 64).

4. J. Philip Wogaman, *The Great Economic Debate: An Ethical Analysis* (Philadelphia: Westminster, 1977), 43.

5. E. Calvin Beisner, *Prosperity and Poverty: The Compassionate Use of Resources in a World of Scarcity* (Westchester, Ill.: Crossway, 1988), 54.

6. Cf. William Frankena, "The Concept of Social Justice," in *Social Justice,* ed. R. Brandt (Englewood Cliffs, N.J.: Prentice-Hall, 1962), 18–21.

7. Cf. further Stephen Charles Mott, *A Christian Perspective on Political Thought* (New York: Oxford, 1993), 77–88.

8. Our translation.

9. Cf. also Isa. 30:18; Jer. 9:24; Hosea 2:19; 12:6; Micah 6:8.

10. Mott's translation. Cf. also Pss. 40:10; 43:1–2; 65:6; 71:1–2, 24; 72:1–4; 116:5–6; 119:123; Isa. 45:8; 46:12–13; 59:11, 17; 61:10; 62:1–2; 63:7–8 (LXX); and frequently with *pillēt* for "deliver": Pss. 31:1; 37:28, 40.

11. Cf. Job 29:12, 14; Prov. 24:11.

12. *Triumphs* in the NRSV translates the word for *justice (sᵉdāqāh)* in the plural—i.e., "acts of justice" (cf. the NIV, "righteous acts").

13. Cf. Pss. 107; 113:7–9.

14. Literally! See the collection (about two hundred pages of biblical texts) in Ronald J. Sider, *For They Shall Be Fed* (Dallas: Word, 1997).

15. Cf. Norman H. Snaith, *The Distinctive Ideas of the Old Testament* (London: Epworth, 1944), 68, 71–72; James H. Cone, *God of the Oppressed* (New York: Seabury Press, 1975), 70–71.

16. This is not to ignore the fact that there are many causes of poverty, including laziness and other sinful choices (see Sider, *Rich Christians in an Age of Hunger* [Dallas: Word, 1997], chap. 6). God wants people who are poor because of their own sinful choices to repent and be changed by the power of the Holy Spirit.

17. Ps. 72:1–4; Prov. 31:8–9; Isa. 1:10, 17, 23, 26; Jer. 22:2–3, 14–15; Dan. 4:27.

18. The following section is adapted from Ronald J. Sider, *Living like Jesus: Eleven Essentials for Growing a Genuine Faith* (Grand Rapids: Baker, 1999), 141–44.

19. Mott's translation. See Mott and Sider, "Economic Justice."

20. Hans Walter Wolff, *Anthropology of the Old Testament* (Philadelphia: Fortress, 1974), 68. The NIV translates: "becomes poor and is unable to support himself."

21. C. Spicq, *Les Épîtres Pastorales, Études Bibliques* (Paris: Gabalda, 1969), 190 (on 1 Tim. 6:8).

22. Leslie Poles Hartley, *Facial Justice* (London: Hamish Hamilton, 1960; Oxford: Oxford Univ. Press, 1987).

23. The following paragraphs are taken from Sider, *Rich Christians in an Age of Hunger*, 68ff.

24. See the discussion and the literature cited in Stephen Charles Mott, *Biblical Ethics and Social Change* (New York: Oxford, 1982), 65–66; and Stephen Charles Mott, "Egalitarian Aspects of the Biblical Theory of Justice," in *American Society of Christian Ethics, Selected Papers 1978*, ed. Max Stackhouse (Newton, Mass.: American Society of Christian Ethics, 1978), 8–26.

25. For a survey of the literature on Leviticus 25, see R. Gnuse, "Jubilee Legislation in Leviticus: Israel's Vision of Social Reform," *Biblical Theological Bulletin* 15 (1983): 43–48.

26. On the centrality of the land in Israel's self-understanding, see Christopher J. H. Wright, *An Eye for an Eye: The Place of Old Testament Ethics Today* (Downers Grove, Ill.: InterVarsity Press, 1983), especially chaps. 3 and 4. Walter Brueggemann's *The Land* (Philadelphia: Fortress Press, 1977) is also a particularly important work on this topic.

27. Some scholars interpret the text differently; see Mott and Sider, "Economic Justice," n. 65.

28. John Calvin, *The Harmony of the Last Four Books of Moses*, Eighth Commandment, on Deuteronomy 15:1, following the translation of Harro Höpfl, *The Christian Polity of John Calvin* (Cambridge: Cambridge Univ., Studies in the History and Theory of Politics, 1982), 158. *Mediocris* would seem to mean here "avoiding the extremes."

29. See especially John Mason's excellent article, "Assisting the Poor: Assistance Programmes in the Bible," *Transformation* (April–June 1987): 1–14.

30. Ibid., 7.

31. Ibid., 9.

32. Ibid.

33. Ronald H. Nash, *Freedom, Justice and the State* (Lanham, Md.: University Press of America, 1980), 27.

34. John Calvin, *Institutes of the Christian Religion,* Library of Christian Classics 20–21, ed. J. McNeill (Philadelphia: Westminster, 1960), 4.20.3, 4, 22 (1488, 1490, 1510); cf. Höpfl, *Christian Polity of John Calvin,* 44–46. Similarly for Luther, government is an inestimable blessing of God and one of God's best gifts; cf. W. D. J. Cargill Thompson, *The Political Thought of Martin Luther,* ed. P. Broadhead (Sussex: Harvester, 1984), 66.

35. Meredith G. Kline, *Kingdom Prologue* (Hamilton, Mass.: Meredith G. Kline, 1983), 34, citing Dan. 4:27 in support.

Chapter 3: A Comprehensive Strategy

1. Tim and Rosemary are fictional characters, but I could document every segment of this story from actual events and persons I know. See, for example, my *Cup of Water, Bread of Life* (Grand Rapids: Zondervan, 1994), especially chaps. 4 and 8.

2. This chapter owes a special debt to Stephen V. Monsma's fine essay, "Poverty, Civil Society, and the Public Policy Impasse," in *Toward a Just and Caring Society: Christian Responses to Poverty in America,* ed. David P. Gushee (Grand Rapids: Baker, 1999), chap. 2.

3. *A Call to Civil Society: Why Democracy Needs Moral Truths* (New York: Institute for American Values, 1998), 6.

4. Monsma, "Poverty."

5. Quoted in ibid.

6. Allen E. Bergen, "Values and Religious Issues in Psychotherapy and Mental Health," *The American Psychologist* 46 (1991): 401.

7. David B. Larson and Susan S. Larson, "Is Divorce Hazardous to Your Health?" *Physician* (June 1990).

8. Michael Sandel, "Making Nice Is Not the Same as Doing Good," *The New York Times,* 29 December 1996, p. E9.

9. See the fine summary of a number of studies showing these tendencies in Amy E. Black, *For the Sake of the Children: Reconstructing American Divorce Policy,* Crossroads Monograph, no. 2 (Wynnewood, Pa.: Evangelicals for Social Action, 1995), 22–31. Also see David Blankenhorn, *Fatherless America: Confronting Our Most Urgent Social Problem* (New York: Basic Books, 1995); Eric F. Dubow and Tom Lester, "Adjustment of Children Born to Teenage Mothers: The Contribution of Risk and Protective Factors," *Journal of Marriage and the Family* 52 (1990): 393–404; Richard Gill, "For the Sake of the Children," *Public Interest* (summer 1992): 81–96; Sara McLanahan and Gary Sandefur, *Growing Up with a Single Parent: What Hurts, What Helps* (Cambridge: Harvard Univ. Press, 1994); Judith S. Wallerstein and Sandra Blakeslee, *Second Chances: Men, Women, and Children a Decade after Divorce* (New York: Ticknor and Fields, 1989); Barbara Dafoe Whitehead, "Dan Quayle Was Right," *The Atlantic Monthly* (April 1993): 47–84; and Nicholas Zill, Donna Morrison, and Mary Jo Coiro, "Long-Term Effects of Parental Divorce on Parent-Child Relationships, Adjustment, and Achievement in Young Adulthood," *Journal of Family Psychology* (1993): 91–103.

10. Sylvia Ann Hewlett and Cornel West, *The War against Parents: What We Can Do for America's Beleaguered Moms and Dads* (Boston: Houghton Mifflin, 1998).

11. Lawrence M. Mead, *The New Politics of Poverty* (New York: Basic Books, 1992), 183.

12. Ibid., 238. More recently, Mead has expressed openness to the role of faith-based groups. See his "The Poverty Debate and Human Nature," in *Welfare in America: Christian Perspectives on a Policy in Crisis,* ed. Stanley W. Carlson-Thies and James W. Skillen (Grand Rapids: Eerdmans, 1996), 209–42.

13. See Sider, *Good News and Good Works: A Theology for the Whole Gospel* (Grand Rapids: Baker, 1999), chaps. 6, 9, 10, and the marvelous statement in the new *Catechism of the Catholic*

Church (New York: Image, 1995), 514 (sect. 1888) on the relationship between inner conversion and social change.

14. See Meredith Ramsay, "Redeeming the City: Exploring the Relationship between Church and Metropolis," *Urban Affairs Review* (May 1998): 595–625.

15. *Call to Civil Society*, 8.

16. Ed Rubenstein, "Right Data: Policy or Hypocrisy?" *National Review* (11 September 1995); George Barna, *What Americans Believe* (Ventura, Calif.: Regal Books, 1991), 226.

17. See the scores of studies in Patrick F. Fagan, "Why Religion Matters: The Impact of Religious Practice on Social Stability," *Backgrounder* 1064 (25 January 1996), The Heritage Foundation, Washington, D.C.; and John J. DiIulio Jr., "Supporting Black Churches," *Brookings Review* (spring 1999): 42–45.

18. Richard B. Freeman, "Who Escapes?" in *The Black Youth Employment Crisis*, ed. Richard B. Freeman and Harry J. Holzer (Chicago: Univ. of Chicago Press, 1986), 354.

19. For a variety of studies, see Ronald J. Sider and Heidi Rolland Unruh, "Correcting the Welfare Tragedy," in *Welfare in America*, 465–66.

20. Rebecca M. Blank's "sophistication criterion" reinforces my argument. In *It Takes a Nation: A New Agenda for Fighting Poverty* (Princeton, N.J.: Princeton Univ. Press, 1997), 241–45, she shows how narrowly targeted programs (e.g., teen pregnancy-prevention programs that focus only on technical sexual information and ignore peers, parents, etc.) are usually unsuccessful. Programs that deal only with the physical/economic side of problems and ignore the personal/spiritual are also too narrowly focused and fail her "sophistication criterion."

21. See the distinction between four different types of "faith"-based programs in Ronald J. Sider and Heidi Rolland Unruh, "Charitable Choice and the First Amendment," *Brookings Review* (spring 1999): 46–49; and at greater length, Sider and Unruh, "An (Ana)Baptist Theological Perspective on Church-State Cooperation: Evaluating Charitable Choice," in *Welfare Reform and Faith-Based Organizations*, ed. Derek Davis and Barry Hankins (Waco: J. M. Dawson Institute of Church-State Studies, Baylor University, 1999).

22. Daniel Patrick Moynihan, *Miles to Go: A Personal History of Social Policy* (Cambridge: Harvard Univ. Press, 1996), 230.

23. Stanley W. Carlson-Thies and the Center for Public Justice have played an important role in Charitable Choice; see his very useful booklet, *Guide to Charitable Choice* (Washington, D.C.: Center for Public Justice, 1997); see also Sider and Unruh (n. 19).

24. Quoted in Joe Laconte, "The Bully and the Pulpit," *Policy Review* (November–December 1998): 35.

25. There is surprisingly little hard data on the actual number of churches, synagogues, and mosques. *The Yearbook of American and Canadian Churches* suggests that there are 350,000 "local communities of faith." Nancy T. Ammerman et al., *Studying Congregations: A New Handbook* (Nashville: Abingdon, 1998), 8. Independent Sector estimated 258,000 religious congregations (1992) with an average annual budget of $150,000; Blank, *It Takes a Nation*, 205, 308–9. Drawing on his research in the 1998 National Congregations Study (conducted in conjunction with the National Opinion Research Center at the University of Chicago), Mark Chaves concludes that current knowledge does not allow us to go beyond the estimate of between 290,000 and 350,000; "How Many Congregations Are There?" (unpublished memo, 29 January 1999). I use 325,000 as a reasonable estimate.

26. In 1998, the federal government alone was projected to spend $93.9 billion on food stamps, SSI, TANF, and EITC, plus $105 billion on Medicaid; Committee on Ways and Means, *1998 Green Book* (Washington, D.C.: U.S. Government Printing Office, 1998), 1359.

27. These are estimates based on preliminary results from Mark Chaves's study (see n. 25) shared in a personal memo, 2 February 1999.

28. Center on Budget and Policy Priorities (8 April 1999), 1. The exact figures are 47.6 percent and 11.9 percent.

29. Center on Budget and Policy Priorities (17 March 1998).

30. Ronald J. Sider, "Evaluating the Triumph of the Market," in *The Jubilee Challenge: Utopia or Possibility?* ed. Hans Ucko (Geneva: WCC Publications, 1997), 112–33.

31. *A Call to Civil Society*, 24.

32. See below, p. 177.

33. Joseph A. Maciariello, "Business and Empowerment," in *Toward a Just and Caring Society*, chap. 13.

34. Ibid.

35. See Lt. Col. David Grossman, *On Killing: The Psychological Cost of Learning to Kill in War and Society* (New York: Little, Brown and Co., 1996).

36. Quoted in *Christianity Today*, 10 August 1998, 34–35.

37. Quoted in Monsma, "Poverty."

38. Quoted in Joe Klein, "In God They Trust," *The New Yorker*, 16 June 1997, 44.

39. David B. Larson has pioneered some of the most important analysis; see David B. Larson and Susan S. Larson, *The Forgotten Factor in Physical and Mental Health: What Does the Research Show?* (Rockville, Md.: National Institute for Health Care Research, 1994). See also the vast number of studies cited in Patrick F. Fagan, "Why Religion Matters," *Backgrounder* 1064 (25 January 1996), The Heritage Foundation, Washington, D.C.

40. See John and Sylvia Ronsvalle, *The State of Church Giving through 1995* (Champaign, Ill.: Empty Tomb, 1998); and John and Sylvia Ronsvalle, "Giving to Religion," *Christian Century* (June 3–10, 1998): 579–81.

41. See Blank, *It Takes a Nation*, 194–95.

42. Stanley W. Carlson-Thies and James Skillen sketch a similar framework in "A New Vision for Welfare Reform" in their *Welfare in America*, 553–79.

43. Available from Call to Renewal, 2401 Fifteenth Street NW, Washington, D.C. 20009.

Chapter 4: If I Work, Can I Earn a Family Income?

1. Slight adaptation from Mary Jo Bane and David T. Ellwood, *Welfare Realities* (Cambridge: Harvard Univ. Press, 1994), 143.

2. See chap. 1, n. 6.

3. Rebecca M. Blank, *It Takes a Nation: A New Agenda for Fighting Poverty* (Princeton, N.J.: Princeton Univ. Press, 1997), 31.

4. Sylvia Ann Hewlett and Cornel West, *The War against Parents: What We Can Do for America's Beleagured Moms and Dads* (Boston: Houghton Mifflin, 1998), 76 (1990 figures).

5. Daniel T. Lichter and Erica L. Gardner, "Welfare Reform and the Poor Children of Working Parents," *Focus* (UW-MIRP) 18, no. 2 (fall/winter 1996–97): 65. The figures are from 1990.

6. Ibid., 69.

7. From 11.4 percent to 17.8 percent. Michael Tanner, *The End of Welfare* (Washington, D.C.: Cato Institute, 1996), 21.

8. The majority of part-time workers, of course, *want* part-time work. Lawrence M. Mead, *The New Politics of Poverty* (New York: Basic Books, 1992), 76, says that in 1985, only 12 percent wanted full-time work.

9. Telephone call, 12 February 1999, with the Bureau of Labor Statistics. For earlier years, see the Bureau of Labor Statistics, Current Population Survey, "Employed Persons by Full/Part-Time (Economic and Non-Economic Status) Annual Averages, 1968–97." Juliet B. Schor, *The Overworked American* (New York: HarperCollins, 1992), 39–40, argues that the problem is much greater than these figures would suggest.

10. Blank, *It Takes a Nation*, 32.

11. Robert Rector and William F. Lauber, *America's Failed $5.4 Trillion War on Poverty* (Washington, D.C.: The Heritage Foundation, 1995), 26. See also Mead, *New Politics of Poverty*, 8.

12. Blank, *It Takes a Nation*, 58.

13. Ibid., 62.

14. For women, only high school dropouts lost ground. Ibid., 63.

15. Ibid., 69.

16. Ibid. See also, Sheldon H. Danziger and Peter Gottschalk, *America Unequal* (Cambridge: Harvard Univ. Press, 1995), 12.

17. Mead, *New Politics of Poverty*, 83. Robert Rector blames the welfare system; Rector and Lauber, *War on Poverty*.

18. Danziger and Gottschalk, *America Unequal*, 91ff.

19. Ibid., 102.

20. Ibid., 103–8.

21. Ibid., 108.

22. Interestingly, Michael Tanner of the Cato Institute briefly acknowledges this point in passing; *End of Welfare*, 23.

23. Furthermore, some people will always lack the ability to be educated for high-skill jobs.

24. In her careful analysis of what welfare mothers really needed, Kathryn Edin discovered that a total income of about 130 percent of the poverty level was necessary to achieve financial independence and avoid significant hardship (i.e., hunger, eviction from housing, inability to afford medical care). See Christopher Jencks and Kathryn Edin, "Do Poor Women Have a Right to Bear Children?" *The American Prospect* 20 (winter 1995): 43–52. See also Kathryn Edin and Laura Lein, *Making Ends Meet* (New York: Russell Sage Foundation, 1997).

25. Regional differences should be taken into account. For childless couples and single adults between the ages of twenty-five and sixty-four, I advocate a goal of at least 100 percent of the poverty level achieved via the most effective combination of wages, EITC, and food stamps.

26. 22 October 1986 in *Public Papers of the President: Ronald Reagan* (Washington, D.C.: U.S. Government Printing Office, 1989), vol. 2, 1415. Reagan was speaking of the entire bill, several features of which (including the expansion of the EITC) helped the working poor.

27. Even a conservative like Eric D. Schansberg who opposes the vast majority of government interventions in the economy favors the EITC. *How Poor Government Policy Harms the Poor* (Boulder, Colo.: Westview Press, 1996), 55–58.

28. For an overview of the EITC, see Kathryn Porter, Wendell Primus, Lynette Rawlings, and Esther Rosenbaum, *Strengths of the Safety Net* (Washington, D.C.: Center on Budget and Policy Priorities, 1998), 19–27; Danziger and Gottschalk, *America Unequal*, 158–65; John E. Anderson, "Taxation and Economic Justice," in *Toward a Just and Caring Society: Christian Responses to Poverty in America*, ed. David P. Gushee (Grand Rapids: Baker, 1999), chap. 9.

29. Schansberg, *Poor Policy*, 131.

30. Porter et al., *Strengths of the Safety Net*, 21–23.

31. Robert Greenstein and Isaac Shapiro, "New Research Findings on the Effects of the Earned Income Tax Credit," Center on Budget and Policy Priorities (15 March 1998), 7, 5.

32. Anderson, "Taxation and Economic Justice."

33. See Rob Norton, "The Minimum Wage Is Unfair," *Fortune* (27 May 1996): 53; Blank, *It Takes a Nation*, 111–16.

34. Greenstein and Shapiro, "Earned Income Tax Credit," 8–13.

35. See table 3 on p. 115.

36. See also Anderson, "Taxation and Economic Justice." Danziger and Gottschalk (*America Unequal*, 60–62) also call for an expansion. For childless couples and single adults, see n. 25 above.

37. Danziger and Gottschalk, *America Unequal*, 165–66.

38. Nicholas Johnson et al., *State Income Tax Burdens on Low-Income Families in 1997*, Center on Budget and Policy Priorities (April 1998), and a press release from CBPP, 13 April 1998.

39. See the EITC "Campaign Outreach Strategy Guide" available from the Center on Budget and Policy Priorities (see list of organizations).

40. Bread for the World Institute, *The Changing Politics of Hunger: Hunger 1999* (Silver Spring, Md.: Bread for the World Institute, 1999), 59.

41. The projected expenditures for 1998 were food stamps ($24.5 billion); EITC ($21.7 billion); TANF ($21.8 billion). Committee on Ways and Means, *1998 Green Book* (Washington, D.C.: U.S. Government Printing Office, 1998), 1359.

42. See BFWI, *Hunger 1999*, 57–61.

43. Correspondence, Kim Wade, Bread for the World Institute, 15 March 1999.

44. Schansberg, *Poor Policy*, 55–58; Blank, *It Takes a Nation*, 114. The Heritage Foundation says that because of the 1996 increase, 128,000 less entry-level job opportunities were available to teenagers; D. Mark Wilson, "Increasing the Mandated Minimum Wage," *Backgrounder* 1162 (5 March 1998): 2.

45. Blank, *It Takes a Nation*, 115. In 1986, 37 percent were teenagers, 20 percent were wives whose husbands worked, and 59 percent were under twenty-five (Mead, *New Politics of Poverty*, 20).

46. *The New York Times*, 31 March 1996, sect. 4, p. 3.

47. Danziger and Gottschalk, *America Unequal*, 196, n. 14.

48. *The New York Times*, 31 March 1996, sect. 4, p. 3.

49. There is also an important more technical problem. If the EITC is huge, then work disincentives are substantial at the income levels at which the EITC is phased out. Robert Greenstein, "Raising Families with a Full-Time Worker Out of Poverty," Center on Budget and Policy Priorities (8 May 1996), 2.

50. In 1968, the minimum wage in 1997 dollars was $6.81 (U.S. Department of Labor, Bureau of Labor Statistics, 15 January 1998). See the data in Blank, *It Takes a Nation*, 115.

51. Mead (*New Politics of Poverty*, 120–23) thinks this claim is greatly overstated.

52. Blank, *It Takes a Nation*, 262.

53. Daniel Moynihan, *Miles to Go: A Personal History of Social Policy* (Cambridge: Harvard Univ. Press, 1996), 47.

54. Sylvia Ann Hewlett and Cornel West, *The War against Parents*, 49.

55. For details of the law, see *1998 Green Book*, 678–81.

56. Danziger and Gottschalk, *America Unequal*, 163.

57. Ibid., 162–65; Blank, *It Takes a Nation*, 262–63. (Blank does not advocate an increase, but she does urge a program of assured child support, which I discuss and reject in the way she proposes it in my chapter on the family.)

58. With this, the EITC and the Home Ownership Tax Credit all being phased out over the same approximate range, there would be a substantial disincentive to earn more money.

59. For workers with more than two children, a portion is refundable.

60. Blank, *It Takes a Nation*, 58.

61. Between the ages of sixteen and sixty-four; Center for the Study of Social Policy, *World without Work: Causes and Consequences of Black Male Joblessness* (Washington, D.C.: Center for the Study of Social Policy, December 1994), 1.

62. Telephone call, 12 February 1999, with the Bureau of Labor Statistics.

63. Mead, *New Politics of Poverty*, 94. Figures are for the years 1970–90.

64. See William Julius Wilson, *The Truly Disadvantaged* (Chicago: Univ. of Chicago Press, 1987); and William Julius Wilson, *When Work Disappears: The World of the New Urban Poor* (New York: Knopf, 1996), especially 37–42.

65. Blank, *It Takes a Nation*, 189.

66. For example, Mead, *New Politics of Poverty*, ix, 85.

67. Ibid.

68. *Implementing Welfare in America's Cities: A 34-City Survey* (November 1997).

69. Mead, *New Politics of Poverty,* 59.

70. It is true that one such program (CETA) in the 1970s had serious problems, but evaluation shows that even that program also had significant success. See Clifford M. Johnson and Ana Carricchi Lopez, "Shattering the Myth of Failure," Center on Budget and Policy Priorities (5 December 1997), 22; and Danziger and Gottschalk, *America Unequal,* 170–71. Politically, of course, we must deal with the perceived failure of CETA; see Sheldon H. Danziger, Gary D. Sandefur, and Daniel H. Weinberg, eds., *Confronting Poverty: Prescriptions for Change* (Cambridge: Harvard Univ. Press, 1994), 12.

71. Johnson and Lopez, "Shattering the Myth," 23–24.

72. Ibid., 2–4. See also Danziger and Gottschalk's suggestion on how to correct past weaknesses (*America Unequal,* 170–71).

73. I largely follow and agree with Danziger and Gottschalk; ibid., 171–74. Many policy experts favor such a proposal—e.g., Michael Kaus, *The End of Equality* (New York: Basic Books, 1995), chap. 8; and David T. Ellwood, *Poor Support: Poverty in the American Family* (New York: Basic Books, 1988), 1242–45.

74. Danziger and Gottschalk, *American Unequal,* 171.

75. Johnson and Lopez, "Shattering the Myth," 20.

76. We need to experiment to find the optimal number of weeks people must first search for regular work, but they should not have to wait more than six to twelve weeks to become eligible for PSE. We should also carefully consider requiring everyone in PSE to take ten hours a week in improving job skills. The training should cost participants only a nominal fee.

77. $4.68 per hour (85 percent of minimum wage of $5.50) for 2,000 hours = $9,360. The 1998 poverty level for one person was $8,480.

78. A single mom who works thirty hours a week and has one child: $7,020 (wages) + $2,389 (EITC) + $1,486 (food stamps) + $1,125 (Dependent Care Tax Credit) + $400 (Child Tax Credit) = $12,420 - $537 (Social Security Taxes) = $11,883 (i.e., $648 above the poverty level). Two-parent family of four with parents working a combined forty hours: $9,360 (wages) + $3,756 (EITC) + $3,132 (food stamps) + $3,000 (Dependent Care Tax Credit) + $800 (Child Tax Credit) = $20,048 - $716 (Social Security Taxes) = $19,332 (i.e., $2,802 above the poverty level).

79. Danziger and Gottschalk, *America Unequal,* 171–72.

80. Blank, *It Takes a Nation,* 118.

81. Ibid., 177. See also her call for continued experimentation in chap. 7 of Danziger, Sandefur, and Weinberg, *Confronting Poverty,* 200–201.

82. *Christianity Today* (7 September 1998), 21.

83. Skip Long, "The Jobs Partnership," *Call to Renewal Newsletter* 3, no. 2 (1998), 3, 7.

84. This story was supplied by Rev. Skip Long, executive director of Jobs Partnership.

85. See Joseph A. Maciariello, "Business and Empowerment," in *Toward a Just and Caring Society,* chap. 13.

86. Ibid.

87. Charles Colson, "Not Just a Janitor," *Breakpoint* (9 December 1991).

88. See the brief history of Christian participation in the emergence of unions in Perry Bush, "To Follow the Carpenter of Nazareth," *Sojourners* (September–October 1998): 28–32; William Bole, "Religion and Labor," *Working USA* (November–December 1998): 42–49; and William Bole and George Higgins, *Organized Labor and the Church* (New York: Paulist Press, 1993).

89. Pat McDonnell Twain, "In the Lap of Luxury," *Sojourners* (September–October 1998): 34–35.

90. Ibid., 35.

91. Helene Slessarev, "Organizing the Poor," in *Toward a Just and Caring Society,* chap. 12. ACORN—the Association of Community Organizations for Reform Now (117 W. Harrison Street, Chicago, IL 60605; tel.: 312-939-7488)—has a national campaign on the living wage.

92. Danziger and Gottschalk, *America Unequal,* 130.

93. Quoted in Patrick O'Neill, "Where No Union Has Gone Before," *Sojourners* (September–October 1998): 43. For further information write to Maria Rodriguez-Winter, FLOC, 1221 Broadway Street, Toledo, OH 43609.

94. Slessarev, "Organizing the Poor."

95. See Ronald J. Sider, *Rich Christians in an Age of Hunger* (Dallas: Word, 1997), 245–46.

Chapter 5: Broken Families and Rising Poverty

1. Carol J. DeVita, "The United States at Mid-Decade," *Population Bulletin* 50, no. 4 (March 1996): 38.

2. For this chapter, I rely especially upon David P. Gushee's fine chapter, "Rebuilding Marriage and the Family," in *Toward a Just and Caring Society: Christian Responses to Poverty in America,* ed. David P. Gushee (Grand Rapids: Baker, 1999), chap. 15. When not otherwise indicated, statistics used in my chapter are from Gushee's carefully documented piece.

3. William A. Galston, "Putting Children First," *The American Educator* (summer 1992): 12.

4. David Popenoe, "The Controversial Truth," *The New York Times,* 26 December 1992; Gushee, n. 39.

5. William J. Bennett, John J. DiIulio Jr., and John P. Walters, *Body Count: Moral Poverty . . . and How to Win America's War against Crime and Drugs* (New York: Simon and Schuster, 1996), 201.

6. Quoted in Daniel Moynihan, *Miles to Go: A Personal History of Social Policy* (Cambridge: Harvard Univ. Press, 1996), 152. Moynihan's 1965 report ("The Negro Family") is reprinted in Lee Rainwater and William L. Yancey, *The Moynihan Report and the Politics of Controversy* (Cambridge: MIT Press, 1967). Moynihan was using 1963 statistics (p. 54).

7. The figure was 33 percent in 1994 and 32 percent in 1995; table 1347, *Statistical Abstract of the United States 1998* (Department of Commerce).

8. Moynihan, *Miles to Go,* 227, citing 1994 data from the June 1996 Monthly Vital Statistics Report of the National Center for Health Statistics.

9. *Fatherhood Today* (winter 1998–99), 9.

10. Moynihan, *Miles to Go,* 227.

11. Quoted in ibid., 224.

12. See the excellent monograph by David Orgon Coolidge, *Same-Sex Marriage?* Crossroads Monograph, no. 9 (Wynnewood, Pa.: Evangelicals for Social Action, 1996), available from ESA, 10 E. Lancaster Avenue, Wynnewood, PA 19096; tel.: 800-650-6600.

13. That includes rejecting the slander that gays and lesbians are largely responsible for the decline of the family. The family has declined largely because of the failures and sins of the 95 to 97 percent majority that are heterosexual. See the excellent book by Stanley Grenz, *Welcoming but Not Affirming* (Nashville: John Knox/Westminster, 1999).

14. I owe this story to Cathy Brechtelsbauer.

15. For the extensive literature on biblical feminism, the equality of women, and mutual submission in marriage, see Rebecca Merrill Groothuis, *Good News for Women* (Grand Rapids: Baker, 1997); Gretchen Gaebelein Hull, *Equal to Serve* (Grand Rapids: Baker, 1998); Elaine Storkey, *What's Right with Feminism* (London: SPCK, 1985); Craig Keener, *Paul, Women and Wives* (Peabody, Mass.: Hendrickson, 1992). See also the extensive bibliographies and other publications of Christians for Biblical Equality, 122 West Franklin Avenue, Suite 218, Minneapolis, MN 55404-2451.

16. Committee on Ways and Means, *1998 Green Book* (Washington, D.C.: U.S. Government Printing Office, 1998), 1256.

17. Gushee, "Rebuilding Marriage."

18. Charts 96 and 97, *Statistical Abstract of the United States 1997* (Department of Commerce), 78.

19. William Raspberry, "Hollowed Communities," *Washington Post,* 19 November 1993. When I tried to confirm this with the Census Bureau, I was told the data is not available. Charles Murray, *Losing Ground: American Social Policy, 1950–1980* (New York: Basic Books, 1984), 129, cites similar decennial census figures for 1950 (78%) and 1940 (77%). See also, ibid., 262.

20. Robert Rector and William F. Lauber, *America's Failed $5.4 Trillion War on Poverty* (Washington, D.C.: The Heritage Foundation, 1995), 31.

21. Moynihan, *Miles to Go,* 227.

22. Table 66, *Statistical Abstract of the United States 1998,* 60.

23. *Fatherhood Today* (winter 1998–99), 9.

24. 1996 figures; *Statistical Abstract of the United States 1997,* 63, chart 75.

25. Nancy Dreher, "Divorce and the American Family," *Current Health* 2 (November 1996): 6.

26. See, for example, Christopher Jencks, *Rethinking Social Policy, Race, Poverty and the Underclass* (New York: Harper Perennial, 1992), 133–36; and Moynihan, *Miles to Go,* 150 (for high school texts).

27. Sylvia Ann Hewlett and Cornel West, *The War against Parents: What We Can Do for America's Beleaguered Moms and Dads* (Boston: Houghton Mifflin, 1998), 35 (their italics).

28. See Rebecca M. Blank, *It Takes a Nation: A New Agenda for Fighting Poverty* (Princeton, N.J.: Princeton Univ. Press, 1997), 37–38.

29. Lester C. Thurow, *The Future of Capitalism: How Today's Economic Forces Will Shape Tomorrow's World* (New York: W. Morrow, 1996), 31. See all of 31–34 and his conclusion that "changes within capitalism are making the family and the market less and less compatible" (p. 34).

30. William Julius Wilson, *When Work Disappears: The World of the New Urban Poor* (New York: Knopf, 1996), chap. 4, especially 95–98.

31. Juliet B. Schor, *The Overworked American* (New York: HarperCollins, 1992), 10–13 and elsewhere.

32. Hewlett and West, *The War against Parents,* 99.

33. Ibid., 103–4, using Eugene Steuerle, "The Tax Treatment of Households of Different Size," in *Taxing the Family,* ed. Rudolph G. Penner (Washington, D.C.: American Enterprise Institute, 1983), 74. The expanding EITC has partially offset this loss at the lower-income end.

34. Hewlett and West, *The War against Parents,* 108–9.

35. Ibid., 76–83.

36. *1998 Green Book,* table G-11, 1256 (1995 figures).

37. Ibid., table H-1, 1299 (1996 figures).

38. Quoted in Gushee, "Rebuilding Marriage."

39. See the studies cited in *Propositions* 1 (spring 1998): 7–9.

40. Gushee, "Rebuilding Marriage."

41. Richard R. Peterson, "A Re-Evaluation of the Economic Consequence of Divorce," *American Sociological Review* 61 (June 1996): 528–36. See the discussion (including William Galston's similar findings) in Gushee, "Rebuilding Marriage."

42. William A. Galston, "Putting Children First," 13.

43. Judith S. Wallerstein and Sandra Blakeslee, *Second Chances: Men, Women, and Children a Decade after Divorce* (New York: Ticknor and Fields, 1989), 18.

44. Gushee, "Rebuilding Marriage."

45. See in addition to Wallerstein and Blakeslee's *Second Chances,* Paul R. Amato and Alan Booth, *A Generation at Risk* (Cambridge: Harvard Univ. Press, 1998); and David B. Larson et al., *The Costly Consequences of Divorce* (Rockville, Md.: National Institute for Health Care Research, n.d.).

46. Deborah A. Dawson, "Family Structure and Children's Health and Well-Being," *Journal of Marriage and the Family* 53, no. 3 (August 1991): 573ff.

47. Irwin Garfinkel and Sara S. McLanahan, *Single Mothers and Their Children* (Washington, D.C.: Urban Institute, 1986), 31.

48. Hewlett and West, *War against Parents,* 165.

49. Moynihan, *Miles to Go,* 149, refers to this argument, which he rejects! See also *Propositions* 1 (spring 1998): 4–8, and the literature cited there.

50. Quoted in Moynihan, *Miles to Go,* 150.

51. M. Anne Hill and June O'Neill, *Underclass Behaviors in the United States* (New York: City Univ. of New York, Baruch College, 1993), cited in Rector and Lauber, *War on Poverty,* 30, n. 62.

52. Cynthia C. Harper and Sara S. McLanahan, "Father Absence and Youth Incarceration," paper presented at the annual meeting of The American Sociological Association, San Francisco, August 1998; discussed in *Propositions* (fall 1998): 9–10.

53. *Propositions* (fall 1998): 10.

54. Quoted in Moynihan, *Miles to Go,* 149.

55. Quoted in ibid., 149–50.

56. Gushee, "Rebuilding Marriage."

57. Other religious communities—Jews, Muslims, etc.—can also play significant roles.

58. John W. Kennedy, "True Love Waits," *Power for Living* (27 December 1998), 1–7. For more information on True Love Waits, write to Richard Ross, Southern Baptist Sunday School Board, 901 Commerce Street, Nashville, TN 37203.

59. For example, The National Coalition against Pornography led by Dr. Jerry Kirk (800 Compton Road, Suite 9224, Cincinnati, OH 45231; tel.: 513-521-6227).

60. *A Call to Civil Society: Why Democracy Needs Moral Truths* (New York: Institute for American Values, 1998), 20.

61. Michael McManus, *Marriage Savers* (Grand Rapids: Zondervan, 1993). You can contact him at: Marriage Savers, 9311 Harrington Drive, Potomac, MD 20854. In addition to the books and organizations cited by McManus, see also Ronald J. Sider, *Living like Jesus* (Grand Rapids: Baker, 1999), chap. 3; and Glen Stassen and David P. Gushee, *Christian Ethics as Following Jesus* (Downers Grove, Ill: InterVarsity Press, 1999), chap. 9.

62. Hewlett and West, *War against Parents,* 242.

63. William A. Galston, "The Reinstitutionalization of Marriage: Political Theory and Public Policy," in *Promises to Keep: Decline and Renewal of Marriage in America,* ed. David Popenoe, Jean Bethke Elshtain, and David Blankenhorn (Lanham, Md.: Rowman and Littlefield, 1996), 285–87. See also the excellent monograph by Amy E. Black, *For the Sake of the Children: Reconstructing American Divorce Policy,* Crossroads Monograph, no. 2 (Wynnewood, Pa.: Evangelicals for Social Action, 1995).

64. One of the many factors that undermines educational opportunity for the poor is that poor families move frequently, thus requiring their children to switch schools often.

65. Quoted in Robert D. Carle and Louis A. DeCaro Jr., eds., *Signs of Hope in the City: Ministries of Community Renewal* (Valley Forge, Pa.: Judson Press, 1997), 138–39.

66. Including phase-out provisions.

67. *Call to Civil Society,* 25.

68. See Hewlett and West, *War against Parents,* 253.

69. *Call to Civil Society,* 24.

70. Ibid., 19.

71. Mark Wilson, "Flex Time for Families," F.Y.I. #132, The Heritage Foundation (26 February 1997).

72. See Blank, *It Takes a Nation*, 263–66 (who proposes limiting it to poor moms); and Sheldon H. Danziger and Peter Gottschalk, *America Unequal* (Cambridge: Harvard Univ. Press, 1995), 174–75.

73. See, for example, Mary Jo Bane and David T. Ellwood, *Welfare Realities* (Cambridge: Harvard Univ. Press, 1994), 154–57.

74. Quoted in Perry Glanzer, *Failing to Provide: Christian Reflection on America's Child Support Policies*, Crossroads Monograph, no. 6 (Wynnewood, Pa.: Evangelicals for Social Action, 1996), 39. This monograph provides a good overview of Assured Child Support proposals.

75. See 1996 welfare legislation; 1996 *Congressional Quarterly Almanac*, 6–16 to 6–17.

76. Glanzer, *Failing to Provide*, 43.

77. I would also favor extending the EITC to noncustodial fathers (who actually pay child support) at the same level it goes to single moms with children—up to at least 50 percent of the child support they pay. (The same should apply in the far less frequent cases of noncustodial mothers.)

Chapter 6: Does Justice Include Health Care for the Poor?

1. Census Bureau, Current Population Reports, P60-202, 1 September 1998. For this and much of the data in this chapter I am using the carefully documented chapter by Clarke E. Cochran, "Health Policy and the Poverty Trap," in *Toward a Just and Caring Society: Christian Responses to Poverty in America*, ed. David P. Gushee (Grand Rapids: Baker, 1999), chap. 8, and also Cochran's *Health Care Policy: Where Do We Go from Here?* Crossroads Monograph, no. 17 (Wynnewood, Pa.: Evangelicals for Social Action, 1997).

2. Katherine Swartz, "Dynamics of People without Insurance," *Journal of the American Medical Association* 271 (5 January 1994): 64–66.

3. Census Bureau, Current Population Report, P60-202, 1 September 1998.

4. 1995 figures; Committee on Ways and Means, *1998 Green Book* (Washington, D.C.: U.S. Government Printing Office, 1998), 1105.

5. See *1998 Green Book*, 1109.

6. Ibid., 1110.

7. Bureau of Labor Statistics, Contingent and Alternative Work Arrangements Survey, February 1997.

8. See the data cited in Cochran, "Poverty Trap."

9. Swartz, "Dynamics of People without Insurance," 64.

10. See the studies cited in Cochran, "Poverty Trap," and Cochran, *Health Care Policy*, 31, especially the review of the literature in *Health Affairs* 16 (January–February 1997): 90–105. See also Laurie Kaye Abraham, *Mama Might Be Better Off Dead: The Failure of Health Care in Urban America* (Chicago: Univ. of Chicago Press, 1993).

11. *The New York Times*, 9 April 1999, pp. A1, A16.

12. See the several studies cited in Cochran, "Poverty Trap," especially *Journal of the American Medical Association* 279 (3 June 1998): 1703–8.

13. See the studies in Cochran, "Poverty Trap."

14. Every other OECD nation except Canada (10.3 percent) spends less than 10 percent of GDP on health care; the United States spends 14.1 percent (1995); *1998 Green Book*, 1115.

15. See my *Good News and Good Works: A Theology for the Whole Gospel* (Grand Rapids: Baker, 1999), chap. 5.

16. See chap. 2, pp. 59–60.

17. See chap. 2, pp. 59–61.

18. See Daniel Callahan's attempt to define "basic services": *What Kind of Life?* (New York: Simon and Schuster, 1990), chap. 7; cf. also Cochran, "Poverty Trap."

19. *1998 Green Book,* 1109.

20. And the related flexible spending accounts for other medical expenses.

21. Eric D. Schansberg, *How Poor Government Policy Harms the Poor* (Boulder, Colo.: Westview Press, 1996), 75–76. See similarly Michael Kaus, *The End of Equality* (New York: Basic Books, 1995), 90.

22. Ibid., 76.

23. See Cochran, *Health Care Policy,* 41–44 for a short concise summary of Medicare and Medicaid.

24. Rebecca M. Blank, *It Takes a Nation: A New Agenda for Fighting Poverty* (Princeton, N.J.: Princeton Univ. Press, 1997), 165–66.

25. Frank J. Thompson and John J. DiIulio Jr., eds., *Medicaid and Devolution* (Washington, D.C.: Brookings Institution Press, 1998), 6.

26. Cochran, *Health Care Policy,* 49.

27. For a more extended analysis of next steps, I recommend two recent publications by Clarke E. Cochran, a specialist in health organization management: *Health Care Policy* and "Poverty Trap." Both are available from ESA, 10 E. Lancaster Avenue, Wynnewood, PA 19096; tel.: 800-650-6600.

28. According to the estimates of the Congressional Budget Office; see Cindy Mann and Jocelyn Guyer, "Overview of the New Child Health Block Grant," Center on Budget and Policy Priorities (6 January 1998), 18. CHIP's complex provisions are lucidly explained in this paper.

29. The basic health plan in Washington State offers something of a model at the state level. See James R. Tallon Jr. and Lawrence D. Brown, "Who Gets What?" in *Medicaid and Devolution,* 251–52.

30. David T. Ellwood, *Poor Support: Poverty in the American Family* (New York: Basic Books, 1988), 107, proposes something of this sort. Christopher Jencks, *Rethinking Social Policy, Race, Poverty and the Underclass* (New York: Harper Perennial, 1992), 234, suggests a premium set at 5 percent of income.

31. Steven A. Schroeder, "Doctors and Diversity: Improving the Health of Poor and Minority People," *Chronicle of Higher Education* (1 November 1996): B5.

32. See the several studies cited in the analysis of MSA's in a 21 July 1998 report from the Center on Budget and Policy Priorities, 2, n. 1.

33. A story given to me by Carl Holland, professor of social work, Illinois State University.

34. David Hilfiker, *Not All of Us Are Saints: A Doctor's Journey with the Poor* (New York: Hill and Wang, 1994).

35. Christian Community Health Fellowship, P.O. Box 23429, Chicago, IL 60623; tel.: 773-843-2700.

36. This includes federal and state expenditures. The figures in chap. 3, p. 87 refer only to *federal* expenditures.

Chapter 7: Quality Education for Everyone

1. Quoted in Daniel Moynihan, *Miles to Go: A Personal History of Social Policy* (Cambridge: Harvard Univ. Press, 1996), 140.

2. This chapter owes a special debt to Charles L. Glenn, professor of education at Boston University. See his "Family Choice of Schools: Making It Fair" (unpublished paper); and "Just Schools: Doing Right by Poor Kids," in *Toward a Just and Caring Society: Christian Responses to Poverty in America,* ed. David P. Gushee (Grand Rapids: Baker, 1999), chap. 10.

3. Quoted in Jonathan Kozol, *Savage Inequalities* (New York: Harper, 1991), 172.

4. Ibid.

5. Ibid., 138–39.

6. Quoted in ibid., 149.

7. Quoted in ibid., 167.

8. Quoted in ibid., 168.

9. Ibid., 167.

10. Quoted in ibid., 145.

11. In this chapter, I have chosen to focus on grades 1–12. Higher education, of course, is also important. Among other things, we ought to expand Pell grants to low-income college students.

12. Paul E. Peterson and Jay P. Greene, "Race Relations and Central City Schools: It's Time for an Experiment with Vouchers," *Brookings Review* (spring 1998): 34.

13. Paul E. Peterson and Bryan C. Hassel, eds., *Learning from School Choice* (Washington, D.C.: Brookings Institution Press, 1998), 13.

14. Kozol, *Savage Inequalities,* 58.

15. Ibid., 118.

16. National Center for Education, *Dropout Rates in the United States: 1996* (Washington, D.C.: U.S. Department of Education, 1997), 14.

17. 1992 data; U.S. Department of Education, *The Educational Progress of Hispanic Students* (1995), 5; *The Educational Progress of Black Students* (1995), 4.

18. *Progress of Hispanic Students,* 18; *Progress of Black Students,* 16.

19. E. D. Hirsch Jr., *The Schools We Need: Why We Don't Have Them* (New York: Doubleday, 1996), 42. The Coleman Report in 1966 showed that minority students started school with an educational deficiency compared to white students and the gap increased as they continued in school. Moynihan, *Miles to Go,* 169.

20. Hirsch, *The Schools We Need,* 42.

21. U.S. Department of Labor News, 1 May 1998. The precise figures are 19.8 percent, 11.1 percent, and 2.1 percent.

22. Hirsch, *The Schools We Need,* 43.

23. Ibid., 45.

24. Ronald F. Ferguson, "Shifting Challenges: Fifty Years of Economic Change toward Black-White Earnings Equality," *Daedalus* 124 (winter 1995): 66–67.

25. *Educational Progress of Hispanic Students,* 8–9.

26. *Educational Progress of Black Students,* 9.

27. Deborah A. Dawson, "Family Structure and Children's Health and Well-Being," *Journal of Marriage and the Family* 53, no. 3 (August 1991): 573ff.

28. *Statistical Abstract of the United States 1997* (Department of Commerce), 78.

29. Tufts University School of Nutrition Science and Policy, *The Link Between Nutrition and Cognitive Development in Children* (1998), 3, 5.

30. See the studies cited in Glenn, "Just Schools."

31. John E. Chubb and Terry M. Moe, *Politics, Markets and America's Schools* (Washington, D.C.: Brookings Institution Press, 1990), 186–87.

32. Ibid., 212–15.

33. "Choice System Helps Schools in East Harlem," *The New York Times,* 24 February 1998, p. B1.

34. Chester E. Finn, quoted in Glenn, "Just Schools."

35. See Glenn, "Just Schools."

36. See for this story, Kozol, *Savage Inequalities,* 214–29.

37. *The New York Times,* 3 October 1989; Kozol, *Savage Inequalities,* 225, 253.

38. CDF, *State of America's Children 1998,* 50. This figure is adjusted for regional differences and extra (outside) funds for special needs.

39. *Inequalities in Public School Revenues,* 11. This report adjusts the figures on general revenues available to each district by (a) factoring in differing costs in divergent regions, and (b) adding state and federal funds targeted for special needs. I use the adjusted figures.

40. Ibid., 23.

41. Ibid., 13, 21.

42. Linda Darling-Hammond, "Unequal Opportunity: Race and Education," *Brookings Review* (spring 1998): 31.

43. CDF, *State of America's Children 1998,* 50.

44. *Wall Street Journal,* 17 December 1993, p. A14.

45. Glenn, "Just Schools." See also The Coleman Report (1966); Hirsch, *The Schools We Need,* 21; Susan Mayer, *What Money Can't Buy* (Cambridge: Harvard Univ. Press, 1998).

46. Eric A. Hanushek, "Outcomes, Costs and Incentives in Schools," in *Improving America's Schools: The Role of Incentives,* ed. Eric A. Hanushek and Dale W. Jorgensen (Washington, D.C.: National Academy Press, 1996), 40–41.

47. Joel Belz, "Separating Church, State," *World* (4 March 1995), 3.

48. Laura Lippmann, Shelley Burns, and Edith McArthur, *Urban Schools: The Challenge of Location and Poverty* (Washington, D.C.: U.S. Department of Education, 1996), 2–3, 29, 39; Glenn, "Just Schools."

49. The federal government could provide some of the funding, but the states should retain their constitutional responsibility and authority for education. After I completed this chapter, the *Atlantic Monthly* published "A Bold Experiment to Fix City Schools" (July 1999): 15–31, calling for a "major multi-year test of vouchers."

50. Personal correspondence and telephone call. For the AFT's proposals, write to American Federation of Teachers, 555 New Jersey Avenue NW, Washington, D.C. 20001.

51. Harvard professor Paul E. Peterson offers an excellent overview of both sides in "School Choice: A Report Card," in *Learning from School Choice,* 3–32.

52. Peterson, "School Choice," 11.

53. Peterson and Greene, "Race Relations," 34–35. See the additional polls cited in Glenn, "Family Choice."

54. 1997 National Opinion Poll—Children's Issues, The Joint Center for Political and Economic Studies, 1090 Vermont Avenue NW, Suite 1100, Washington, D.C. 20005.

55. Susan P. Choy, *Public and Private Schools* (Washington, D.C.: National Center for Education Statistics, 1997), 5–6. See Glenn, "Family Choice," 1–4.

56. James S. Coleman and Thomas Hoffer, *Public and Private High Schools* (New York: Basic Books, 1987), 213. See also Glenn, "Family Choice," 12–14.

57. Glenn, "Family Choice," 13.

58. Anthony S. Bryk, Valerie E. Lee, and Peter B. Holland, *Catholic Schools and the Common Good* (Cambridge: Harvard Univ. Press, 1993), 57, 247.

59. Peterson, "School Choice," 23.

60. Jay P. Greene and Paul E. Peterson, "School Choice Data Rescued from Bad Science," *Wall Street Journal,* 14 August 1996. An earlier methodologically flawed study (widely cited by the AFT) said this program had no positive results. See the longer study by Jay P. Greene, Paul E. Peterson, and Jiangtao Du, "School Choice in Milwaukee," in *Learning from School Choice,* 335–56.

61. Choy, *Public and Private Schools,* 10–13, 16.

62. Ibid., 8, 14, 18.

63. Peterson, "School Choice," 17.

64. Choy, *Public and Private Schools,* 19. See the similar findings on the Cleveland voucher experiment; *The New York Times,* 18 September 1997, p. A16.

65. National Center for Education Statistics, *Digest of Education Statistics 1997,* tables 61, 168. In Catholic schools, tuition covers about 62 percent of the total costs at the elementary school level and about 75 percent at the secondary level; *United States Catholic Elementary and Secondary Schools, 1997–1998* (Washington, D.C.: National Catholic Educational Association, 1998),

14. It is also important to recognize that one significant aspect of the lower costs in private schools is the very low teachers' salaries, which ought to be raised.

66. *Newsweek*, 2 September 1996, 27.

67. Peterson and Greene, "Race Relations," 36.

68. "Review and Outlook," *Wall Street Journal*, 25 October 1993, p. A20.

69. See the evidence cited in John E. Brandl, "Governance and Educational Quality," in *Learning from School Choice*, 55–82.

70. Glenn, "Just Schools."

71. *Rapport sur l'état de la liberté d'enseignement dans le monde* (Geneva: Organisation internationale pour le développement de la liberté d'enseignement, 1995). Most Canadian provinces fund some parental choice of religious schools, but the situation varies widely from generous support in British Columbia and Quebec to little support in the Maritime provinces.

72. Peterson and Greene, "Race Relations," 36–37.

73. Christian Smith and David Sikkink, "Is Private School Privatizing?" *First Things* (April 1999): 16–20.

74. Alan Peshkin, *God's Choice: The Total World of a Fundamentalist Christian School* (Chicago: Univ. of Chicago Press, 1989), 329, 274, 332–34.

75. Glenn, "Family Choice," 29.

76. Peterson and Greene, "Race Relations," 36.

77. *Private Schools in the United States: A Statistical Profile, 1990–91* (Washington, D.C.: National Center for Education, 1995), table 2.5.

78. Peterson, "School Choice," 27.

79. Quoted in ibid., 26.

80. See Stephen Monsma, *When Sacred and Secular Mix* (Lanham, Md.: Rowman and Littlefield, 1996); and the two articles by Sider and Unruh cited in chap. 3, n. 21.

81. See, for example, decisions in *Witters* (1986), *Zobrest* (1993), *Rosenberger* (1995), *Agostini* (1997), and the decision *not* to hear an appeal against the Milwaukee voucher plan in 1998. See further Section Five on constitutional issues in Peterson and Hassel, *Learning from School Choice*, 395–428.

82. Available from ESA, 10 E. Lancaster Avenue, Wynnewood, PA 19096.

83. Peterson, "School Choice," 28.

84. Quoted in ibid., 28.

85. Further information about this proposal is available from ESA, 10 E. Lancaster Avenue, Wynnewood, PA 19096.

Chapter 8: Could Welfare Empower the Poor?

1. Janice A. Cardano, "Reflections of a Child on Welfare," in Bread for the World Institute, *The Changing Politics of Hunger: Hunger 1999* (Silver Spring, Md.: Bread for the World Institute, 1999), 81. Janice has an M.A. from UCLA and works at Bread for the World Institute. For an excellent account of how welfare mothers struggle, see Kathryn Edin and Laura Lein, *Making Ends Meet: How Single Mothers Survive Welfare and Low-Wage Work* (New York: Russell Sage Foundation, 1997). For a vivid portrayal of different types of people on welfare, see Jill Duerr Berrick, *Faces of Poverty: Portraits of Women and Children on Welfare* (New York: Oxford Foundation, 1995).

2. April 10, 1999, press release by the Administration for Children and Families, U.S. Department of Health and Human Services; www.acf.dhhs.gov/news/stats/aug-sep.htm.

3. BFWI, *Hunger 1999*, 65.

4. See Sharon Parrott, "How Much Do We Spend on 'Welfare'?" Center on Budget and Policy Priorities (4 August 1995).

5. Calculations based on tables 1–6, Committee on Ways and Means, *1998 Green Book* (Washington, D.C.: U.S. Government Printing Office, 1998), 1359.

6. "What Corporate Welfare Costs You," *Time*, 9 November 1998, cover story.

7. The projected total for 1998 was $93.9 billion; *1998 Green Book*, 1359.

8. For good overviews, see David T. Ellwood, *Poor Support: Poverty in the American Family* (New York: Basic Books, 1988), 26–44; Mary Jo Bane and David T. Ellwood, *Welfare Realities* (Cambridge: Harvard Univ. Press, 1994), 1–27; and, more briefly and tendentiously, Robert Rector and William F. Lauber, *America's Failed $5.4 Trillion War on Poverty* (Washington, D.C.: The Heritage Foundation, 1995), 11–22.

9. Quoted in Michael Kaus, *The End of Equality* (New York: Basic Books, 1995), 109.

10. Quoted in ibid., 110 (Kaus's italics).

11. Ibid., 111.

12. Ellwood, *Poor Support*, 63.

13. Many other factors, of course, contributed to this result. See chap. 5.

14. James Patterson, *America's Struggle against Poverty, 1900–1980* (Cambridge: Harvard Univ. Press, 1980), 179.

15. Ellwood, *Poor Support*, 32, 38–39 (1984 dollars).

16. 1994 dollars; Rebecca M. Blank, *It Takes a Nation: A New Agenda for Fighting Poverty* (Princeton, N.J.: Princeton Univ. Press, 1997), 99–100.

17. Bane and Ellwood, *Welfare Realities*, 15–19.

18. Edin and Lein, *Making Ends Meet*.

19. Bane and Ellwood, *Welfare Realities*, 23–27.

20. *1998 Green Book*, 402, 413.

21. Ellwood, *Poor Support*, 23. See further David T. Ellwood and Mary Jo Bane, "The Impact of AFDC on Family Structure and Living Arrangements," *Research in Labor Economics* 7 (1985): 137–207; Robert Moffitt, "Incentive Effects of the U.S. Welfare System: A Review," *Journal of Economic Literature* 20 (March 1992): 1–61; the critique of Marvin Olasky in Kurt C. Schaefer, "The Privatizing of Compassion," in *Toward a Just and Caring Society: Christian Responses to Poverty in America*, ed. David P. Gushee (Grand Rapids: Baker, 1999), chap. 5; Blank, *It Takes a Nation*, 142–61; Peter Gottschalk, Sara McLanahan, and Gary D. Sandefur, "The Dynamics and Inter-generational Transmission of Poverty and Welfare Participation," in *Confronting Poverty: Prescriptions for Change*, ed. Sheldon H. Danziger, Gary D. Sandefur, and Daniel H. Weinberg (Cambridge: Harvard Univ. Press, 1994), chap. 4.

22. Rector and Lauber, *War on Poverty*, 27 (see all of 23–33); Michael Tanner, *The End of Welfare* (Washington, D.C.: Cato Institute, 1996), 69–94, especially the recent studies on out-of-wedlock births on 78–80.

23. Quoted in Daniel Moynihan, *Miles to Go: A Personal History of Social Policy* (Cambridge: Harvard Univ. Press, 1996), 32.

24. Ellwood, *Poor Support*, 22.

25. Quoted in Moynihan, *Miles to Go*, 29.

26. See the detailed summaries in the *Congressional Quarterly 1996 Almanac* (Washington, D.C.: Congressional Quarterly, 1997), 6-13 to 6-21; *Congressional Quarterly 1997 Almanac*, 2-57 to 2-58, 6-31 to 6-36; and Stanley W. Carlson-Thies, "Transforming American Welfare," in *Toward a Just and Caring Society*, chap. 14.

27. BFWI, *Hunger 1999*, 61.

28. *Congressional Quarterly 1997 Almanac*, 6-31.

29. Carlson-Thies, "Transforming American Welfare."

30. See n. 2 and *1998 Green Book*, 413.

31. *1998 Green Book*, 413.

32. Raymond Hernandez, "Most Dropped from Welfare Don't Get Jobs," *The New York Times*, 23 March 1998, pp. A1, B6; Barbara Vobejda and Judith Haveman, "Sanctions," *Washington Post*, 23 March 1998, pp. A1, A10; Jason DeParle, "What Welfare-to-Work Really Means," *The New York Times Magazine*, 20 December 1998, 50–89. A 1998 report prepared by

the Children's Defense Fund and the National Coalition for the Homeless says that many who have moved from welfare to work are worse off than before: *Welfare to What? Early Findings on Family Hardship and Well-Being.*

33. From a survey of Catholic parishes by Catholic Charities USA (19 March 1999). The U.S. Conference of Mayors' 1998 survey discovered a similar patter (http://www.bread.org /action/hunger.html 4/1/99).

34. See the excellent analysis in Heidi Rolland Unruh, "Welfare Reform's First Birthday," *PRISM* (January–February 1999): 8–11, 17–18.

35. See Carlson-Thies's critique in "Transforming American Welfare."

36. Unfortunately, careful studies have discovered that large numbers of people eligible for transitional Medicaid as they moved from welfare to work actually lost their Medicaid coverage. Robert Pear, "Poor Workers Lose Medicaid Coverage Despite Eligibility," *The New York Times,* 12 April 1999, pp. A1, A21.

37. For an excellent foundational examination of welfare policy, see Stanley W. Carlson-Thies and James W. Skillen, eds., *Welfare in America: Christian Perspectives on a Policy in Crisis* (Grand Rapids: Eerdmans, 1996). See also Warren R. Copeland, *And the Poor Get Welfare* (Nashville: Abingdon, 1994).

38. While they are not to blame for the way I adapt their material, this section depends significantly on Ellwood, *Poor Support,* 11–12, and Bane and Ellwood, *Welfare Realities,* 28–66.

39. The word *healthy* in categories 2, 3, and 4 does not overlook the fact that some people struggle with significant physical and emotional problems, but it means that they are not sufficiently disabled to be eligible for disability payments (category 5 people are eligible).

40. 1990 data; Daniel T. Lichter and Erica L. Gardner, "Welfare Reform and the Poor Children of Working Parents," *Focus* (UW-MIRP) 18, no. 2 (fall/winter 1996–97): 65.

41. Ellwood, *Poor Support,* 103. Government transfers include EITC, food stamps, etc. The situation is somewhat improved since 1988 when Ellwood wrote this, thanks to significant increases in the EITC in the 1990s.

42. Bane and Ellwood, *Welfare Realities,* 157.

43. Ibid., 54.

44. Ibid., 61.

45. Ellwood, *Poor Support,* 148.

46. Bane and Ellwood, *Welfare Realities,* 39.

47. Ibid.

48. Ibid., 48.

49. Ibid., 40–41.

50. *1998 Green Book,* 532.

51. Blank, *It Takes a Nation,* 103–5.

52. $24 billion (SSI) in 1996 compared to $17.6 billion for AFDC; *1998 Green Book,* 1359.

53. Lawrence M. Mead, *The New Politics of Poverty* (New York: Basic Books, 1992), 238–39.

54. The following is my argument, not Mead's. For Mead, see his "The Poverty Debate and Human Nature," in *Welfare in America,* 209–42.

55. For the following, see Joseph A. Maciariello, "Business and Empowerment," in *Toward a Just and Caring Society,* chap. 13, and the material in n. 58.

56. GSM is actually one of the four Love, Inc., affiliates in Ottawa County (together the four affiliates relate to 250 churches), but GSM was asked to coordinate the mentoring services for all four. Love, Inc., is a part of World Vision, U.S. For their work on welfare, see www.churchesatwork.org.

57. Bill Raymond in a speech in Philadelphia on 12 December 1998.

58. An unpublished packet of informational materials on GSM, 14, available from Good Samaritan Ministries, 513 E. Eighth Street, Suite 25, Holland, MI 49423.

59. Amy L. Sherman, "Getting to Work: Church Based Responses to Welfare Reform," *PRISM* (January–February 1999): 12–16.

60. Write to Bridge of Hope, P.O. Box 1223, Coatesville, PA 19320; tel.: 610-380-1360. The details and quotations used above come from personal correspondence with the executive director, Edith Yoder. See also their book of stories: Valerie Weaver, *Amazing Hope: A Ministry of Friendship to Homeless Families* (Morgantown, Pa.: Masthof Press, 1998).

61. For a list, see Sherman, "Getting to Work"; and the Welfare Information Network at www.welfareinfo.org/faith.htm, especially Jessica Yates's March 1998 report "Partnerships with the Faith Community in Welfare Reform." See also Amy L. Sherman's "Establishing an Effective, Church-Based, Welfare-to-Work Mentoring Ministry: A Practical 'How-To' Guide," Trinity Presbyterian Church, P.O. Box 5102, Charlottesville, VA 22905.

62. See Amy L. Sherman's helpful suggestions in *Restorers of Hope: Reaching the Poor in Your Community with Church-Based Ministries That Work* (Wheaton: Crossway, 1997), and World Vision's Churches at Work web site at www.churchesatwork.org.

63. See Luis E. Lugo, *Equal Partners: The Welfare Responsibility of Governments and Churches* (Washington, D.C.: Center for Public Justice, 1998).

64. See the excellent (unpublished working) paper, Wendell E. Primus and Esther Rosenbaum, "Increasing Child Well-Being by Increasing Earnings of Non-custodial Parents and Encouraging Stronger Attachment to Their Children," Center on Budget and Policy Priorities (1998); and Wendell E. Primus and Charita L. Castro, "A State Strategy for Increasing Child Support," Center on Budget and Policy Priorities (22 February 1999).

65. See some beginning programs described in Jason DeParle, "Welfare Overhaul Initiatives Focus on Fathers," *The New York Times*, 3 September 1998, pp. A1, A28.

66. See Ellwood's discussion of transitional assistance, *Poor Support*, 121–23, 178–83.

67. This is not always the case. Edin and Lein *(Making Ends Meet)* found that if mothers worked at very low wages, their families experienced more hardship than families on welfare.

68. Mothers with young children between the ages of one and six should not have to work more than twenty to thirty hours a week.

69. Bane and Ellwood, *Welfare Realities*, 160; Ellwood, *Poor Support*, 180.

70. Ellwood, *Poor Support*, chap. 6. And the situation is worse now than in 1988 when he published this book.

71. 1996 figures; *1998 Green Book,* 1299.

72. Blank, *It Takes a Nation*, 28–29 (Blank's figures are from 1990).

73. Ellwood, *Poor Support,* 214. See also Glenn C. Loury, "Discrimination in the Post–Civil Rights Era," *Journal of Economic Perspectives* 12, no. 2 (spring 1998).

74. See Ronald J. Sider, *Cup of Water, Bread of Life* (Grand Rapids: Zondervan, 1994), chaps. 4 and 8, for detailed accounts.

75. Many are newer and therefore smaller than Lawndale and Circle. For information, write to Christian Community Development Association, 3848 W. Ogden Avenue, Chicago, IL 60623.

76. For example, Joe Klein, "In God They Trust," *The New Yorker* (16 June 1997): 40–48.

77. "Supporting Black Churches," *Brookings Review* (spring 1998): 47.

78. Details of this story come from personal conversation with Mary Nelson, founder and executive director of Bethel New Life. For more information see their web site at www.bethel newlife.org.

Chapter 9: Other Important Issues Affecting the Poor

1. For this translation, see chap. 2, pp. 59–60.

2. There are, of course, many other subjects that I do not even mention: for example, housing for the poor, gambling, and the concentration of toxic sites and environmental pol-

lution in poorer neighborhoods. On housing, see Karen Hosler Kispert, "Affordable Housing Zone Ahead," Crossroads Monograph, no. 7 (Wynnewood, Pa.: Evangelicals for Social Action, 1996). On toxic waste in poor communities, see Robert D. Bullard, ed., *Unequal Protection: Environmental Justice and Communities of Color* (San Francisco: Sierra Club, 1994); Philip J. Landrigan, "Children's Health and the Environment—the Vital Connection," *Creation Care* (spring 1999).

3. William J. Bennett, John J. DiIulio Jr., and John P. Walters, *Body Count: Moral Poverty . . . and How to Win America's War against Crime and Drugs* (New York: Simon and Schuster, 1996), 22.

4. Ibid., 35–36.

5. Ibid., chap. 2, especially 60–64.

6. Ibid., 61–62.

7. I owe most of the following to John J. DiIulio Jr., although I am responsible for my adaptation of his ideas.

8. Quoted in *Newsweek,* 1 June 1998, 25.

9. See the "Ten Point Plan to Mobilize the Churches" available from Ella J. Baker House, 411 Washington Street, Dorchester, MA 02124.

10. For information, write to Dr. Dean Trulear, One Commerce Square, 2005 Market Street, Suite 900, Philadelphia, PA 19103; tel.: 215-557-4400.

11. Table 1364, *Statistical Abstract of the United States 1998,* 841 (1996 data).

12. Iris J. Lav, "Information and Misinformation about Federal Tax Burdens," Center on Budget and Policy Priorities (21 January 1999). It is true that total federal tax revenues have increased as a percent of the GDP, but that is because the soaring stock market has greatly increased capital gains income and therefore tax revenues, but capital gains income is not counted in the GDP. Ibid.

13. Robert Greenstein and Iris J. Lav, "Proposed 10% Tax Cut," Center on Budget and Policy Priorities (21 January 1999), and "Proposed 10% Income Tax Rate Cut," Citizens for Tax Justice (20 January 1999).

14. For this section, I am summarizing John E. Anderson, "Taxation and Economic Justice," in *Toward a Just and Caring Society: Christian Responses to Poverty in America,* ed. David P. Gushee (Grand Rapids: Baker, 1999), chap. 9.

15. 820 First Street NE, Suite 510, Washington, D.C. 20002; tel.: 202-408-1080; www.cbpp.org.

16. Center on Budget and Policy Priorities (17 March 1998).

17. Kathryn Porter, Wendell Primus, Lynette Rawlings, and Esther Rosenbaum, *Strengths of the Safety Net* (Washington, D.C.: Center on Budget and Policy Priorities, 1998), 29.

18. The Congressional Research Service of the Library of Congress has two excellent short overviews: *Social Security: Brief Facts and Statistics* (94-27 EPW; updated 2 November 1998) and *Current Social Security Issues* (96-43 EPW; updated 21 May 1998). Your congressperson can get you a free copy. In fact, ask for the full Congressional Research Service's packet on Social Security.

19. Wendell Primus, "The Strengths of Social Security," Center on Budget and Policy Priorities (n.d.).

20. It is actually more complex. Current payroll taxes provide a surplus ($2 out of every $15) that is invested in U.S. treasury bonds.

21. *Current Social Security Issues,* 2.

22. From a draft statement on Social Security by the Catholic bishops; for a copy, contact the United States Catholic Conference, Nancy Wisdo, Director, Office of Domestic Social Development, 3211 Fourth Street NE, Washington, D.C. 20017; tel.: 202-541-3187.

23. *Social Security: Brief Facts and Statistics,* 10.

24. Center on Budget and Policy Priorities (8 April 1999), 1–2; and *The New York Times,* 9 April 1999, p. A16.

25. Two widely discussed reports by the Heritage Foundation argued the opposite, but a careful analysis of their work by the Office of the Chief Actuary of the Social Security Administration pointed out many flaws and concluded that "the non-white population actually enjoys the same or better expected rates of return from Social Security than for the white population." Quoted in Kilolo Kijakazi, "African-Americans, Hispanic Americans and Social Security," Center on Budget and Policy Priorities (8 October 1998), 2.

26. African Americans are 11 percent of the labor force but account for 18 percent of workers receiving disability. Ibid., 4.

27. Primus, "Strengths of Social Security."

28. For a pro-privatization argument from a libertarian perspective, see Peter J. Ferrara and Michael Tanner, *A New Deal for Social Security* (Washington, D.C.: Cato Institute, 1998).

29. Senator Rick Santorum emphasizes this point. Santorum wants to direct from 2 to 5 percent of the current 12.4 percent payroll tax into personal retirement accounts. He says his proposal would guarantee minimum benefits similar to existing ones even if one's personal account did poorly. But it is not clear how all that can be done without raising taxes.

30. Studies by Henry Aaron at the Brookings Institution and Peter Diamond of M.I.T. See Kilolo Kijakazi, "The Shortcomings of Individual Accounts," Center on Budget and Policy Priorities (n.d.).

31. Gary L. Bauer, "Save Social Security, Save Our Families," *The New York Times,* 23 January 1997, op-ed page.

32. By adjusting the inflation indicator so it is more accurate, having an independent board invest some of the surplus trust funds in the private stock and bond market, slightly reducing benefits, and modestly expanding the earnings base subject to taxation, the Social Security Trust Fund can be made solvent through 2070. See Primus, "Strengths of Social Security," and many other documents from the Center on Budget and Policy Priorities.

33. Lawrence Mishel, Jared Bernstein, and John Schmitt, *The State of Working America, 1998–99* (Ithaca, N.Y.: Cornell Univ. Press, 1999), 262, 270.

34. Ibid., 271.

35. Michael Sherraden, *Assets and the Poor: A New American Welfare Policy* (Armonk, N.Y.: M. E. Sharpe, 1991); Jeffrey R. Gates, *The Ownership Solution: Toward a Shared Capitalism for the Twenty-First Century* (Reading, Mass.: Addison-Wesley, 1998); Bruce A. Ackerman and Anne Alstott, *The Stakeholder Society* (New Haven: Yale Univ. Press, 1999); and Richard B. Freeman, *The New Inequality: Creating Solutions for Poor America* (Boston: Beacon Press, 1999).

36. See John D. Mason, "The Good City: Inner-City Poverty and Metropolitan Responsibility," in *Toward a Just and Caring Society,* chap. 11.

37. See, for example, P. Jargowsky, *Poverty and Place: Ghettoes, Barrios, and the American City* (New York: Russell Sage Foundation, 1997), chap. 2.

38. Helene Slessarev, "Organizing the Poor," in *Toward a Just and Caring Society,* chap. 12.

39. The best known are Industrial Areas Foundation (220 W. Kinzie, Chicago, IL 60610; 312-245-9211) with fifty local organizations involving 1.5 million people; the Gamaliel Foundation (203 N. Wabash Avenue, Suite 808, Chicago, IL 60601; 312-357-2639) working especially in the Midwest; The Pacific Institute for Community Organizations (171 Santa Rosa Avenue, Oakland, CA 94610; 510-655-2801) active in seventy cities; and Direct Action and Resource Training (P.O. Box 370791, Miami, FL 33137; 305-576-8020).

40. Christians Supporting Community Organizing, 2444 Washington Street, Suite 202, Denver, CO 80205; 303-860-7747.

41. Quoted in Slessarev, "Organizing the Poor."

Chapter 10: We Can End the Scandal

1. Sylvia Ann Hewlett and Cornel West, *The War against Parents: What We Can Do for America's Beleaguered Moms and Dads* (Boston: Houghton Mifflin, 1998), 42–43.

2. Wayne L. Gordon, *Real Hope in Chicago* (Grand Rapids: Zondervan, 1995).

3. Ibid., 155–66.

4. See John Perkins, ed., *Restoring At-Risk Communities* (Grand Rapids: Baker, 1995). CCDA member organizations are listed in the appendix by state. CCDA, 3848 W. Ogden Avenue, Chicago, IL 60623. Not all six hundred members are as large as LCC.

5. See Catherine O. Sweeting, "Thus Far by Faith," in *Signs of Hope in the City: Ministries of Community Renewal,* ed. Robert D. Carle and Louis A. DeCaro Jr. (Valley Forge, Pa.: Judson Press, 1997), chap. 5 (there are many holistic models in this book); and Floyd Flake and Donna Marie Williams, *The Way of the Bootstrapper: Nine Action Steps for Achieving Your Dreams* (San Francisco: HarperSanFrancisco, 1999).

6. Samuel G. Freedman, *Upon This Rock: The Miracles of a Black Church* (New York: Harper, 1993).

7. G. Willis Bennett, *Guidelines for Effective Urban Church Ministry* (Nashville: Broadman, 1983).

8. See chap. 3, n. 21.

9. The Center for the Study of Values at Harvard Divinity School has produced a useful "Research Report on Faith-Based Organizations and Social Service Provision," February 1999.

10. See Ronald J. Sider, *Good News and Good Works: A Theology for the Whole Gospel* (Grand Rapids: Baker, 1999), especially chaps. 1 and 2, and Allen Sholes's "With Action and in Truth," *Moody* (November–December 1997), 21–28.

11. *Christianity Today* (16 June 1997), 60.

12. *Washington Post,* 18 October 1997.

13. Write to Tom Pelton, March for Jesus USA, P.O. Box 3216, Austin, TX 78764.

14. For example, Stephen Carter, *The Culture of Disbelief: How American Law and Politics Trivialize Religious Devotion* (New York: Basic Books, 1993).

15. See my forthcoming book (Baker) on how one moves from the Bible to political conclusions. Also, a six-lesson study guide (for Sunday school classes) called *Politics and the Bible* is available from ESA, 10 E. Lancaster Avenue, Wynnewood, PA 19096.

16. Hillary Rodham Clinton, *It Takes a Village* (New York: Simon and Schuster, 1996); Kay C. James, *Transforming America: From the Inside Out* (Grand Rapids: Zondervan, 1995); and Kay C. James, "Transforming America," *Imprimis* (February 1996): 1–7.

17. For more information, write to Southern Sector Initiative: Dallas Working Together, 2001 Ross Avenue, Suite 3500, Dallas, TX 75201-2997.

18. See the document, "We Hold These Truths," which has been frequently reprinted. See *PRISM* (September–October 1997): 23–24, 42.

19. For information on Call to Renewal, contact Call to Renewal, 2401 Fifteenth Street NW, Washington, D.C. 20009.

20. For another example of converging interest in the poor, see the book by the charismatic leader John Dawson, *Healing America's Wounds* (Ventura, Calif.: Regal Books, 1994).

21. See, for example, R. A. Clemetson and R. Coates, eds., *Restoring Broken Places and Rebuilding Communities: A Casebook on African-American Church Involvement in Community Economic Development* (Washington, D.C.: National Congress for Economic Development, 1995); Diane Cohen and Robert Jaeger, *Sacred Places at Risk: New Evidence on How Endangered Older Churches and Synagogues Serve Communities* (Philadelphia: Partners for Sacred Places, 1997); Virginia Hodgkinson, Murray Weitzman, Arthur Kirsch, Stephen Norga, and Heather Gorski, *From Belief to Commitment: The Activities and Finances of Religious Congregations in the United States* (Washington, D.C.: Independent Sector, 1993).

22. Ronald J. Sider, *For They Shall Be Fed* (Dallas: Word, 1997) contains two hundred pages of biblical texts on the poor.

Bibliography

General Works

Abraham, Laurie Kaye. *Mama Might Be Better Off Dead: The Failure of Health Care in Urban America.* Chicago: Univ. of Chicago Press, 1993.

Ackerman, Bruce A., and Anne Alstott. *The Stakeholder Society.* New Haven: Yale Univ. Press, 1999.

Amato, Paul R., and Alan Booth. *A Generation at Risk.* Cambridge: Harvard Univ. Press, 1998.

Are States Improving the Lives of Poor Families? A Scale Measure of State Welfare Policies. Medford, Mass.: Tufts School of Nutrition Science and Policy, 1998.

Bane, Mary Jo, and David T. Ellwood. *Welfare Realities.* Cambridge: Harvard Univ. Press, 1994.

Beckmann, David, and Arthur Simon. *Grace at the Table: Ending Hunger in God's World.* Downers Grove, Ill.: InterVarsity Press; and New York: Paulist Press, 1999.

Beisner, E. Calvin. *Prosperity and Poverty: The Compassionate Use of Resources in a World of Scarcity.* Westchester, Ill.: Crossway, 1988.

Berrick, Jill Duerr. *Faces of Poverty: Portraits of Women and Children on Welfare.* New York: Oxford, 1995.

Black, Amy E. *For the Sake of the Children: Reconstructing American Divorce Policy.* Crossroads Monograph, no. 2. Wynnewood, Pa.: Evangelicals for Social Action, 1995.

Blank, Rebecca M. *It Takes a Nation: A New Agenda for Fighting Poverty.* Princeton, N.J.: Princeton Univ. Press, 1997.

Blankenhorn, David. *Fatherless America: Confronting Our Most Urgent Social Problem.* New York: Basic Books, 1995.

Bread for the World Institute. *The Changing Politics of Hunger: Hunger 1999.* Silver Spring, Md.: Bread for the World Institute, 1999. An important annual publication.

Brown, Larry J., and H. F. Pizer. *Living Hungry in America*. New York: Macmillan, 1987.

Bullard, Robert D., ed. *Unequal Protection: Environmental Justice and Communities of Color*. San Francisco: Sierra Club, 1994.

Callahan, Daniel. *What Kind of Life?* New York: Simon and Schuster, 1990.

Carle, Robert D., and Louis A. Decaro Jr., eds. *Signs of Hope in the City: Ministries of Community Renewal*. Valley Forge, Pa.: Judson Press, 1997.

Carlson-Thies, Stanley W. *Guide to Charitable Choice*. Washington, D.C.: Center for Public Justice, 1997.

Carlson-Thies, Stanley W., and James W. Skillen, eds. *Welfare in America: Christian Perspectives on a Policy in Crisis*. Grand Rapids: Eerdmans, 1996.

Center on Hunger and Poverty, The. *Hidden Hunger, Fragile Futures: A Report on Child Hunger*. Tufts University, 1998.

Choy, Susan P. *Public and Private Schools*. Washington, D.C.: National Center for Education Statistics, 1997.

Chubb, John E., and Terry M. Moe. *Politics, Markets and America's Schools*. Washington, D.C.: Brookings Institution Press, 1990.

Citro, Constance F., and Robert T. Michael, eds. *Measuring Poverty: A New Approach*. Washington, D.C.: National Academy Press, 1995.

Cobb, John. *For the Common Good: Redirecting the Economy Toward Community, the Environment and a Sustainable Future*. Boston: Beacon Press, 1989.

Committee on Ways and Means. *1998 Green Book*. Washington, D.C.: U.S. Government Printing Office, 1998. (www.access.gpo.gov/congress/wmooi.html)

Coolidge, David Orgon. *Same-Sex Marriage?* Crossroads Monograph, no. 9. Wynnewood, Pa.: Evangelicals for Social Action, 1996.

Copeland, Warren R. *And the Poor Get Welfare*. Nashville: Abingdon, 1994.

Danziger, Sheldon H., and Peter Gottschalk. *America Unequal*. Cambridge: Harvard Univ. Press, 1995.

Danziger, Sheldon H., Gary D. Sandefur, and Daniel H. Weinberg, eds. *Confronting Poverty: Prescriptions for Change*. Cambridge: Harvard Univ. Press, 1994.

Davis, Derek, and Barry Hankins, eds. *Welfare Reform and Faith-Based Organizations*. Waco: J. M. Dawson Institute of Church-State Studies, Baylor University, 1999.

Economic Justice for All: Pastoral Letter on Catholic Social Teaching and the U.S. Economy. Washington, D.C.: National Conference of Catholic Bishops, 1986.

Eisinger, Peter K. *Toward an End to Hunger in America*. Washington, D.C.: Brookings Institution Press, 1998.

Ellwood, David T. *Poor Support: Poverty in the American Family*. New York: Basic Books, 1988.

Ferrara, Peter J., and Michael Tanner. *A New Deal for Social Security*. Washington, D.C.: Cato Institute, 1998.

Flake, Floyd, and Donna Marie Williams. *The Way of the Bootstrapper: Nine Action Steps for Achieving Your Dreams*. San Francisco: HarperSanFrancisco, 1999

Freedman, Samuel G. *Upon This Rock: The Miracles of a Black Church*. New York: Harper, 1993.

Freeman, Richard B. *The New Inequality: Creating Solutions for Poor America*. Boston: Beacon Press, 1999.

Gates, Jeffrey R. *The Ownership Solution: Toward a Shared Capitalism for the Twenty-First Century*. Reading, Mass.: Addison-Wesley, 1998.

Glenn, Charles L. *The Ambiguous Embrace: Government and Faith-Based Schools and Social Agencies*. Princeton, N.J.: Princeton Univ. Press, 1999.

Gordon, Wayne L. *Real Hope in Chicago*. Grand Rapids: Zondervan, 1995.

Grossman, David. *On Killing: The Psychological Cost of Learning to Kill in War and Society*. New York: Little, Brown and Co., 1996.

Gushee, David P., ed. *Toward a Just and Caring Society: Christian Responses to Poverty in America.* Grand Rapids: Baker, 1999.

Halteman, James. *The Clashing Worlds of Economics and Faith.* Scottdale, Pa.: Herald Press, 1995.

Harrington, Michael. *The Other America: Poverty in the United States.* New York: Macmillan, 1962.

Hewlett, Sylvia Ann, and Cornel West. *The War against Parents: What We Can Do for America's Beleaguered Moms and Dads.* Boston: Houghton Mifflin, 1998.

Hilfiker, David. *Not All of Us Are Saints: A Doctor's Journey with the Poor.* New York: Hill and Wang, 1994.

Hill, M. Anne, and June O'Neill. *Underclass Behaviors in the United States.* New York: City Univ. of New York, Baruch College, 1993.

Hirsch, E. D. Jr. *The Schools We Need: Why We Don't Have Them.* New York: Doubleday, 1996.

Jargowsky, P. *Poverty and Place: Ghettoes, Barrios, and the American City.* New York: Russell Sage Foundation, 1997.

Jencks, Christopher. *Rethinking Social Policy: Race, Poverty and the Underclass.* New York: Harper Perennial, 1992.

Kaus, Michael. *The End of Equality.* New York: Basic Books, 1995.

Korten, David C. *When Corporations Rule the World.* West Hartford, Conn.: Kumarian Press, 1996.

Kozol, Jonathan. *Savage Inequalities.* New York: Harper, 1991.

Kutzner, Patricia. *Who's Involved with Hunger: An Organization Guide for Education and Advocacy.* Washington, D.C.: World Hunger Education Service. Bread for the World Institute, 1995.

Larson, David B. et al. *The Costly Consequences of Divorce.* Rockville, Md.: National Institute for Health Care Research, n.d.

Linthicum, Robert C. *Empowering the Poor.* Monrovia, Calif.: MARC, 1991.

Mayer, Susan E. *What Money Can't Buy.* Cambridge: Harvard Univ. Press, 1998.

Mead, Lawrence M. *The New Politics of Poverty.* New York: Basic Books, 1992.

Mishel, Lawrence, Jared Bernstein, and John Schmitt. *The State of Working America, 1998–99.* Ithaca, N.Y.: Cornell Univ. Press, 1999.

Monsma, Stephen. *When Sacred and Secular Mix.* Lanham, Md.: Rowman and Littlefield, 1996.

Moynihan, Daniel. *Miles to Go: A Personal History of Social Policy.* Cambridge: Harvard Univ. Press, 1996.

Murray, Charles. *Losing Ground: American Social Policy, 1950–1980.* New York: Basic Books, 1984.

Newman, Katherine S. *No Shame in My Game: The Working Poor in the Inner City.* New York: Russell Sage Foundation/Knopf, 1999.

Olasky, Marvin. *The Tragedy of American Compassion.* Wheaton: Crossway, 1992.

Perkins, John, ed. *Restoring At-Risk Communities.* Grand Rapids: Baker, 1995.

Peterson, Paul E., and Bryan C. Hassel, eds. *Learning from School Choice.* Washington, D.C.: Brookings Institution Press, 1998.

Physicians' Task Force on Hunger in America. *Hunger in America: The Growing Epidemic.* Boston: Harvard Univ. School of Public Health, 1985.

Poppendieck, Janet. *Sweet Charity: Emergency Food and the End of Entitlement.* New York: Viking Press, 1998.

Private Schools in the United States: A Statistical Profile, 1990–91. Washington, D.C.: National Center for Education, 1995.

Rector, Robert, and William F. Lauber. *America's Failed $5.4 Trillion War on Poverty.* Washington, D.C.: The Heritage Foundation, 1995.

Schansberg, Eric D. *How Poor Government Policy Harms the Poor.* Boulder, Colo.: Westview Press, 1996.

Schlossberg, Herbert, Vinay Samuel, and Ronald J. Sider, eds. *Christianity and Economics in the Post–Cold War Era: The Oxford Declaration and Beyond.* Grand Rapids: Eerdmans, 1994.

Schor, Juliet B. *The Overworked American*. New York: HarperCollins, 1992.

Sherman, Amy L. "Establishing an Effective, Church-Based Welfare-to-Work Mentoring Ministry: A Practical 'How To' Guide." Trinity Presbyterian Church, P.O. Box 5102, Charlottesville, VA 22905.

———. *Restorers of Hope: Reaching the Poor in Your Community with Church-Based Ministries That Work*. Wheaton: Crossway, 1997.

Sherman, Arloc. *Wasting America's Future: The Children's Defense Fund Report on the Costs of Child Poverty*. Boston: Beacon Press, 1994.

Sherraden, Michael. *Assets and the Poor: A New American Welfare Policy*. Armonk, N.Y.: M. E. Sharpe, 1991.

Sider, Ronald J. *Rich Christians in an Age of Hunger*. Dallas: Word, 1997.

Stackhouse, Max L. et al. *On Moral Business: Classical and Contemporary Resources for Ethics in Economic Life*. Grand Rapids: Eerdmans, 1995.

Stassen, Glen, and David P. Gushee. *Christian Ethics as Following Jesus*. Downers Grove, Ill.: InterVarsity Press, 1999.

The State of America's Children: Yearbook 1998. Washington, D.C.: Children's Defense Fund, 1998.

Tanner, Michael. *The End of Welfare*. Washington, D.C.: Cato Institute, 1996.

Wallis, Jim. *Faith Works: Lessons from an Activist Preacher*. New York: Random House, 2000.

Weicher, John. *The Distribution of Wealth*. Washington, D.C.: AEI Press, 1996.

Wilson, William Julius. *The Truly Disadvantaged*. Chicago: Univ. of Chicago Press, 1987.

———. *When Work Disappears: The World of the New Urban Poor*. New York: Knopf, 1996.

Wogaman, J. Philip. *The Great Economic Debate: An Ethical Analysis*. Philadelphia: Westminster, 1977.

Wolff, Edward. *Top Heavy: A Study of Increasing Inequality of Wealth in America*. New York: Twentieth Century Fund, 1995.

Woodson, Robert L., Sr. *The Triumphs of Joseph: How Today's Community Healers Are Reviving Our Streets and Neighborhoods*. New York: Free Press, 1998.

Lifestyle

Alexander, John. *Your Money or Your Life: A New Look at Jesus' View of Wealth and Power*. San Francisco: Harper & Row, 1986.

Bascom, Tim. *The Comfort Trap: Spiritual Dangers of the Convenience Culture*. Downers Grove, Ill.: InterVarsity Press, 1993.

Clapp, Rodney, ed. *The Consuming Passion: Christianity and the Consuming Culture*. Downers Grove, Ill.: InterVarsity Press, 1998.

Fuller, Millard. *The Theology of the Hammer*. Macon, Ga.: Smyth & Helwys, 1994.

Sine, Tom. *Why Settle for More and Miss the Best?* Waco: Word, 1987.

Wuthnow, Robert. *God and Mammon in America*. New York: Free Press, 1994.

Theology, Biblical Studies, and the Church

Baum, Gregory. *The Priority of Labor: A Commentary on Laborem Exercens; Encyclical Letter of Pope John Paul II*. New York: Paulist Press, 1982.

Brueggemann, Walter. *The Land*. Philadelphia: Fortress Press, 1977.

Clapp, Rodney. *A Peculiar People: The Church As Culture in a Post-Christian Society*. Downers Grove, Ill.: InterVarsity Press, 1996.

Cone, James H. *God of the Oppressed*. New York: Seabury Press, 1975.

Dayton, Donald W. *Discovering an Evangelical Heritage*. New York: Harper & Row, 1976.

Greenway, Roger S., ed. *Discipling the City: A Comprehensive Approach to Urban Mission*. 2d ed. Grand Rapids: Baker, 1992.

Mott, Stephen Charles. *Biblical Ethics and Social Change*. New York: Oxford, 1982.

———. *A Christian Perspective on Political Thought*. New York: Oxford, 1993.

Mott, Stephen Charles, and Ronald J. Sider. *Economic Justice: A Biblical Paradigm*. Crossroads Monograph, no. 26. Wynnewood, Pa.: Evangelicals for Social Action, 1999.

Perkins, John. *With Justice for All*. Glendale, Calif.: Regal Books, 1982.

Reed, Gregory J. *Economic Empowerment through the Church*. Grand Rapids: Zondervan, 1993.

Ronsvalle, John, and Sylvia. *Behind the Stained Glass Window: Money Dynamics in the Church*. Grand Rapids: Baker, 1996.

Sider, Ronald J. *Cup of Water, Bread of Life*. Grand Rapids: Zondervan, 1994.

———. *Good News and Good Works: A Theology for the Whole Gospel*. Grand Rapids: Baker, 1999.

———. *Living like Jesus*. Grand Rapids: Baker, 1999.

———. *For They Shall Be Fed*. Dallas: Word, 1997.

Swartley, Willard M., and Donald B. Kraybill, eds. *Building Communities of Compassion: Mennonite Mutual Aid in Theory and Practice*. Scottdale, Pa.: Herald Press, 1998.

Villafane, Eldin. *The Liberating Spirit: Toward an Hispanic American Pentecostal Social Ethic*. Grand Rapids: Eerdmans, 1993.

Wright, Christopher J. H. *An Eye for an Eye: The Place of Old Testament Ethics Today*. Downers Grove, Ill.: InterVarsity Press, 1983.

Wuthnow, Robert. *Acts of Compassion: Caring for Others and Helping Ourselves*. Princeton: Princeton Univ. Press, 1991.

———. *The Crisis in the Churches: Spiritual Malaise, Fiscal Woe*. New York: Oxford Univ. Press, 1997.

———. *God and Mammon in America*. New York: Free Press, 1994.

Yamamori, Tetsunao, Bryant L. Myers, and Kenneth L. Luscombe, eds. *Serving with the Urban Poor*. Monrovia, Calif.: MARC, 1998.

Periodicals and Newspapers

First Things, 156 Fifth Avenue, Suite 400, New York, NY 10010.

Multinational Monitor, 1530 P Street NW, Washington, D.C. 20005. Funded by Ralph Nader; it reports on large corporations.

PRISM, 6 Lancaster Avenue, Wynnewood, PA 19096; 800-650-6600. Regular articles on justice and the poor.

Seeds, P.O. Box 6170, Waco, TX 76706.

Sojourners, 2401 Fifteenth Street NW, Washington, D.C. 20009; 202-328-8842. A biblical magazine with regular articles on economic justice, discipleship, and community.

Numerous other religious journals regularly carry related items: *America, Christian Century, Christianity and Crisis, Christianity Today, Commonweal, Engage/Social Action, National Catholic Reporter, World, Worldview*.

Major newspapers such as *The New York Times, Wall Street Journal, Washington Post*, and *Christian Science Monitor* are especially good for keeping up with public policy.

The following magazines are especially helpful for public policy issues: *The American Prospect, Brookings Review, The Economist, Congressional Quarterly* (the best place to get detailed, weekly information on what is happening in Congress), *The New Republic, Weekly Standard, Wash-*

ington Monthly, National Review, Bread for the World's *Newsletter,* Focus on the Family's *Citizen,* Baptist Joint Committee's *Report from the Capitol,* American Baptist Churches' *Advocate,* Ethics and Christian Liberty Commission's *Insight* and *Light* (Southern Baptist), and the Heritage Foundation's *Policy Review.*

List of Organizations

ACORN (Association of Community Organizations for Reform Now), 117 W. Harrison Street, Chicago, IL 60605; 312-939-7488.

Alternatives, P.O. Box 429, 5263 Bouldercrest Road, Ellenwood, CA 30049; 404-961-0102. Publishers of a newsletter on simple living, *Alternative Celebrations Catalog*, and so on.

American Enterprise Institute for Policy Research, 1150 Seventeenth Street NW, Washington, D.C. 20036. An influential conservative think tank on a wide range of public policy issues including hunger.

American Friends Service Committee, 1501 Cherry Street, Philadelphia, PA 19102; 215-241-7060. An established Quaker relief, development, and justice agency.

Baptist Joint Committee on Public Affairs, 200 Maryland Avenue NE, Washington, D.C. 20002; 202-544-4226.

Bread for the World, 1100 Wayne Avenue, Suite 1000, Silver Spring, MD 20910; 301-608-2400; 800-82-BREAD; http://www.bread.org. An effective Christian citizens' lobby.

Bridge of Hope, P.O. Box 1223, Coatesville, PA 19320; 610-380-1360.

Call to Renewal, 2401 Fifteenth Street NW, Washington, D.C. 20009; 202-328-8842.

Canning Hunger, 131 E. Grove Avenue, Orange, CA 92865; 714-279-6570.

Catholic Charities, U.S.A., 1731 King Street, Suite 200, Alexandria, VA 22314.

Catholic Relief Services, 209 W. Fayette Street, Baltimore, MD 21201; 410-625-2220; 800-235-2772. The major Catholic relief and development agency.

CATO Institute, 1000 Massachusetts Avenue NW, Washington, D.C. 20001; http://www.Cato.org.

Center on Budget and Policy Priorities, 820 First Street NE, Suite 510, Washington, D.C. 20002; 202-408-1080; http://www.cbpp.org.

Children's Defense Fund, 25 E. Street NW, Washington, D.C. 20001.

Christian Community Development Association, 3848 W. Ogden Avenue, Chicago, IL 60623; 773-762-0994.

Christian Community Health Fellowship, P.O. Box 23429, Chicago, IL 60623; 773-843-2700.

Christians Supporting Community Organizing, 2444 Washington Street, Suite 202, Denver, CO 80205; 303-860-7747.

Church World Service—The CROP WALK People, 28606 Phillips Street, P.O. Box 968, Elkhart, IN 46515; 219-264-3102; 800-456-1310. CWS is the relief, development, refugee, and global education arm of the thirty-three Protestant, Orthodox, and Anglican denominations of the NCCC. Educational resources and free-loan videos available.

Common Ground, 1160 Old Johnson Ferry Road NE, Atlanta, GA 30319.

Compassion International, Box 7000, Colorado Springs, CO 80933; 800-336-7676.

Congressional Research Service. The Library of Congress prepares excellent "CRS info packs" for members of Congress on a wide range of topics. Your congressman will be glad to send you a free copy if you ask.

Cooperative League of the U.S.A., 59 E. Van Buren Street, Chicago, IL 60605.

Council on Economic Priorities (CEP), 30 Irving Place, New York, NY 10003; 800-729-4CEP; http://www.accesspt.com/cep/. Provides social and environmental research on corporations for consumers, investors, managers, employees, and activists.

Dwelling House Savings and Loan, 501 Herron Avenue, Pittsburgh, PA 15219; 412-683-5116.

Environmental Defense Fund, 162 Old Town Road, East Setauket, NY 11733; 800-225-5333.

Ethics and Christian Liberty Commission (Southern Baptist), 901 Commerce, Suite 550, Nashville, TN 37203; 615-244-2495.

Evangelical Environmental Network, 10 E. Lancaster Avenue, Wynnewood, PA 19096; 800-650-6600.

Evangelicals for Social Action, 10 E. Lancaster Avenue, Wynnewood, PA 19096; 610-645-9391; Esa@esa-online.org. ESA's magazine, *PRISM,* has a regular Washington update in each issue.

Family Research Council, 801 G Street NW, Washington, D.C. 20001; 202-393-2100.

Focus on the Family, 8605 Explorer Drive, Colorado Springs, CO 80920; 719-531-3400.

Friends Committee on National Legislation, 245 Second Street NE, Washington, D.C. 20002; 202-547-6000. Issues a monthly newsletter and weekly legislative update.

Generous Christians Campaign, 10 E. Lancaster Avenue, Wynnewood, PA 19096; 800-650-6600.

Good Samaritan Ministries, 513 E. Eighth Street, Suite 25, Holland, MI 49423.

Habitat for Humanity, 121 Habitat Street, Americus, GA 31709; 800-HABITAT.

Harvest for Humanity, 213 S. Wheaton Avenue, Wheaton, IL 60187; 603-510-3737; dhfh@ix.netcom.com. Helps poor farm workers become owners.

Heritage Foundation, 214 Massachusetts Avenue NE, Washington, D.C. 20002; 202-546-4400.

Industrial Areas Foundation, 220 W. Kinzie, Chicago, IL 60610; 312-245-9211.

Institute for Consumer Responsibility, 3618 Wallingford Avenue N., Seattle, WA 98103; 206-632-5230.

Interfaith Center on Corporate Responsibility, 475 Riverside Drive, Suite 566, New York, NY 10027.

Jeremiah Project, The, Center for Civic Innovation, The Manhattan Institute, 52 Vanderbilt Avenue, New York, NY 10017; 212-599-7000.

Jobs Partnership, P.O. Box 31768, Raleigh, NC 27622.

Lutheran Services in America, 2177 Youngman Avenue, St. Paul, MN 55116; 800-664-3848.

March for Jesus USA, P.O. Box 3216, Austin, TX 78764.

Marriage Savers, 9311 Harrington Drive, Potomac, MD 20854.

Mennonite Central Committee, 21 S. Twelfth Street, Akron, PA 17501.

Mennonite Economic Development Associates (MEDA), Domestic Division Office, 302-280 Smith Street, Winnipeg, Manitoba, Canada R3C 1K2; 204-944-1995.

National Association of Christians in Social Work, P.O. Box 121, Botsford, CT 06404.

National Association of Community Development Loan Funds, 924 Cherry Street, Second Floor, Philadelphia, PA 19107; 215-923-4754.

National Association of Evangelicals, 450 Gundersen Drive, Carol Stream, IL 60188; 708-665-0500.

National Center for Neighborhood Enterprise, 1424 Sixteenth Street NW, Suite 300, Washington, D.C. 20036; 202-518-6500.

National Coalition Against Pornography, 800 Compton Road, Suite 9224, Cincinnati, OH 45231; 513-521-6227.

National Council of Churches, 475 Riverside Drive, New York, NY 10027.

National Faith-Based Demonstration Project, One Commerce Square, 2005 Market Street, Suite 900, Philadelphia, PA 19103; 215-557-4400.

National Fatherhood Initiative, One Bank Street, Suite 160, Gaithersburg, MD 20878; 301-948-0599.

National Interfaith Committee for Worker Justice, 1020 West Bryn Mawr, Fourth Floor, Chicago, IL 60660; 773-728-8400; http://www.igc.org/nicwj.

Network, 224 D Street SE, Washington, D.C. 20005. A citizen lobby staffed by Catholic Sisters who publish a monthly newsletter, a quarterly, and a hunger packet.

OPPORTUNITY International, Box 3695, Oakbrook, IL 60522; 708-279-9300. An excellent microenterprise development organization.

Prison Fellowship, P.O. Box 17500, Washington, D.C. 20041; 703-478-0100.

Public/Private Ventures, One Commerce Square, 2005 Market Street, Suite 900, Philadelphia, PA 19103; 215-557-4400.

Salvation Army, P.O. Box 269, Alexandria, VA 22313; 703-684-5500.

Teen Challenge USA, P.O. Box 1015, Springfield, MO 65801.

True Love Waits, Southern Baptist Sunday School Board, 901 Commerce Street, Nashville, TN 37203.

Union of Gospel Rescue Missions, 1045 Swift Street, Kansas City, MO 64116.

Welfare Information Network. http://www.welfareinfo.org/faith.htm.

World Relief Corporation, P.O. Box WRC, Wheaton, IL 60187; 708-665-0235, 800-535-5433; WorldRelief@xc.org. The anti-poverty arm of the National Association of Evangelicals.

World Vision Inc., P.O. Box 9716, Federal Way, WA 98063-9716; 800-423-4200. See their Churches at Work web site: http://www.churchesatwork.org.

Subject Index

Scripture Index

Ronald J. Sider (Ph.D., Yale University), professor of theology and culture at Eastern Baptist Theological Seminary in Philadelphia, is president of Evangelicals for Social Action and publisher for *Prism* and *Creation Care* magazines. He is the author of over twenty books, including *Living like Jesus* and the best-selling *Rich Christians in an Age of Hunger*.

Persons interested in further information about meetings, programs, and materials that seek to implement this book's call for holistic mission are invited to contact:

Ron Sider
President
Evangelicals for Social Action
10 E. Lancaster Avenue
Wynnewood, PA 19096
215-645-9390
800-650-6600
Fax: 215-649-3834

Also by Ronald J. Sider

Rich Christians in an Age of Hunger
Karlstadt's Battle with Luther
Christ and Violence
For They Shall Be Fed, editor
Completely Pro-Life
Preaching about Life in a Threatening World
Non-violence: An Invincible Weapon?
Cup of Water, Bread of Life
Living like Jesus
Good News and Good Works

If you've been challenged by *Just Generosity*, you'll want to share Ron Sider's insights with others!

Now you can discuss and experience *Just Generosity: A New Vision for Overcoming Poverty in America* with any small group. *Just Generosity: A Study and Action Guide*, written by experienced world-relief agency worker Susan Weaver Van Lopik, is easy to use and highly interactive. It provides:

- ten stimulating sessions, one on each chapter of *Just Generosity*
- suggestions for opening and closing the sessions
- helpful chapter summaries
- Bible studies
- questions for discussion
- action-learning suggestions

This study guide is available for $2.95 from Evangelicals for Social Action (1-800-650-6600) or CRC Publications (1-800-333-8300, ISBN 1-56212-493-5).

Enables any small group to share Ron Sider's rich insights

a study and action guide

FOREWORD BY CHARLES W. COLSON & JOHN J. DIIULIO JR
AFTERWORD BY EUGENE RIVERS

JUST
GENEROSITY

A New Vision for overcoming poverty in America

Ronald J. Sider
AUTHOR OF RICH CHRISTIANS IN AN AGE OF HUNGER

BY SUSAN WEAVER VAN LOPIK

EVANGELICALS FOR SOCIAL ACTION

ESA is a national association of Christians dedicated to empowering the poor and living like Jesus in every area of our lives.

Jesus is Lord of our whole lives, and our lives must be subject to the whole of his gospel. ESA provides a network and resource for Christians committed to this kind of "holistic" discipleship and ministry in our lost and hurting world. Together we can share the good news of Jesus Christ through word and deed.

Join ESA and become a part of an exciting movement including . . .

PRISM> ESA's bimonthly magazine will equip, empower, inform, and inspire you to care about the poor and live more like Jesus, growing a genuine faith in every part of your life. PRISM offers insightful, biblical reflection on the world in which we live and is full of stories and strategies for effective outreach and ministry.

Christian Citizenship> ESA helps Christians to be active, engaged, and responsible citizens. PRISM features a regular "Washington Update," providing a biblical perspective on the latest political developments in our nation's capital. Our Crossroads program brings together Christian scholars for a deeper look at important issues of public policy.

Caring for Creation> ESA hosts the Evangelical Environmental Network (EEN), a network of Christian organizations making care for creation an integral part of their work. World Vision, Habitat for Humanity, and InterVarsity Christian Fellowship are among the members of this environmental network. ESA also produces *Creation Care* magazine, a biblical, environmental quarterly.

Ministry Networks> Becoming a member of ESA makes you a part of a dynamic network of Christians throughout America. Network 9:35 is our exciting new network of churches and pastors committed to the genuine faith and holistic ministry described in Matthew 9:35. ESA's Generous Christians Campaign is a growing movement of individuals giving sacrificially of their time and resources to help share Jesus' love with the poor, the hungry, and the outcast.

Join Us!

Evangelicals for Social Action • 10 E. Lancaster Avenue • Wynnewood, PA 19096
1-800-650-6600 • esa@esa-online.org

Other Baker Books
by Ronald J. Sider

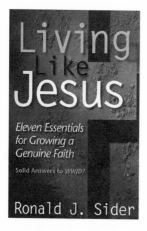

Living like Jesus
*Eleven Essentials for Growing
a Genuine Faith*
Ronald J. Sider

By contrasting nominal Christianity with
the power of the authentic gospel, *Living
like Jesus* challenges believers to reexam-
ine their commitment and return to the
basics of faith.

0-8010-5843-0   9.99p

Good News and Good Works
A Theology for the Whole Gospel
Ronald J. Sider

This "biblical theology of the whole
gospel" affirms that the church must
address both personal and social sin and
engage in both evangelism and social
action in order to fulfill its mission.

0-8010-5845-7   12.99p